THE FELL TERRIER

THE FELL TERRIER

D. BRIAN PLUMMER

COCH-Y-BONDDU BOOKS

First published by The Boydell Press 1983
Reprinted by Coch-y-Bonddu Books 1997
© 1983 David Brian Plummer
All rights reserved.

ISBN 0 9528510 7 5

Published & distributed by
COCH-Y-BONDDU BOOKS
MACHYNLLETH, POWYS, SY20 8DJ
Tel 01654 702837   Fax 01654 702857

CONTENTS

5

ILLUSTRATIONS

TERRIER BLOODLINES

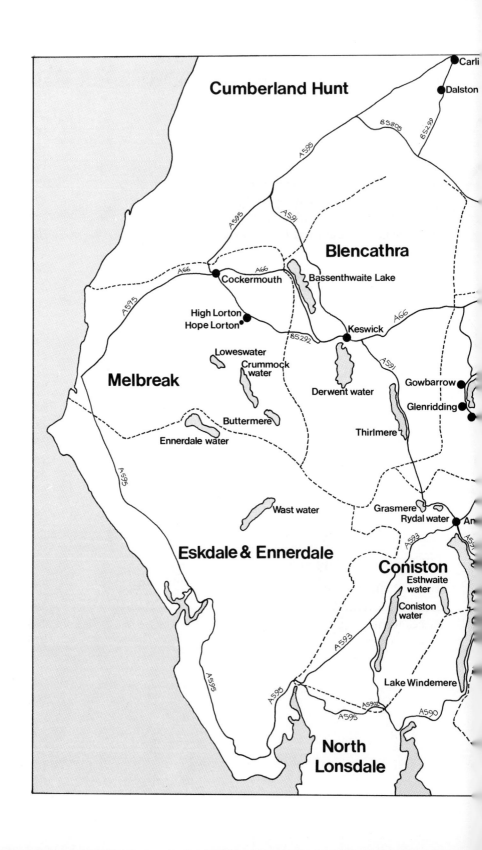

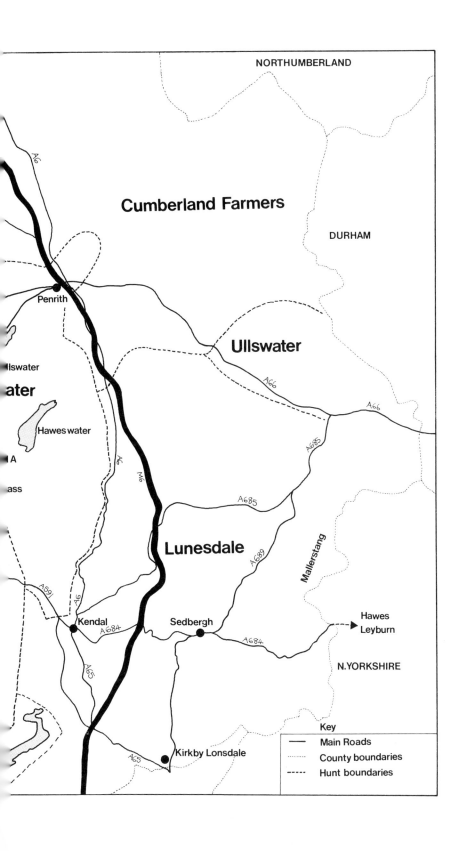

NORTHUMBERLAND

Cumberland Farmers

DURHAM

Ullswater

A66

A66

Penrith

Ilswater

ater

Haweswater

A

ass

A6

M6

A685

A685

A689

Mallerstang

Lunesdale

A591

A6

Kendal

A684

Sedbergh

A684

Hawes
Leyburn

N.YORKSHIRE

A65

A65

Kirkby Lonsdale

Key

— Main Roads

····· County boundaries

‑‑‑‑‑ Hunt boundaries

I DEDICATE this book to Eddie Pool, my guide during my repeated stays in the Lake District, and to John Winch, who set me out on this marathon paper chase.

PHOTOGRAPHS BY
DAVID HANCOCK

THE FELL TERRIER

Introduction

Take the M6 and journey north, away from Birmingham. It will be a long journey, and tedious, too. Believe me, I know. I've made this trip 210 times during the last five years. Pass Walsall quickly, for I still teach there, and continue north along that straight, unchanging road: Stafford, Newcastle, Stoke and still further. There will be little to interest you, and seemingly little to justify your trip. In due course you come to a sign which says Holmes Chapel. Nuttall lives there: a soft-spoken, articulate ex-gamekeeper, trying desperately to keep Cyril Breay's and Frank Buck's strain of terrier relatively pure. But do not stop. Your real journey has just begun.

North again, and the air becomes smoky as the wind blows in from the heavily industrialized areas of Lancashire. Don't turn off on the M56, which will only take you to Manchester, though some say the black smooth fell terrier originated here. Avoid also the M62, which gives a choice of Liverpool or the inevitable Manchester. Straight on now to Lancaster and beyond, and you have left the smell of towns and industry behind. By Lancaster your trip is nearing its end. Don't turn for Carnforth, though there are signs to it in plenty. Terrier men abound in this district. There'll be a sign for Kirkby Lonsdale in a minute. Breay lived there: a baffling enigma of a man, and everything I'd like to be if I'd the courage to try, but I haven't, so I still while away my days as an unsuccessful school teacher.

On yet a while, however, for there'll be time enough to talk of Breay and his curious, fascinating life. Travel still further north. There's a sign ahead that says Kendal and Sedbergh. Leave the motorway here. Careful, there's a sheep grid just ahead, a noisy device to ensure the M6 doesn't become a morass of fur and mutton pulp. Left is Sedbergh, home of Lunesdale Foxhounds, and their huntsman, John Nicholson, a great houndsman by any standards. Further on still there is Hawes, with Maurice Bell and his outlaw Wensleydale Pack. A controversial figure, Bell – one who received considerable unjust publicity. Forget the left turn and its route through fell and limestone country, a death-trap for terriers and pot-holers alike. Turn right to Kendal. Middleton lives here, trying to preserve the terrier strain bred by Fred Barker in 1920; and Keith Clement, who breeds a now unfashionable Breay type of terrier; and Harold Watson, born 1907, a font of hunting wisdom and a man who can tell a tale to fascinate.

Drive carefully as you go through Kendal. It is a hard place to negotiate and you can easily miss the A591 that takes you through to Windermere, a long thin lake which disappointed me when I first saw it. Down therefore into Windermere, past the bed and breakfast signs that seem to jut out of every garden, past the gift shops with their curious souvenirs and the sickly-sweet Kendal mint cake. Windermere was called Onudr by the Vikings. There's a railway station, though Wordsworth tried his damnedest to stop it being built, for Wordsworth, like many lakelanders, tried hard to prevent indus-trialization ruining the lakes. It's a tourist town now, for many of the orange kagools seen here have arrived by train to visit the Lake District. Many of their owners will see only Windermere, as there is much to view in both lake and village.

Turn away from the town, however, and keep on the A591, past the sign that says Troutbeck. Clapham lived here for a while – a strange, aloof man who told tales of his adventures with Canadian fur trappers and wrote a book that attracted a different type of tourist to the lake. Pass the road that would take you to Patterdale and Glenridding, for we will arrive there by another route. On now to Ambleside. The Vikings called it Hamelsaldr, 'the seat of Hamel', a Viking leader who held his rustic earthy court in this lake village, the passage of time having corrupted the Nordic sound to Ambleside. Stop here a while. It is worth the stay. You are in the heart of the Coniston Hunt country, in the midst of a lunar landscape, a land straight out of a forbidding Oz, or perhaps a Rider Haggard tale. The Coniston Hunt is at Ambleside (not at Coniston, as the name might suggest), on a stone-built hunt yard perched on a hill off a winding road that leads up to the Kirkstone Pass. Ogilvie is the huntsman, a fascinating, soft-spoken chap, a poet as well as a huntsman, eloquent but unassuming. He is not a native of the Lakes, but is rapidly becoming one.

Up that steep and narrow road now, with its 1 in 3 gradient, or so it seems, up and still up towards the Kirkstone Pass, chilly in summer and bitterly cold in winter, a land scarred by quarrying and ice. In fine weather there will be orange kagools in plenty, in winter very few. Only fools go up there in winter – fools or fell pack followers, that is. There's a pub at the top of the pass – an inn called the Kirkstone Pass Inn, a hostel beloved by Clapham, who wrote some of the notes for his book *Foxhunting in the Lakeland Fells* on the tables of this pub. It is a pub that has changed little since 1920, a pub that only recently took down its photograph of Tommy Dobson, who died in 1910. Stop a while, listen to the locals ridiculing the odd tourist out hiking in the icy cold of winter. 'Should be locked up,' they murmur, staring into their beers, yet tomorrow you will find these self-same locals, men well beyond

16

their prime, running like chamois over those self-same fells across which agile kagool-clad youngsters are now struggling and panting.

It's a hard land. Ask the Chapmans. They should know. Father and son, George and Anthony, have hunted this land with the Coniston since 1908, and Anthony still lives there, writing his memoirs, recalling better times perhaps. Looking down at Ambleside you may catch a glimpse of Dr Arnold of *Tom Brown's Schooldays* summer house, though Arnold seldom ventured up Kirkstone way. It's not the place for a man with angina pectoris, or for any man on a winter's day.

On now towards Patterdale, past the Brotherswater Hotel. Glance up at the hillside at the enormous excavations on your right. Butcher and Badger, two fell terriers, were buried there, and men toiled for fourteen days to get them out, the Currys writing a poem about the dig. You are in a land rich in ballads of hunting and songs of mining disasters. Black smooth-coated fell terriers are sometimes called Patterdales – wrongly, as it happens, and as we will emphasize throughout this book.

Supposedly St Patrick came to preach at Patterdale, the tiny village originally being called Patricdale – except that Patrick never preached here, and probably never came to the Lakes. Anthony Barker does live here, however: Anthony Barker, the son of Fred Barker who hunted the Pennine Pack at Ousby. He is a hard, tough, often silent sort of man, but a wonder with terriers. A man with earthy yet stinging comments. It was Anthony Barker who hunted the Ullswater during the Second World War, caretaking it, so to speak, for Joe Wear, and he who also worked Jim Fleming's Myrt, the *magna mater* of all modern fell terriers. His house is on the side of the hill going into Patterdale, and there he lives, a great raconteur and even greater hunter. Nimrod grown old maybe, but Nimrod nevertheless.

Past Patterdale and you are into Ullswater Hunt country, a wild and scenic country hunted by Dennis Barrow, a genial powerful man who lives at Glenridding, a now fashionable district, where a one-up, one-down house was recently sold for £20,000. It's not always been fashionable. Once it was a boom town for miners who came here after copper and lead, undermining the mountain-side, ripping out the metallic bowels of the earth. I stayed in Glenridding for the night once, at a bed and breakfast farmhouse, only to hear my landlady tell of an old mine shaft that had suddenly appeared in her back yard after a wet spell. Ask Eddie Pool of Glenridding, he'll tell you. His ancestors came north as tramp miners to mine that copper and lead. Few people know this land, its legends, its history, like Eddie. He knew Joe Wear, a famous huntsman with the Ullswater Hunt, 'as great a huntsman as Joe Bowman', so Eddie says. Eddie will tell you about mining these hills and of the mining disaster that saw off four close friends in one morning. He could keep an audience enthralled for hours, and no one can tell a tale of fell terriers like Eddie Pool.

There aren't any spoil piles on the hills now, or none to speak of. Nature has taken care of that, though the Ullswater still has a high lead level, maybe as a result of the mining. It may even be a poisonously high level, though Bowman drank the waters of the feed streams, and he went on for ever. In Glenridding I met Sylvia Shepherd, who wrote *Brocky*, a lovely, warm Gavin Maxwell type of book. I'd read and re-read her book – she'd never heard of me.

Out of Ullswater, climb up along the A5091, now a good road and an easy gradient, before you join the A66 and turn towards Keswick. You are in Blencathra country now, and in the village of Threlkeld in a tiny wooden bungalow lives Johnny Richardson, huntsman of the Blencathra, aided and abetted by Barry Todhunter, once the youngest whip in the fell packs. 'A boy with big boots and a whip,' was how one local described the fifteen-year-old youth when he became whip. Richardson is worth more than a minute or so of anyone's time. He's one of the great fell hunters, and will maybe go down alongside Bowman, Wear and Peel in years to come. Richardson's worth a book, or maybe two, for few have lived such exciting lives. Few men are as unassuming either – he's seldom heard to blow his own trumpet, is Johnny. Threlkeld: a Viking name, but one of the earliest prehistoric settlements in this part of the world.

Along the A66 again, towards Cockermouth, formerly not only the home of William Wordsworth, but also of John Walker, who pioneered Jenner's vaccination programme when Jenner was becoming a figure of fun among cartoonists in the nineteenth century, and of Fletcher Christian of *Mutiny on the Bounty* fame. Cockermouth is a curious, antique town where I spent a whole day in a café rather antisocially trying to rid myself of flu before attempting to interview Harry Hardasty at Hope Lorton, the home of the Melbreck Foxhounds. 'Prich' Bland, Harry's son-in-law, hunts the hounds now, and lives in a house next to the stone-built kennels that are perched precariously on the side of a hill. Bland is a reticent man by most standards, but Harry even more so. Perhaps it is the land that produces such men, or, again, perhaps not, for Willie Irving, an outgoing, genial, happy sort of chap hunted this pack before Harry. Irving's hunt terriers were some of the best lookers in the country during his time with the Melbreck, and when he retired from hunt service he bred some of the best Kennel Club-registered Lakeland terriers.

Retrace your steps to Keswick now and down the A591 to Ambleside, turning right towards Hawkshead. I first made this trip in summer, and crossed the steep and difficult Wrynose and Hardknott passes: steep, difficult climbs for my tiny Fiat, along a route used by seventeenth-century liquor smugglers and Lake District bootleggers, a route used by Lanty Lee, the same who produced a fiery hell-brew tasting 'twixt vitriol and wood alcohol in Bessycrag Quarry. Later I crossed the passes in midwinter in a blinding, sudden snowstorm after a farmworker called Richard had advised me to turn back, even though the day was bright and sunny. I should have listened to him. Men who live on these hills seem to possess a sixth sense about weather. It took me six hours to cross the passes that night, six hours to battle on into the freezing darkness of the Eskdale and Ennerdale country.

Next day I tried in vain to find Tommy Dobson's grave in Boot Church-yard – a grave identified by a gravestone out of which peeps a curious, cherubic face that would have passed as a ringer for an elderly Dylan Thomas or a Dionysus perhaps. I found it next summer, aided by Arthur Irving, brother of Willie Irving, one of an illustrious family. Arthur once hunted the Eskdale and Ennerdale Hunt at Eskdale Green. Edmund Porter hunts it now, as have three generations of Porters: Edmund, Jack and Willie Porter. That same Willie Porter, acolyte of the Lakeland pixie, the diminutive Tommy Dobson, that same Willie Porter's stamina was legend throughout the Lakes. Clapham met Willie Porter and was impressed by his stamina and rugged determination. Edmund is of the same mould, and with two genera-tions of fell terrier breeders in his pedigree, there are few more knowledge-able men to interview.

This, then, is the Lake District, the reason for my 210 trips up that damnable M6. Today it is fashionable to state that the best fell terriers are bred in the Midlands or in Yorkshire, but reader, I assure you that it was here, in the Lake District, where the strains began.

PART ONE: THE LAND

I was unimpressed by the Lakes during my first visit, possibly because most thirteen-year-old boys are naturally somewhat blasé about most things and would boast that they found a ringside seat at the battle of Waterloo a bit of a drag, but primarily because my guide, a twenty-two-year old intellectual, hot out of college, was rather a twit. To her the Lakes meant Wordsworth, and our coach trip (two bad cases of vomiting and the obligatory anglicized chorus of 'Sospan Fach') flashed straight to Grasmere to Dove Cottage where Wordsworth and his sister once sojourned. Ignoring the landscape, the lakes, the industrial archaeology, the curiously untouched people, we streaked over the Kirkstone Pass towards Patterdale and Glenridding, hell bent for Gowbarrow where Wordsworth wrote the ridiculous and rather inane 'I wandered lonely as a cloud' – for some reason one of the most famous lines in English poetry. We passed the sign for Patterdale, and excitedly I whispered to our guide, 'Patterdale was the old name for a Lakeland terrier.' She treated me to a pitying glance, the sort that is probably taught graduates during their teaching diploma year to bring down a plebeian who talks about anything worldly. 'Really?' she said in as bored a manner as she could manage, and leaped into a couplet about daffodils, miming the fluttering action of the flowers with her hands – an action that caused considerable embarrassment on the bus and amazement to the villagers of Patterdale. What curious affectations, to be sure, are found among members of the teaching profession. As I said, I was unimpressed by my first visit to the Lakes.

Later, much later, at the age of thirty, equipped with a knowledge of geology of the land and its multitude of mineral lodes, an appreciation of the effects of glaciation and a soupçon of the history of Cumbria, I returned to the Lakes and found it a fascinating landscape, and though I still dislike Wordsworth's infernal limp and affected poetry, I find something to interest me every time I visit that country.

It was not always a land of rugged peaks and steep-sided cliffs, acre upon acre of ice-shattered scree and mound upon mound of mining-spoil pile.

Once the area was covered by a shallow sea, a sea so primitive that fish had not been evolved when it existed, though the waters teemed with crustacea and curious antique insects, some of which were so outlandish that they were never destined to survive to present times. It was a muddy and sandy sea during the ages that scientists have labelled the Cambrian and the Ordovician eras, and layers of mudstone and shale sandstone and grit were deposited during this time – stone which in its original form probably resembled the black shales of the pit spoil piles that littered the sides of my mining valley home in South Wales.

Later, however, the land was to see more turbulent times. Shortly after these muds and shales had been consolidated into rocks, it became unstable, hostile even to primitive life forms as a mass of boiling molten magma began to push its way up through the crust of the earth, creating a vast elongated dome covering the whole of the Lake District. The land must have been like hell at that time, with volcanoes pouring out white-hot lavas and showering down vast quantities of hot ash dust of the kind that overwhelmed Pompeii in A.D. 79. For a million years or maybe longer this boiling hell lasted; in the twinkling of an eye, geologically speaking, the rocks laid down in that shallow sea were baked, twisted, laminated and deformed. Shales became slates, soft crumbly sandstones became iron-hard gneisses, while all the while below the surface of that huge dome the granitic magma cooled slowly, a fraction of a degree every thousand years perhaps, but cool it did – granites with such a peculiar crystalline form that I found a piece of this Shap granite shaped into an egg-like paper-weight for sale in a Singapore curiosity shop; granites whose curious physical structure cause such interest that few school-boy geological collections the world over do not contain at least one specimen of the strange pegmatite rock with its huge pink felspar crystals.

The dome that covered the Lake District then cooled, allowing rivers to run which radiated from the elevated centre of the dome – rivers that etched the area so that from the air they resemble the spokes of a giant misshapen cartwheel, rivers that eroded and washed away the baked and twisted shales and slates, sandstones and gneisses at the hub of the wheel, revealing the hard plutonic rocks that lay below the surface of the land. Hard rocks these are, rocks that defy the shovel and pick of any hunter trying to excavate a trapped terrier. Breay could tell tales of this, and Bowman too, or Wear or any Lakeland huntsmen for that matter, for few have not had at some time to dig through those ancient volcanic rocks to extract a trapped terrier that had followed a fox into the fissures of the earth. Frank Buck can tell tales of trapped dogs imprisoned below boulders of this resistant rock, for few people have the Bucks' experience of Lakeland terrier rescues. Buck in his day was a fearless man, a demon with the pick and an expert with dynamite, someone who would crawl into a dangerous fissure to fetch out a trapped dog. Many times was he called into the Lakes to dynamite rock piles to extract trapped fell terriers.

In geological times, however, the volcanic activity, the movement of a

1. Frank Buck (second left) about to blow out a trapped terrier.

magma of molten granite deep below the dome that was to become the Lake District caused other reactions: lodes of metal-bearing rock including galena from which lead is refined, marcasite, chalcopyrites that yields copper, barytes from which barium can be processed, plumbago, an ore composed of carbon and iron, an ore that contains graphite, the type of carbon from which pencil leads are made, and wolfram, from which the steel-hardening tungsten is manufactured, pushed their way into the surrounding rocks, eventually inviting man to mine them, encouraging and daring him to dig deep, narrow crevices into the mountain-sides to extract these minerals. They are crevices which no amount of back stopping with 'spoil' can completely fill, crevices which act as a sanctuary for the Lakeland foxes and badgers, crevices which are deathtraps for the terriers which follow those foxes into those old mine shafts. Ullswater has many such, and at Leverswater, near Coniston, the land is literally honeycombed with them. Bunting, in his book *The Lake District*, states that these shafts can be a dangerous hazard to climbers. How much more of a hazard are they to any terrier which goes to ground in old mine workings where a fox has been 'put in' by hounds.

Not all the land is derived from volcanic rock, however. Kendal and the area south of Kendal stands on limestone – a rock not without its hazards to the terrier to ground on foxes. Nicholson of the Lunesdale Hunt at Sedbergh once told me with characteristic modesty that the Lunesdale country was not as tough a land to hunt since some of it was fairly free of borrans. He then proceeded to show me a photograph of a terrier he had dug out of limestone after a hard five-day dig. Breay lost dogs in limestone country: not often, for Breay was a careful man where terriers were concerned, but he lost one or two in spite of the fact he was always able to call on the excavating and dynamiting skills of Frank Buck. Parkin, former huntsman for the Lunesdale, has photographs which show enormous chasms of excavated rock that had to be removed to excavate his Rock strain of fell terrier. Indeed, there are probably more terriers lost – 'sunk without trace' might be a more appropriate phrase – in limestone country than any other type of land.

Limestone is a peculiar sort of rock. It was originally laid down under fairly deep water, and when the sediment consolidated into rock, the strata cleared and cracked to form huge blocks (Figure 1), some of which can be as

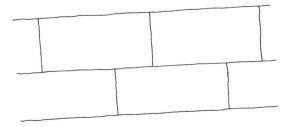

much as several hundred tons in weight. Limestone is slightly soluble in rainwater, charged as it is with carbon dioxide, and thus, after a period of time, the cracks separating the blocks become enlarged and channels appear in the limestone. Sometimes these channels are fairly wide, wide enough for a fox to follow or a stream to disappear into one (Figure 2). Once a stream has

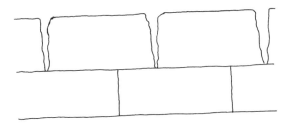

been swallowed up by these crevices, subterranean erosion is increased greatly and potholes, huge crevices and occasionally caves are then formed by the running water.

Many of these underground caves house vast pitch-black lakes whose waters remain at a constant icy temperature (Figure 3). Limestone country is

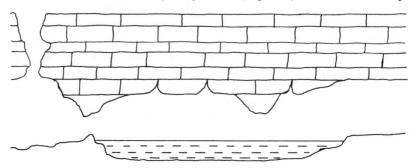

the dream world of the speleologist who, lowered with ropes into the depth of the earth, with torch and canoe, sets out to explore the dark mysteries of this underground world. It is hell for the terrier, on the other hand. Many foxes dive for sanctuary into these swallow-holes when pressed by hounds, falling maybe a dozen feet on to a ledge and sliding like syrup into one of the crevices that has been worked by the passage of hundreds of foxes over the years. Many of these swallow-holes have claimed hounds a-plenty, for when they are excited, close on the heels of the fox, hounds are unable to stop themselves hurtling into the blackness of these chasms, the bottoms of which are littered with the whitened bones of beasts which have stumbled into them over a thousand or so years.

In southern counties, where foxes are hunted for sport and not necessity, a fox going to ground in a hazardous place is given 'neck' and hounds are whipped off to try for another, but in the Lakes and the fell country a fox is considered vermin and killed out of necessity, not for sport. Thus, where a fox goes a terrier must follow, even into these frightful pits, either to bolt the fox or, if it will not bolt, to fight and kill it, battling often as not by lying on its side in the earth, trading blow for blow. Bowman lost the mother of Lil, his gift to Sid Wilkinson in 1924, in such an earth, so some tales tell, and Jummy, one of the Coniston terriers in Clapham's book, supposedly lost an eye in one of the few limestone earths in the Coniston country.

For tales of hunting in limestone country and of the hazards that face a fell terrier working there, one could do no better than to talk to John Nicholson at Sedbergh, who hunts the Lunesdale Foxhounds, or Maurice Bell, a genial giant of a man who hunts a private pack of foxhounds at Hawes – the Wensleydale Foxhounds. Bell's country is predominantly limestone, a country less dramatic and less lunar in appearance than that hunted by Lakeland packs, but a difficult country nevertheless. Bell tells stories of gill earths, holes into which icy streams suddenly disappear, holes into which foxes plunge when pressed by hounds to swim or paddle a little way and then slip into one of the relatively dry crevices above the water level. One of these streams was tested by tipping fluorescine, a chemical which gives water a greenish, iridescent tinge, into the gill as it disappeared into one of the swallow-holes. A stream reappearing three valleys away showed the greenish tinge – and where water will go a fox will follow. Bell puts terriers into what I would consider impossible places and expects a dog to work foxes out of those nightmare earths. Some succeed and come out alive, others do not.

Bell tells a tale of a fox that went into a gill earth followed by a very hard, game terrier. Fighting its fox in icy water, the dog finally succeeded in killing its quarry, but as it emerged, the shock of the icy gill caused a huge chunk of congealed blood to enter its larynx and the terrier choked to death in moments. Such tales are by no means uncommon in the Lakes. Another woolly coated terrier, owned by an associate of Bell, went to ground in a gill earth and after an hour or so of engaging his fox in icy water emerged and collapsed. Bell covered the dog with a coat and raced it down to the near-by farm to place it in front of a fire, but it was dead before he could help it. As I have said, what is a speleologist's dream is often a hunter's nightmare. Pat O'Malley, a likeable Irishman, and a great story-teller, said that he went off woolly coated dogs when he saw such a terrier emerge from a freezing peat earth, shake itself and then keel over in a state of shock.

Such rock formations are bad enough, but to worsen the situation still further, during the Quaternary era in earth's history – an era that began maybe a million or so years ago – the Lake District was covered by an immense glacier, a glacier that continued to function long after the rest of Britain cast off the Ice Age. 'In the beginning was the ice,' an ancient Viking edda begins, and whereas one can question the authenticity of such a statement, certainly the ice shaped the Lake District, for nowhere in England can the effects of glaciation be seen more clearly than in the Lakes. In summer, hosts of students, out on field courses to study the effects of glaciation, join the throngs of orange kagools and poetry-reading Wordsworth lovers.

As I write this (it is 25 December 1981) in my freezing cottage where the waterpipes have burst asunder, I am well aware of the irresistible force of ice, but a glacier on the move is a thing of stupendous magnitude. Whole valleys are straightened as the mass of moving ice chops off spurs of land as a child snaps off a dead twig from a tree, and valleys are deepened, the sides made U-shaped and steeper by the relentless and inexorable movement of a glacier. Earth, clay, trees, boulders of colossal size are torn out as though they were pebbles and dragged along by the ice. Rocks are polished as though by sandpaper and scarred as if some hideously powerful vandal has set to work on them with a gigantic rasp. Sides of mountains are sheered by the action, and perilously rocky crags are formed where the ice plucks out portions of the hills.

Yet glaciers, however powerful, are scarcely eternal, and when they melt they deposit their refuse anywhere and everywhere, like a dustman denied his

Christmas tip. Huge mounds of boulder clay – a mixture of earth clay and rock – were dumped on the floors of Lakeland valleys, creating new lakes and causing the others to be enlarged. Vast areas of hillside were covered in deep screes of rocks, rocks often alien to the substrata on which they stand, and enormous boulders have been left high and dry in seemingly ridiculous places, boulders which rock precariously to and fro with every bad storm.

The retreating ice dropped enormous piles of gigantic boulders piled dozens of feet deep, interlaced with crevices and crannies like the catacombs of Rome. In my own South Welsh coalfield home as a boy, I frequently ran my own terriers through the moraines along the side of our own slightly glaciated valley, heart in mouth lest my terrier, disappearing into the piles of stone, should jam or be injured far below my feet, but those ice-formed screes, those stone piles in Wales, were piddling moraines compared to the borrans of the Lake District, a land which received its full bounty from the ice.

A penny for every terrier that has come to grief in such places would yield a goodly sum in the Lake District, for the borrans or piles of stones seen along the sides of the valleys are bad places to work. When a terrier goes to ground in such places, it is a duel 'twixt dog and fox, with only God as umpire, for the terrier man can do little to aid the dog once it has vanished after a fox into a crevice. Some come to grips with a fox and kill it but are so weakened by the skirmish that they lack the strength to crawl out. In an earth set, such a dog can be dug out; in a borran earth it must do as best it can to escape or be there for ever. Often the boulders which make up the borrans are polished smooth by the action of the ice and afford no purchase to allow a dog to crawl out.

Bowman knew all of the borrans of the Ullswater country. All are dangerous and some are infernal. In Skeldon's *Reminiscences of Joe Bowman*, a book that paints a strangely unreal picture of Bowman, the following story is told about his assault on one of the borrans with a favourite terrier.

> The following is a miner's story. Joe was at a joint meet. Gathered together were a number of miners. When miners are not working or striking they can find time for sport with their dogs. On this occasion they were boasting about their grand terriers. Bowman and Farrer were sitting in a corner 'saying nowt but takken o' in'. After a time Joe congratulated them on having such good terriers and was sorry he himself had none 'worth speaking of', and went on to observe that none of them offered 'to give an auld chap yan'. However, he once did have a good one. The miners were now listening. Hounds had had a meet at the other end of the county and had run a fox to earth in a big rough spot. Eventually huntsman and whip arrived with the terriers. It was a fearful looking spot. Turning to Fury Joe remarked, 'Thee and me's been good pals, but t'times come when we mun part, for if thoo gaas in here ah'll nivver see thee agen.' Fury went in. Soon there were signs of a terrific Waterloo underground. Reynard refused to bolt, and after a while Fury emerged, bitten from ear to ear, and half her mask missing, a deplorable sight. The dog was despatched to the nearest farm for treatment, and tools were sent for. At the end of three hours' working an entrance was effected

into the borran. There were all the signs of a tragic struggle – blood, hair, some belonging to fox, some to Fury. But in the corner, piled one on top of the other, were three large foxes! There was silence amongst the miners for several moments.

One of the most ghastly stories concerning the working of a borran was told to me in 1981. I was visiting Johnny Richardson at the Blencathra Hunt Kennels at Threlkeld after he had had a hard and taxing day's hunting, and it says much for Richardson's hospitality that, exhausted as he was, he answered my rather inane questions accurately and politely. We broached the subject of borrans. There are some dangerous ones in the Blencathra country and I noticed Richardson glance across at his whip, Barry Todhunter. It was a mere glance, but I sensed the whip had a tale to tell, and later, when Richardson had finished answering my questions, Barry told his tale of the 'bad earth'. The fell packs sometimes meet four days a week on foot in bad weather, and on this occasion the hunt had been called out on a lamb-killing meet midweek. Their area covers some of the roughest terrain in Britain, and the hounds had marked to ground in a borran earth near a fast-flowing gill. Todhunter put his best terrier bitch to ground (a puppy from the illustrious Sid Wilkinson's bloodline bred down from Fred Barker's Chowt-faced Rock) and heard the bitch engage the fox far below in the depths of the borran. The followers were attentive for a while, but interest waned after an hour or so, in spite of the fact that the bitch was really 'at her fox' with a vengeance, and anyway, bad weather was coming up – as it does without much warning in that part of the world. Reluctantly Todhunter moved the hounds on and tried for another, but during the afternoon a blinding snowstorm blew up, the sort of storm one sees in films about the Canadian Mounted Police or gold prospecting in the Klondike and hunting was abandoned. That night Todhunter helped to bed down and feed the hounds, but at daybreak was out to retrieve his terrier. He climbed the hill, noting that the gill was unusually short of water, and by the time he reached the borran he realized why. The snow had come down heavily on that part of the fell and a drift had blocked off the gill, diverting it into the borran. Todhunter and a few others worked frantically, shifting tons of huge stones to excavate the terrier. After much digging they came upon a fox perched above the rushing torrent flowing through the borran, but the terrier was nowhere to be found and had presumably been drowned and washed into the borran's depths.

Crags, portions of hillside plucked by passing glaciers until they resemble sections of Monument Valley or stage props for *Star Trek*, can present problems for a terrier, and numerous dogs come to grief in their fissures and crevices. Dogs trapped in such spots are in mortal danger, for there is little the terrier man can do to rescue them, the igneous rock usually being resistant to pick and shovel, the fissures unrelenting even to dynamite. A few years ago I read an account of a terrier trapped in such a fissure when, after all efforts to get the dog out had failed, the RSPCA advised calling in a vet to administer a dose of lethal gas to put an end to the poor devil's misery. The vet pumped in a cyanide-based powder, and the shrill frantic bark of the terrier stilled to a whisper before silencing. There are few fairy-tale happy endings to such stories. It is not that sort of country.

Eddie Pool, my guide and mentor during my stay in the Ullswater country, tells a curious tale of a dog trapped in that most photographed of Lakeland spots, Dove Crag, a hellish place in winter, and one that must have made a lasting impression on Clapham, author of *Foxhunting in the Lakeland Fells*, for he makes frequent mention of the spot and shows one photograph of a particularly bad place near Dove Crag.* Pool has bitter memories of the place. Jock, the son of Pool's Wasp III, crawled up a fissure in Dove Crag, and after bolting his fox the terrier tried to follow the fox out, but fell to his death in doing so.

Bowman, talking to a southern newspaperman who came north to interview that enigma of enigmas, a genuine fell man, after Clapham rediscovered the Lakes and opened up the country even as Service opened up Alaska, once described the country as a hard, tough land inhabited by hard, tough people, and if the land shaped its people, its rigours thinning out its weak, weedy or constitutionally unsound, so did it shape the terriers.

The dogs used by these hunters were tough and constitutionally as hard as iron. Most hunts couple the terriers together during hunts to prevent straying, to reduce the chance of sheep worrying and, above all, to stop dogs diving into earths at a whim. The terriers, however, can cover incredible distances during a day, even though shackled. Dennis Barrow estimates that a coupled pair of terriers will cover between ten and twenty miles during an average day's hunting, after this warm-up often being required to go to ground and kill or bolt a fox. Parkin, a famous fell walker, once walked sixty miles in one day to watch Joe Wear hunt. Chances are that he took his coupled Rock-strain fell terriers with him, dogs bred from Benson's Red Ike with an infusion of Buck's terriers. Sixty miles is an incredible distance to walk even along well-metalled roads. Across U-shaped valleys, over heather, over borrans and screes, crossing icy streams in temperatures often below zero, it is a feat to delight a superman.

Richardson can remember the time when there was no transport other than Shanks's pony to any of the meets, and hounds, huntsmen and terriers tramped their way to the meets, often covering up to thirteen miles before the hunting began. A man needs to be as tough as whipcord to survive this sort of life, and his terriers need to be tougher still. Today it is common practice to infuse the fell strains kept in hunt kennels with pedigree Lakeland terrier blood from dogs whose only test of stamina is to be able to survive a hard day's benching at Cruft's. Richardson, like all the other professional huntsmen of the fells, avoids the cross-bred show blood like the plague, for he fears that terriers bred from such dogs can never be constitutionally sound

* Clapham, *Foxhunting in the Lakeland Fells*, photograph opposite p. 102 .

2. *Walter Parkin with a terrier from the Red Rock strain.*

3. Joe Wear with Ullswater Hunt terriers.

enough to stand a very hard day's hunting, and he has seen pedigree Lakeland terriers near dead from exposure after a bad day in the fells. The Blencathra whip, Barry Todhunter, will not use a terrier stud if he suspects the dog has a 'registered' ancestor in its pedigree.

The land has determined the shape of the terrier as well as its constitution. To slide up the crevices in a crag or to weave its way between the tightly packed stones of a borran, a narrow-chested dog is essential, for it must follow wherever a big fell fox has gone. A deep chest, one with ample space for lungs and heart, is desirable, but a broad stocky dog does not find favour with fell huntsmen. Likewise, a terrier with a strong head and a good neck is desirable, for a terrier must be able to finish his fox should it decide not to bolt. Curiously, some of the best fox-killers I have encountered lacked the bull terrier heads of the type bred by Breay, and some were decidedly mousy in appearance, with narrow, snipey jaws. Bill Crisp once bred an incredibly puny dog that was death to foxes. Winch, president of the Fell and Moorland Working Terrier Club, believes that fox killing is a knack rather than the art of simply biting a fox to death. Fox-killers usually eschew the jaw-to-jaw hold of the type of duel beloved by Lucas, and after preliminary fencing go for a throat hold, throttling the fox by dint of a twisting action rather than by 'power-biting' through to the wind-pipe. Thus a strong-jawed dog is not particularly essential if Winch's theory is correct. However, many of the old fell strains – Jim Fleming's of Grasmere, Breay's of Kirkby Lonsdale, Buck's of Leyburn, for example – produced terriers with bull-terrier like jaws and mouths like steel traps.

A weatherproof jacket would seem the ideal coat to survive the sub-zero temperatures encountered on the fells in mid-winter: a hard, crisp, brush terrier type of coat that can throw off water at a shake and not finish up causing the dog to resemble a ball of mud at the end of each day's hunting. Many fell terrier men place coat as one of the most important qualities in the make-up of a fell terrier. Maurice Bell of Hawes avoids open-coated terriers like the plague, and states that such a jacket is worse than a smooth coat since it holds the water and causes the owner a great deal of distress. Johnny Richardson also rates coat as important. Braithwaite Wilson, whip to Joe Bowman and ultimately huntsman for the Ullswater Foxhounds – a man who could boast of a wide and very chequered experience – was a coat fanatic and kept only terriers with the crisp, hard, waterproof coat of what he called the 'original Patterdale' (but see page 72 for my comments on this). Wilson was interviewed by Sir Jocelyn Lucas while researching his book *Hunt and Working Terriers*, and told Sir Jocelyn that breeders were ruining the original type of terrier by introducing Bedlington blood into the strains (thereby creating a soft linty coat, perhaps). Likewise, C. R. 'Kitty' Farrer, secretary of the Ullswater Hunt, was a stickler for the correct type of jacket and he would never keep a terrier with a poor soft coat. Bowman, however, often used rough shaggy-coated terriers, large terriers with Bedlington terrier blood as well as the terriers bred at the Ullswater Hunt Kennels.

Frank Buck can remember Bowman coming to hunt in Hawes near Buck's junior school – an act that caused Buck to play truant for the day – and he recalls that Bowman's dogs were very shaggy-coated terriers. John Pool of Glenridding, one of a long line of terrier breeders in the Ullswater Hunt country, often mated his fell strains to Bedlingtons to keep the fire in them, as did Tommy Dobson of the Ennerdale and Eskdale Hunt, and both breeders produced dogs which were gutsy, hard and useful, but lacked the crisp coat described by Braithwaite Wilson and 'Kitty' Farrer as 'essential'. Breay of Kirkby Lonsdale and Fleming of Grasmere, for that matter, often bred slape-coated dogs with a thick smooth coat – water-resistant and easily cleaned; and while Maurice Bell says that he has seen Breay's dogs looking decidedly unhappy on a cold day in the Lunesdale country, Breay had his dogs out regularly with Nicholson and Nicholson describes these terriers as the ideal type of dog for the Lunesdale country.

It goes without saying that fell terriers must have courage (and a great deal of guts at that), but the courage must be tempered with discretion. A terrier with a bull-terrier type of disposition, a 'go in and fight to the death' temperament, does not find favour in the Lakes, despite what books say to the contrary. The old fell strains were game, but knew how to handle their foxes without taking too much damage to themselves. When Bland of the Melbreck felt his terriers were losing this discretion, he introduced Border terrier blood from John Dixon of Otterburn, who breeds a very useful strain of Border terrier. Likewise, Richardson will not tolerate an iron-hard, bull-headed sort of terrier. Both Richardson and Bland decry the use of registered Lakeland terrier blood, not because the pedigree blood lacks courage, but because Lakeland terriers are too game – 'damn' fool game' Jim Fleming once described them – and their courage is not tempered with discretion. Furthermore, both Bland and Richardson agree that pedigree Lakelands, or, as Richardson describes them, 'terriers with blood', are often touchy with other dogs, which makes them difficult to handle in couples and bad or impossible to kennel with hounds. Bell is of the same opinion. He dislikes the crazy game dog and states that his best and gamest terrier, a dog called Britt, was a famous fox killer, the sort of dog that killed a fox without giving it a chance to bolt but rarely took severe maulings and was quiet and docile with other dogs. Nicholson likes dogs that are game, but he values discretion and sense more highly than blind courage – he has to. Many of the earths in the Lunesdale country are badger sets, and in such places a headstrong dog soon comes to grief.

Size is a controversial subject, and most books on northern working terriers state that a huge terrier is needed to work the fell earths. Nothing could be further from the truth. I questioned Nicholson of the Lunesdale, Bland of the Melbreck, Barrow of the Ullswater, Ogilvie of the Coniston and Richardson of the Blencathra. Not one of them believes that a dog much bigger than thirteen inches is any use to them, and some have kept quite small terriers. Breay, it is true, did produce a few big terriers from time to time, and some of his blood is probably responsible for the giants that are winning at working terrier shows in the Midlands and the south. Wally Wyld at the Grove and Rufford Foxhounds kept a fairly pure strain of Breay fell terrier, and while Wyld (nor anyone for that matter) could not fault the strain for courage, he found them too big to work the earths in Nottingham. The fox is *Vulpes vulpes* from Land's End to John O'Groats, so Wyld's criticism must hold good for most parts of the country. Now and again, however, a good big one that can do the work in spite of its size is born. In 1932 (some dispute this date, I should add), Albert Benson produced his famous Red Ike. Richardson describes Ike as a big Irish terrier type of dog, but adds that he was a really grand terrier to work in spite of his size, and there is a saying in the Shires that a big terrier can get up close to a fox if he really wants to. But there is time enough to talk about the various fell strains. What about the people who bred them?

PART TWO: THE PEOPLE

We were travelling home from the village of Patterdale, near Ullswater, after interviewing Anthony Barker, the sixty-year-old son of Fred Barker who once hunted a pack of Pennine Foxhounds at Ouseby during the First World War. Kendal loomed on the horizon, and my companions, Theodora Moritz, an American hunting enthusiast who had come over from New Jersey for a night's rat hunting, and David Hancock, my friend and photographer, began to reflect on the day's work. Mrs Moritz had listened to Anthony Barker for nearly ten minutes before she had begun to understand the curious Cumbrian accent, while David had been fascinated with Anthony's photographs of his father and his dogs. Barker had patiently spent three hours telling us tales of hunting in the Lake District, tales which made Clapham's account seem a little like an Enid Blyton description of 'the lake scene', and a further hour filling in a vital gap in my knowledge of the pedigrees of fell terriers. As we travelled home along the M6, heading south to Birmingham, we mused on the stories told by Anthony, tales of the first badger dug in the Ullswater country, stories of wartime hunts when the diminutive but dynamic Barker kept the Ullswater Hounds until Joe Wear returned from the war. We were passing Knutsford service station when David spoke. 'They're a different breed of person,' he uttered and both Mrs Moritz and I could do little else but agree.

Early man settled on the edges of the Lake District, and there is little evidence to suggest that he inhabited the somewhat more hostile and forbidding central area. Near Calder Hall, at a place called Eninside Tarn, evidence of a primitive Stone Age settlement, c. 3000 B.C., has been unearthed – a rare combination of the old and the new, for there is an atomic power station only a matter of miles away from that site, a site which yielded stone tools, fishing spears and the remains of a hollowed-out log that had once been a dug-out canoe.

During Bronze Age times, however, there is evidence of numerous Celtic settlements along the coast, and in all probability these settlers came by boat from Wales. Certainly there is considerable evidence of the Welsh language in the place-names of Cumbria, and the very name Cumbria is derived from Cumry, the Welsh name for Wales. Likewise glen, as in Glenridding, is derived from the Welsh word *glyn*, a valley. The origin of the name Penrith can easily be worked out by any moderately fluent Welsh speaker: *pen* = a head; *ryde* = a ford.

In spite of the fact that the area is rich in minerals and some of its streams are stained with haematite (an ore of iron), the Iron Age seems to have passed the Lake District by, and there is evidence to suggest that when the rest of Britain had perfected the manufacture of iron tools and weapons and had become proficient in smelting iron from the haematite and limonite ores, the Lake District remained an anachronism and still worked in bronze and even, in some districts, in flint. Perhaps the Iron Age people who had come in from southern Europe did not bother to colonize the lakes, or perhaps the lake dwellers, conservative then as now, resisted any change to their way of life. Certainly there is evidence to suggest that, by nature, the lake dweller is mistrustful of innovation and often hostile to strangers. But I run ahead of my tale, I fear.

On the subject of hostility to outsiders, however, the enmity 'twixt the Lake District dwellers and the Scots, an enmity that only ceased in 1603 when James I became King of England and Scotland, dates from Celtic times. The Brigantes, a tribe of Celts who lived in Cumbria, were continuously at war with the Novantae, who lived just across the Scottish border, and raiding expeditions both into Scotland and Cumbria were incessant during the Roman occupation. Some Scottish etymologists even claim that the word 'brigand' is derived from the atrocities inflicted by raiding Brigante tribesmen north of the border, though this view is controversial. Agricola led several punitive expeditions against these Scots, however, but seemingly to little avail, for there existed bitter enmity between Scot and Cumbrian even into the reign of James I.

Viking stock rather than Anglo-Saxon seems to have been the next racial group to settle in the Lakes, since there is little evidence for an Anglo-Saxon colonization of Cumbria. Certainly the use of the Norse language for counting sheep was current in Cumbria up until the beginning of this century, but far from the murder, rape and pillage one has been taught to associate with the Scandinavian invasions, the Viking occupation of the Lake District seems to have been relatively bloodless and the northern invaders seem to have been absorbed by the Celtic inhabitants of Cumbria. These invaders left a considerable mark on the Lake District, however, for over one hundred place-names are derived from the Norse tongue. Thwaite is a derivation of *thveit*, meaning a piece of cleared forest land; dale is derived from *dal*, a valley; fell from *fjall*, a moor. Likewise, mere is simply a corruption of *mjir*, a lake. Various leaders gave their names to places. Hawkswater and Hawkshead are derived from Häkon rather than from the name of a bird, and Ambleside is simply a corruption of Hamil's seat.

By the time of William Rufus (there is little reference to the area known as Cumbria today prior to Rufus's reign) the population of the Lakes consisted of scarcely more than 5,000 people – a sheepherding population of virtually pure Viking and Celtic blood. This population seems to have increased rather slowly until the reign of Elizabeth I – though it received a severe thinning during the reign of Edward II when the Scots came south in force under Bruce, raping, impaling and stealing cattle and sheep. Towers similar to the Martello towers built during the Napoleonic Wars were constructed during this time, and the remains of such a tower can still be seen near Windermere.

Flemish weavers came to the Lakes during the fourteenth century and taught the population new methods of spinning, weaving and dyeing – in fact, a particular shade of green is still referred to as Kendal green after the town where the manufacture of this dye had perfected colour and mordant. Later an engineer, the builder of the first practical steam engine, invented a bobbin machine that revolutionized the cotton industry and bobbin-making became a major occupation in the Lakes. Tommy Dobson, the volatile pixie-sized man who became the Master of the Eskdale and Ennerdale Foxhounds, was a bobbin-maker by profession; and Edmund Porter, the present hunts-man for that hunt, still has Tommy's indenture papers in the hunt archives.

During the first Elizabeth's reign, Lord Burghley, chancellor to the queen, decided that the Lake District had mineral supplies worth exploiting, particularly copper supplies, which were essential in the boat-building industry. But though the supplies of ore were fairly abundant, labour, and above all skilled miners capable of moving this ore, were not, for the Lake District was farmed by families of fiercely independent shepherds like the Nicholsons (the ancestors of John Nicholson of the Lunesdale Foxhounds) who were reluctant to take part in mining activities.

Burghley therefore turned his eyes to the Continent to find his miners and in 1566 imported Daniel Hochstetter, one of a long line of geologists from Germany, to prospect the land. Hochstetter found copper in plenty and large supplies of lead, but was unable to conscript labour for his enterprises. Thus he imported miners from Germany and Holland to dig his mines, among whom were the ancestors of the Pools and the Tysons, two important hunting families in the Lake District. Literally overnight the Lakes became a fac-simile of a Hollywood Yukon set. Hochstetter sunk two lead mines at Dale Head and Goldscope, and a fairly productive copper mine at Ellers. The population reacted violently to the newcomers and a state of near war pre-vailed in the Lake District for a number of years. Things became so bad in the 1570s that Hochstetter had to move his miners to a site on Derwent Isle for their own protection. Most books state that the Lakelanders' attitude towards the German miners was unreasonable, but there is considerable evidence to the contrary. Eddie Pool, a descendant of those same miners, tells tales handed down by his family about their wild nature, and the Lake District received a fairly rough handling from these immigrants, until the population absorbed them. Some books state that the fell hound, a type of dog distinct from the English foxhound, owes at least part of its ancestry to dogs brought in by the German miners, and though I can find no evidence to corroborate the theory, I have met quite a few fell hound breeders who believe the original fell hounds came in with the German settlers.

Dutch miners again invaded the fells in 1690, prospecting for copper, and opening new shafts and reopening those of Hochstetter to mine for copper. Both the German and the Dutch miners sank their shafts in peculiar ways – ways, in any case, that must seem peculiar to modern miners, who are used to pumps to drain the workings of the water that seeps in from the surrounding rock. They sank their shafts into the hills, drilling upwards from the base of the hill so as to allow surplus water to drain out of the workings. John Gordon, in his book *The Dandie Dinmont Terriers*, mentions one theory concerning the origin of that dog and its cousin the Bedlington. At one time it was supposed that the Dutch miners brought this type of terrier to the north, but there is more convincing evidence to suggest that these were dogs bred by Romany families such as the Jeffersons and the Faas, and by Scottish tinker families such as the Jacksons, who plied their trades on both sides of the border. These families were called muggers in Scotland (I have been unable to find the origin of this name) and potters in the Lakes (some of them travelled in potcart types of caravan). Johnny Richardson can remember several of these potters who travelled with lurchers and Bedlington terriers, buying second-grade wool from the Lakeland farms. I believe that these and not the Dutch miners were the first breeders of the Dandie Dinmont and Bedlington terriers.

In 1830, however, John Barrett, a Cornwall-based mining engineer, came north with teams of workers and opened the Coniston Mining Company near Leverswater, and the hills around this area are literally undermined with excavations. Barrett brought revolutionary mining methods to the Lake District. Before the Cornish invasion, mines were simply holes burrowed upwards into the hills to allow water to drain away from the working. Now, however, the methods of mining employed in Cornwall, using an extra-ordinary pumping device constructed of dozens of joined solid oak spars, allowed mining to proceed far more easily and to be worked in difficult lodes. Barrett sank dozens of shafts near Coniston, and every few years some climber or rambler seems to discover yet another old 'Barrett' shaft. I believe this Cornish invasion of the fells to be most important, for there is con-siderable evidence that many of the miners brought terriers with them from the West Country and these terriers entered into the pedigrees of the fell terriers of the Lakes.

In 1841, yet another emigré population began to settle in the west Lakes. The potato famine of Ireland drove many smallholders and crofters to sell up their land and leave Ireland. America took the vast majority, but some settled in the Lake District, some at Ravenglass (curiously, there is a historical theory that the Romans constructed a port at Ravenglass in order to invade Ireland), but the majority seemingly near Egremont and Cleator Moor. Alan Johnston, a Lakeland terrier breeder from Egremont, grandson of the famous Alf Johnston, once told me that Cleator Moor still has a strong Irish tradition, and there are some fairly hectic celebrations there on St Patrick's Day. Winch believes that these immigrants brought terriers with them, and these terriers too entered into the bloodlines of the fell terriers of the Lake District.

Few of the mines of the Lake District are worth working today, and the traditional mining families, such as the Pools, now work at other employments. Slate quarrying, however, is still practised in the Lakes at the Old Man of Coniston, Broughton Moor, Kirkstone (the Kirkstone quarry is a huge but, oddly enough, not an unsightly working) and Burlington, and roughly one in nine of the male population of the Lake District still finds employment in the slate quarries.

Sheep farming remains an important occupation in the Lake District, though the land is so unproductive that only the small hardy Herdwick sheep (sheep reputedly introduced by the early Viking settlers, though I have my doubts) are profitable, and the grazing is so poor that the hills can sustain less than one sheep an acre. The fox hunts in the south of England are largely social events and perform few useful functions, no matter what hunt supporters say to the contrary. In the fells, however, the fell packs play an important part in the economy, and both sheep farmers and hunt servants function almost symbiotically. Most of the huntsmen and whips of the fell packs come from sheep-farming families. The Chapmans, who hunted the Coniston Hunt (George and his son Anthony), come from a long line of sheep farmers, as do the Nicholsons, and early agricultural show records show many class winners for Herdwick sheep owned by various members of the Nicholson family. Likewise, Johnny Richardson is from farming stock. Hardasty of the Melbreck retired from hunt service and returned to sheep farming, leaving the hunt in the capable hands of Richard Bland, his son-in-law. The Porter family, Willie, Jack and Edmund, are of farming stock, and the Irvings, Arthur (who hunted the Eskdale and Ennerdale), Harry (the secretary of the Eskdale and Ennerdale) and Willie (who hunted the Melbreck) were all originally trained as shepherds. Barrow of the Ullswater and Ogilvie of the Coniston are some of the few fell-pack huntsmen who have no sheep farms in the pedigree, for Barrow is from a family of quarrymen and Ogilvie a doctor's son. Maurice Bell of Hawes is also from sheep-farming stock and I recently heard he had resigned from his job as a construction worker and was buying a sheep farm near Hawes.

It is perhaps vital that the huntsman of the fell packs should know something at least of sheep farming, for not only are they required to control sheep-worrying foxes, but the fell pack committees have a rather curious, almost feudal system concerning the employment of hunt servants. The hunt servants of the mounted packs to the south are full-time hunt servants and are kept on a full pay during the summer months. Not so the fell huntsman and whip. At the end of the season, the hounds are put out to near-by farms if possible, but servants are thanked and paid a tiny retainer fee, then literally cast adrift to find employment during the summer months.

Most, if not all, find summer-time work in the near-by sheep farms, dipping and shearing as well as farm maintenance work. All in all, few jobs are as taxing or as financially unrewarding as the job of a fell pack hunt servant, yet there are applicants in plenty when posts fall vacant. Perhaps there is more to the Lakeland way of life than the acquisition of wealth, or maybe the theology of making a fast buck has not yet become the official religion of Cumbria.

4. Fell huntsmen, 1953. Left to right: Harry Hardasty (Melbreck), Walter Parkin (Lunesdale), Joe Wear (Ullswater), Anthony Chapman (Coniston), Johnny Richardson (Blencathra) and Arthur Irving (Eskdale and Ennerdale).

PART THREE: THE TERRIERS

1. The Quarry

Few areas in Europe have as rich a fauna as the Lake District. Perhaps the terrain is conducive to wildlife, or maybe the fact that the Lake District has a population of less than a hundred residents to the square mile (a ninth of the national average) has something to do with it. Certainly it is a district where near-extinct animals not only hang on to their precarious existence but, given a chance, actually increase.

At the Ullswater Hotel one night I listened attentively as two local farmers talked excitedly of a pine marten that had appeared on a stand of trees near one of their farmhouses. Martens are admittedly uncommon in the Lake District, but then they are extinct in the rest of Britain, for any animal with a worth-while pelt would find itself running the gauntlet of extinction in a country such as ours. I was recently sent a letter by a young man called O'Brien from Millom, Cumbria, with a photograph of Willie Porter standing in a doorway with Tommy Dobson. I already had this photograph, but Mr O'Brien stated that he had heard tell how Willie Porter (*c*. 1912) often hunted these marten, or marten cats as they were once called, in the Lake District with the Eskdale and Ennerdale Hounds. While I doubt there is documentary evidence to support the statement, ample evidence exists that taxidermists, catering for the whims of private collectors at the turn of the century in an age that appreciated stuffed animals with glass eyes peering sightlessly out of glass cases, often approached Robinson, a stone worker who lived near Egremont, to obtain marten pelts and cadavers. Robinson was a renowned hunter and was known for being one who could obtain a good terrier or so. No doubt working those lonely roads gave him ample opportunity to be with (and enter his terriers to) a variety of quarry.

Polecats or foulmartens (once called foumarts in the Lakes), so called because they give off a foul, pungent odour when upset – an odour that

(Tommy Dobson) (Willie Porter)
Eskdale and Ennerdale Forkounds.

5. *Tommy Dobson and Willie Porter with some of Dobson's Bedlington/fell hybrids.*

instantly distinguishes them from the less obnoxious pine martens or sweet-martens – were also found in the Lakes at the turn of the century. In fact, my earliest memory of writing anything about terriers was of copying an epitaph for a very game fell terrier into my school roughbook, the appraisal of the dog reading that he could face a foumart and draw a brock – no mean feat for a terrier, believe me, and quite a few southern terrier men used polecats to test the mettle of young terriers. Polecats, when roused, not only release a foul, sickening, persistent odour that clings to clothes and fur for weeks, but also bite with incredible speed and savagery. Their interest in poultry (polecat = poule cat = hen cat) virtually guaranteed their extinction in the farmlands of Britain, but they are reputedly still found in the Lake District. A dark musteline flashed in front of my car on the road between Penrith and Keswick in August 1981, but whether it was a polecat or simply an escaped ferret or wild mink I did not have time to see.

In spite of the high lead content of many Cumbrian streams – a lead content so high that some authorities state the water to be dangerous – fish abound in some of the brooks and rivers of the Lake District, and at one time the country could boast an extraordinary number of otters. Two packs of otter hounds controlled – if controlled is the correct word – the otter popula-tion of the Lakes, these being the Carlisle and the Kendal and District Hounds. (The Kendal was disbanded in 1978–9, but at the time of writing the pack of magnificent hounds is still being kept at the expense of its former master, Stephen Hollins-Gibson, and its former huntsman, Tom Harrison, a superb hound and terrier man.) Jack Nanson worked his terriers to otter with the Kendal and District Otterhounds during Lucas's visit to the hunt in 1930, and Nanson used a somewhat refined strain of Lakeland terrier – a neat type of dog, by all accounts, with obvious fox-terrier blood. Glaister, the deputy master of the Carlisle Otterhounds, kept a strain of pedigree fox terrier and Border terriers, and also used what Lucas describes as cross-breds, which were in all probability the rough-and-ready fell terriers being bred around the Carlisle area at that time. In fact, it has to be said that Lucas's background research in his chapter on the Lakeland terrier is some-what sparse.

So numerous were otters at the turn of the century that miners and farmers often spent Sunday mornings hunting them. G. H. Long, an octogenarian born at Egremont but now living in Bedford, recalls these hunts. The miners, quarrymen and farmers congregated near Egremont each Sunday during the summer and ran a mixed pack of fell terriers and beagles (put out from a local pack for the summer months) at otter – and not without success, by the sound of it. Long's tales of pre-First World War hunting in the Lake District are fascinating, and one could easily swamp a book of this size with his stories.

Badgers are not nearly so numerous in the Lake District as one might imagine, though there is evidence to suggest that they are increasing in numbers in Cumbria and around Troutbeck are very numerous. Some

41

6. *Armstrong's Rock and other terriers hunting otter on the river Lune.*

districts have a fair number of badgers, but in other districts they are very rare. The dig organized by John Pool and Anthony Barker (see accompanying photograph) was the first badger that John Pool (an inveterate hunter) had ever seen in Ullswater, and certainly neither Clapham nor Bowman make reference to badgers in Ullswater Hunt country. Robert Robertson of Newcastle upon Tyne once told me that when he visited the Lake District to hunt there, most of the terrier men were somewhat less than ready to put their dogs to ground to a badger, the reasons being obvious. Some places, particularly the borran earths, are undiggable, and a badly mauled terrier can find it very difficult to scale up the smooth-sided, near-perpendicular boulders that make up many borrans.

7. *Anthony Barker, Frank Buck (?) and John Pool with the first badger taken in Ullswater Hunt country. The near-black terrier at their feet is Fleming's Myrt, ancestor of most modern working fell terriers.*

Robertson hunted a strain of Russells which he obtained from a hunt kennel in Ireland – terriers used to nip, bark at and bolt foxes for hounds. Lake District fell terriers during Robertson's days were a little too hard to deal with badgers effectively, for some closed with the badger as they would a fox and the result was predictable if horrendous. Fell strains were simply not bred for badger hunting, and in fact the first dog I ever saw dismembered by a badger was a wheaten fell terrier that a man from Southerndown, South Wales, had brought back from Troutbeck in 1948. He called it a Lakeland terrier, and with schoolboy cleverness I informed him that Lakeland terriers were really black and tan and resembled small Welsh terriers. I can still remember his face as I gave him my words of wisdom. Indeed, there is a lot to be said about keeping *enfants terribles* in suspended animation until they have outgrown the 'knowledge'.

Badgers, at any rate, are quite numerous in the Lake District at present, though whether they have simply spread from surrounding areas or been brought there by terrier enthusiasts eager to provide sporting quarry closer to home is an open question. Many Lakeland hunters start their dogs on badger today to teach them discretion, that is, to hold back at quarry and not race in and tackle it. A few quick skirmishes with a badger allows a terrier puppy to understand that life below ground is far from beer and skittles, teaching him to bay at his quarry rather than tackle it full tilt. Thus, when the dog enters to fox, he holds back a little, for he understands that creatures found below ground can give him trouble. Most southern hunters try their dogs to badger after they have had considerable experience of dealing with fox, but fell hunters usually enter their dogs to badger to train them for the legitimate sport of fox hunting.

On the subject of Lakeland foxes – the traditional quarry of the fell terrier, the beast they have been bred to tackle, so to speak – a great deal of unscientific nonsense has been spoken and written. Even Clapham falls into the trap – a trap well littered by other writers better supplied with enthusiasm than scientific informativeness – of stating that the fell fox was a distinct variety of fox during John Peel's day (Peel having died in 1854). This is incorrect, and there is no evidence to suggest that the fell fox was in any way different from its lowland cousin in type, colour, courage or size. Clapham goes on to relate how the fell fox was once a large animal, but infusions of foxes brought into areas around the Lakes to restock for adequate hunting reduced the size of the fell fox considerably, the so-called 'greyhound foxes' now being rarely seen.

Clapham must be forgiven his error, however, for not only was this folk-lore belief probably instilled in him by his seniors, but a fox running from hounds across a bleak and forbidding fell does look enormous. Most foxes have a hard time making ends meet in such places, especially in the rabbit-free times of today. Breay once took over 1,000 rabbits in a winter off just one fell which he hunted. Today one would be hard pushed to take twenty from that same fell. But even during the time of Clapham's research, the fells were

8. *Salters Hall Wood badger dig. Left to right: Peter Long, Jim Kitchen, Jones Snr., Charlie Wear, Dick Tomlinson, Dick Jones, Harold Tomlinson, Pat Flusky, Charlie Suddart, Moss Rothery, Bill Tomlinson and Rawlinson, whose dog, the old-type Bedlington, was killed by a badger. Dogs, left to right: Grip, Bess, Floss, Nettle, Tess, Gillert, Grip.*

45

9. *A fragment of a photograph taken in 1941 showing Breay out hunting with Blitz.*

not rich in provender for predators, and most fox scats indicated that beetles sustained the fox population during summer months. Thus the fell fox had a much leaner time than his cousins in the Quorn or the Belvoir country and his frame was thinly fleshed. Such a gaunt animal, running over cover-free fells, would appear large even to the experienced eye, and Jim Blake of Burnley, a good hunter by any standards, is one of those who still believes that huge foxes of a different type inhabit Cumbria. Large foxes are, of course, taken from time to time in the fells. Maurice Bell, hunting on the edge of the Lunesdale country, took a twenty-three-pound fox as recently as 1980 – an animal considerably larger than Clapham's pair of eighteen pounders taken by the Coniston Foxhounds hunted by Anthony Chapman's father, the late George Chapman, at High Dale Park in 1913. Even so, much larger foxes than these are taken by southern packs from time to time, and a twenty-eight-and-a-quarter-pound giant was killed in Worcester some two decades back. Fell foxes are not a different species, and a fox of average weight taken by, say, the Ullswater Foxhounds during the season would be no different from the same average fox taken by the Quorn or the Meynell.

What makes the fell fox a distinct animal from the fox of the south is the nature of the terrain over which he runs, which is why the fell packs hunt on foot, for no horse could possibly negotiate the sides of those U-shaped valleys or travel across the acres of scree and borran.

Of course, the piles of stone that are the result of ice or the quarryman's pick and dynamite make ideal breeding spots for foxes and also act as sanctuaries into which a fox can dart when pressed by hounds. At the risk of sounding a little unscientific myself, I believe that a race of stone-dwelling foxes may be being created in the Lakeland fells – a race that shuns the rabbit earths used by most foxes and which breeds and hides in the huge piles of stone that litter the hills. Such earths are not diggable, and in certain places a terrier can do little good against a fox, jammed between two huge boulders deep in the earth. Rabbit-earth skulking foxes are usually – and I have to say 'usually' with tongue in cheek in the light of my own experiences – dug, and therefore do not perpetuate their lines, whereas the borran-dwelling fox often defeats all attempts to kill him and therefore lives to run and fight another day. If there is a difference in type, a dichotomy between the lowland and fell fox, I believe it is this interest in skulking in stone piles. Some of these stone piles have to be seen to be believed. Early in 1981, David Hancock and I hunted with Bell at Penn Hill, and a moderate-sized fox was found skulking beneath the rocks on a hillside. After a gargantuan dig involving shifting blocks weighing two hundredweight or more, Laurie Dent succeeded in dislodging the fox, which bolted and was killed by hounds. Bell viewed the havoc wrought by the dig and said quietly, 'Easy day this, some places is quite bad!'

Clapham states that when a Lakeland fox is hard pressed, he often makes for the crags rather than for a spot beneath the borrans, and lies up on a ledge out of reach of the hounds, much as a cat perches on a town dweller's window-sill to escape the attentions of street curs. Hounds attempting to follow foxes along these narrow ledges often come to grief. Clapham recalls a young hound who pursued his fox along a narrow ledge and crashed to earth with the fox, falling 200 feet – an event he describes as 'not a pleasant sight'. He also mentions a fell fox in the Blencathra country which fell forty feet and ran off, badly shaken by its fall but still alive.

Foxes are not seen here simply as the sporting beasts that the mounted hunters of the south consider them to be, though a fox run by a pack of fell hounds gives sport a-plenty, I can assure you. Fell packs are kept to control the number of foxes in the country they hunt, and are inclined to be treated as adjuncts to the shepherds' livelihood. For instance, the Blencathra hunt three or four times a week, but are often called out to hunt a lamb-killing fox on rest days. In fact it might be said that the fell packs function symbiotically with the shepherd, for the hounds take the fallen sheep (some hunts will not feed mutton since it is too fattening, and Maurice Bell is very antipathetic to the feeding of sheep to his hounds), and in turn hunt down marauding vixen abroad on killing lamb during the early months of the year. Thus hunting in the Lake District does not stop as soon as the vixens are in cub, as in other hunt counties to the south, but continues until mid April. On the subject of breeding vixens, some vixens do litter down with other vixens in borran and rock earths. Maurice Bell once took fourteen cubs – too large a litter for one vixen and quite possibly the litters of maybe three vixens – from a rock earth a few years ago. He showed me photographs of the cubs, and Buck commented to me that this is by no means uncommon in the Lakes. But the time has come to leave the subject of the quarry and deal with the meat of the book: namely, the terriers themselves.

2. Origins and Bloodlines

It is not surprising that, with the amount of huntable, small, predatory beasts living in the Lake District, Cumbria should have produced a race of excellent, hard-working terriers. Funnily enough, although volumes have been written on the histories and origins of the Bedlington and Dandie Dinmont terriers (containing some serious research, but mostly given to rather absurd make-believe), the cynologist will find little relevant historical data relating to that Cinderella of northern working terriers, the fell or Lakeland terrier.

Miss Irene Morris of Stroud, Gloucester, an authority on the Kennel Club registered Lakeland terrier, believes that the original fell terriers were simply relatively unadulterated forms of the now extinct rough-coated, black-and-tan terrier, the sort of terrier kept at most foxhound kennels before the white-bodied terrier supposedly bred from Colonel Thornton's dog Pitch (see Sidney Castle's *Monograph on the Fox Terrier*) became popular. Indeed, Daniel's *Rural Sports* (1807) shows a decidedly Lakeland type of terrier of the kind sometimes bred by Fleming of Grasmere at the end of the Second World War, baying rather incongruously at a fox which has its head outside the mouth of the earth. Another interesting print from Daniel's book shows 'The Old Earth Stopper' with a pair of terriers, one of which would certainly pass for one of the Ullswater terriers during Joe Bowman's reign as huntsman (the sort of dog that may also have given rise to the Border terrier). This type of terrier was worked in England and Wales, and eventually (with improvements brought about by mating the black and tan terrier with fox terriers) gave rise to the modern Welsh terriers. Certainly long after the English fox-hunt kennels had forsaken the old black-and-tan, rough-coated terrier in favour of the more elegant fox terrier, some hunts in Wales kept the strains of black and tan alive. The Ynysfor terrier depicted in Lucas's *Hunt and Working Terriers* is a fairly typical specimen of the old rough-coated, black-and-tan terrier, and would fit unnoticed into a group of fell terriers in Clapham's book. The evidence against Miss Morris's theory is, quite simply, that few of the old fell terriers were black and tan. Most were wheaten, red or blue and tan, and few photographs of very early fell terriers resemble the dog baying at the fox in Daniel's *Rural Sports*. However, most of the early fell-terrier photographs are of wheaten-and-tan animals, and few black-and-tan terriers were found in the early fell-pack kennels. Yet, by type, the early fell terrier is identical to the old rough-coated, black-and-tan animals.

Archie Kirk, in his tiny but interesting book, *The Lakeland Terrier*, states his belief that the Lakeland terrier is the result of crossing rough-coated, black-and-tan terriers, Irish terriers and Dandie Dinmont terriers, offering as proof of his theory the fact that, while the ideal jacket of the Lakeland terrier is the hard, crisp, water-repellent coat of the Irish terrier, now and again a puppy with the soft open coat and silky topknot of the Dandie Dinmont appears in litters of pedigree Lakeland terriers. Miss Morris of Kelda Kennels breeds a puppy fitting this description in some of her litters, and she showed me an animal of the type when I visited her kennels at Stroud in 1981. Certainly the bitch shown me could well have been bred down from a Dandie Dinmont type or from terriers with a strong trace of Bedlington in their not too distant bloodlines.

There have been terriers in the Lake District for hundreds of years – terriers used to kill and bolt foxes, kill martens and hunt out otters in the rivers which spread like the spokes of a huge cartwheel from the centre of the Lakeland area. But little has been written about these dogs. Winch, an authority on the fell terriers and the instigator of this book, could find only one scanty reference to terriers in the volumes written about that most famous Caldbeck hunter, John Peel. Seemingly these people, literate enough to write books, did not consider data concerning the fell terrier worthy of putting into print, and those who owned the early fell terriers were probably unable to write a book.

Clapham's book, *Fox Hunting in the Lakeland Fells* (1920), now attacked by many as inaccurate, though Clapham was considered to be the authority on fell terriers until the early 1950s, did much to bring the fell terrier to the notice of the outside world. Certainly the photographs – thin sheets stuck by hand into the original book – are fascinating and give an interesting insight into the terrier breed in the days after the First World War. At the end of the nineteenth century, the population of the Lakeland fells was low and the villages where these terriers were bred were very isolated. There were railway lines to Windermere and Coniston, but these had been built to transport rich business tycoons to their summer houses rather than to facilitate contact with the outside world. Thus the terriers bred by the natives of these tiny townships were produced by mating closely related stock, for contact with other strains of terrier was rare. Bands of tinkers, the 'potters' dealing in poor-grade wool, did, it is true, sometimes bring in Bedlington or Dandie Dinmont types, and probably also brought fell terriers from other towns to trade and sell to the hunting enthusiasts, but such visits would have been rare and new terrier blood hard to come by. Thus, by dint of an inbreeding programme, a programme followed by a rigorous culling of inferior stock – stock lacking in courage and of poor constitution – each district tended to produce its own type of terrier.

There is considerable evidence – for example, the photographs of the Pool family and their dogs, the much-photographed Joe Bowman – to support the view that the early Ullswater terriers were wheaten or pale tan in colour, with long loose coats that showed strong traces of Bedlington ancestry. Indeed, both John Pool and his father Anthony before him (the Pools were famous terrier breeders in the Ullswater country) mated their fell terriers to a gutsy strain of Bedlington when they felt the power of the strain was running low. Yet, when Jocelyn Lucas was researching his book, *Hunt and Working Terriers*, he visited the Ullswater Hunt Kennels at Glenridding and was told by Braithwaite Wilson, the huntsman for the Ullswater, that these infusions of Bedlington terrier and white terrier blood were ruining what Wilson called the original Patterdale type. Wilson bred a strain of tight-coated, straight-legged, black-and-tan terrier, most of which had cocked or pricked ears, and he possibly considered these to be the original Patterdale type of terrier. Yet photographs of Bowman taken at one of his early Mardale meets show him with very Bedlington-looking fell terriers, and nowhere can I find photographs of early black-and-tan Ullswater (or 'Patterdale') terriers. (Patterdale lies in the heart of the Ullswater Hunt country.)

In the Eskdale and Ennerdale Hunt country, Tommy Dobson deliberately mated his strain of fell terriers to a very game, gutsy strain of chocolate Bedlington terrier to improve working ability and produce tough game dogs capable of finishing off foxes that refused to bolt. Many tales are told of how Tommy Dobson used a strain of tinker-bred Bedlington to mate to his fell

10. Anthony Pool with old-type lakeland/fell terrier with Bedlington terrier blood.

terriers, but there is little evidence to suggest that Dobson used tinker-bred Bedlingtons for this purpose. In fact, some of the very best working strains of Bedlington were being bred close by at Egremont, so Dobson had little need to seek out tinkers and use their dogs. The first-cross Bedlington/fell terriers were fairly hideous, as photographs often show, but a photograph of Tommy Dobson taken with Dobbie, his favourite terrier, in about 1906, shows him with quite a typey box-headed terrier displaying little of its Bedlington ancestry save for a rather tufted head and a chocolate-coloured coat. Many pedigree Lakeland terrier breeders occasionally throw up a chocolate-coloured puppy in their litters, and most breeders believe that Dobson's chocolate-coloured Bedlington outcross first introduced this colour into the breed. Some breeders even refer to these chocolates as one of Tommy Dobson's chocolates. However, there is another more curious introduction which may have been responsible for this colour appearing in Lakeland terrier litters. I visited the Eskdale and Ennerdale Hunt Kennels last year and photographed Edmund Porter with two fell types of hunt terrier that were nearly identical to the early dogs of Tommy Dobson. While they were black and tan rather than blue, chocolate or wheaten (they had been sired by an N'Beck Kennel male that in turn had been sired by a pedigree Lakeland terrier), their type

11. Tommy Dobson with Dobbie.

and coat was identical to the dogs Dobson bred between 1880 and his death in 1910.

It is my belief that many of the shaggy-coated strains of fell terrier of the type bred by Laurie Dent at Pennhill (see photograph), and called for want of a better name Border/Lakelands, are probably descended from these Bedlington-cross fell terriers bred by Dobson, Pool and other breeders. Certainly many of these strains of Border/Lakeland show very little Border-terrier influence. When Tommy Dobson died, Willie Porter took over the pack and Dobson's terriers and continued to hunt them, if anything more fanatically than Tommy. Few people today have Willie's stamina or tenacity, it seems. At Cruft's in 1982 I met Dobson of the N'Beck Kennels, whose family can boast generations of first-class terrier men. Dobson's grandfather knew Willie Porter quite well, and states Porter would leave home on a Monday with his pack and his terriers and not reappear until the Thursday if scenting conditions were good. Tales of the stamina of Willie Porter are

12. Laurie Dent of Pennhill's strain of border/lakeland.

legion in the Lakes, and while some exaggeration must be allowed for, it is fair to state that Porter must have possessed near-superhuman powers of endurance. One tale I heard in Eskdale was of a hunt that started on a fine sunny day, but by afternoon a blinding snowstorm had blown up – a snowstorm that sent most of the hunt followers scurrying for shelter. Willie, however, continued the hunt, killing his fox and arriving at kennels at 3 a.m., half-frozen but taking food and rest only after he had bedded down and fed his hounds. Dobson's quixotic nature and diminutive shape attracted much publicity, but a whole book, and a good book at that, could truly be written on Willie Porter. Photographs of Willie, taken some ten years after Dobson's death, show him with leggy box-headed terriers which have only a hint of Bedlington blood about them.

The Coniston Hunt terriers were, at the beginning of the twentieth century, a fairly unsightly bunch, though their working ability was beyond question. Clapham's photographs, one of which was taken as early as 1908, nearly twelve years before the book was published, show some rather scruffy hunt terriers, loose coated, out at the elbows and wheaten in colour. One of Clapham's photographs of Jummy, a one-eyed terrier, resembled a rather badly made Norwich terrier rather than a fell terrier. Another photograph, taken outside the Traveller's Rest, shows the Coniston huntsman with tall, rather unsightly houndy terriers with distinct traces of Bedlington and perhaps other breeds as well. Curiously, however, one of the most important bloodlines in the creation of the modern fell terrier was bred by Jim Fleming who lived at Grasmere in the heart of the Coniston country, though it must be admitted that the origin of Fleming's strain is shrouded in some mystery.

The Blencathra Hunt terriers at the turn of the century were a very different kettle of fish, though for some reason Clapham has no photographs of these in his book – possibly Clapham, who was a hound enthusiast, had little interest in fell terriers anyway. He tended to mention even the Coniston Hunt terriers as rather an afterthought. The terriers bred by Jim Dalton were very classy, as the photograph of Turk (c. 1900), his favourite terrier, show. Turk was a typey box-headed terrier, straight-fronted and blue and tan – a terrier of the type which would easily win at a hunt show today. He was an excellent fox killer, was used on many bitches in the Blencathra Hunt

13. *Jim Dalton's Turk – a famous fell terrier with a dash of Major Williams' fox terrier blood – c. 1910. Turk's strain was continued by Johnny Richardson.*

country and produced a number of white puppies – puppies which, far from being destroyed, found a ready market among the rabbit hunters in the Lake District, for G. H. Long states that these rabbit hunters believed their terriers to be better workers or rabbiting and ferreting dogs than the coloured working terriers from which they descended.

One of Turk's most famous puppies was Major, owned by C. R. Farrer, secretary of the Ullswater, a dog which became the ancestor of Gyp in *Hunt and Working Terriers*, Major being bred out of a Patterdale type of bitch which had some white terrier blood in its ancestry. Gyp won a cup for the best working terrier in 1930, but she could not hold a candle to Dalton's dog for looks. However, proof of Turk's ability is the fact that Farrer brought this dog into his own strain and Farrer was a careful breeder who believed only one type of terrier was worth keeping in the breed – that is, the type that is the best.

Certainly it seems very obvious that Jim Dalton used either fox terrier or, for want of a better term, Jack Russell terrier blood in the creation of his strain. Johnny Richardson also believes this to be so, and states that a Colonel or Major (Johnny was uncertain as to the rank or Christian name) Williams was an associate of Dalton, and this gentlemen bred a very typey, box-headed type of Jack Russell that may have entered into Dalton's strain of fell terriers.

Skelton, in his *Reminiscences of Joe Bowman*, mentions this Major Williams, and states that he bred a strain of wire fox terrier in Barrow-in-Furness, and this same Major Williams often infused the local fell terriers with his fox-terrier blood. There were, however, many strains of white terrier in the Lake District at that time and agricultural shows at this time had dozens of Jack Russell types of entry, possibly descended from the days of the Cornish miners who came to the Lakes in about 1830 when Barratt opened the Coniston Mining Company at Leverswater. Winch, who directed me in my researches into the history of the fell terrier, once said to me that there were always more white than fell terriers shown in the early Lake District Agricultural Shows, and there is every reason to believe that Winch is correct.

In the Melbreck Hunt country, a very different type of hunt terrier was being bred: a red (and occasionally a black-and-tan) terrier with a crisp, tight, waterproof coat, a good box-shaped head and a very straight front. Many of the Melbreck terriers were used in the creation of the modern Lakeland. Curiously, for some reason, Clapham does not show any Melbreck terriers in his book, yet Long says the best lookers always came from the Melbreck country. Egremont, however, which at one time was the centre of the Lakeland terrier breeding scene, lies just inside the Eskdale and Ennerdale country. John Winch of the Fell and Moorland Working Terrier Club believes that Irish terrier blood played an important part in the creation of some of these terrier strains, and certainly the western districts of the Lake District did receive a massive infusion of Irish immigrants immediately after the potato famine and again in the early 1900s.

Cleator Moor, near Egremont, has a large population which claims Irish descent. Winch believes that these Irish immigrants brought gutsy, good-coated Irish terriers with them, and these entered into the bloodlines of the dogs bred in the Melbreck country. Certainly the photograph of the Salters Hall Wood badger dig of 1917 shows terriers which closely resemble the Irish terriers kept by crofters in Ireland at the end of the nineteenth century. Joe Mawson of Egremont, a famous breeder of registered Lakeland terriers at one time, showed me a photograph of a terrier bred by his father in 1912, and this terrier had a decidedly early Irish-terrier look about it. Later, so Joe told me, various breeders in Egremont used a terrier with known Irish-terrier ancestry to improve their strains of registered Lakeland terrier. Certainly Archie Kirk believes the Irish terrier played a very important part in the creation of the Lakeland terrier and fell terrier.

Even before 1920, the Melbreck country had a reputation for producing good-looking terriers capable of winning at agricultural shows anywhere in the Lake District, and perhaps it was the presence of such good-quality fell terriers there that persuaded Willie Irving to keep a team of working registered Lakeland terriers at the Melbreck Hunt Kennels at Hope Lorton and later to breed a first-rate kennel of pedigree Kennel Club registered Lakelands. G. H. Long is also convinced that the good-coated, red fell terriers bred around Egremont during his youth owed their type and blind courage to the mixture of the blood of the Irish terrier.

Yet long before the birth of Willie Irving, or G. H. Long for that matter, forces were at work that would alter the appearance and genetic make-up of the fell terrier for ever. In 1859, a gun-maker called W. R. Pape had an idea to publicize his wares and staged the first dog show in Britain, offering double-barrelled shotguns as prizes to the owners of the winning exhibits. It was admittedly a very limited sort of show, in spite of the fact that 'Stonehenge' J. H. Walsh, one of the greatest authorities on sporting dogs, judged. Only pointers and setters were allowed to compete – after all Pape had staged the show only to publicize his wares, not to promote an interest in improving canine eugenics – but the Newcastle show proved to be a great success, and what is more attracted such interest that in 1863 an enormous all-class show was staged at Chelsea. The dog-showing craze spread to the Lakes quite rapidly, and within twenty years of Pape's first show at Newcastle, agricultural shows in the Lake District were staging classes for gun dogs and even terriers. These early terrier shows were fairly extraordinary affairs and were treated very seriously. G. H. Long recalls his father telling him that sometimes these terrier classes had a hundred entries, including coloured working terriers. (As yet the term 'Lakeland terrier' or indeed 'fell terrier' had not been evolved for the dogs which worked with the Lakeland packs, for they were referred to as simply terriers or coloured working terriers.) White terriers usually made up the majority of the class for the fells, which has always boasted a very large Jack Russell type of terrier population, and good-quality Jack Russell types at that, possibly descended from those imported by Barratt's workers in 1830, though this can be only educated guesswork. What is more amazing is that the Lake District terrier owners, terrier men who traditionally kept terriers only for work, keeping and breeding only the gamest and best workers, went overboard with the show craze. Again, I quote an anecdote told to me by G. H. Long, whose tales of those shows are fascinating and need to be recorded now before they are lost for ever. At that time red terriers, wheatens, blacks and blue-and-tan terriers were common in the Lake District, but there were very few good black-and-tan terriers in Cumbria. Most, says Long, were black and with a rather muddy tan grizzle.

In 1924, Peter Long, G. H. Long's father, owned two of these dogs, good typey fox terrier or Irish terrier fell types of excellent conformation but of a poor colour. An Irish dyer lived in Cleator Moor at that time, a man who may have had considerable training as an industrial chemist. He was also an incredible practical joker, for he asked Peter Long to lend him the terriers and returned them to him jet black and fiery red tan. The pair won everywhere that summer, and though the colours were a little too vivid to be natural, and I suppose everyone realized that the coats had been dyed, scarcely a show went by without disgruntled exhibitors trying to remove the colouring with methylated spirits, paraffin and even carbon tetrachloride. All failed. What the Cleator Moor dyer used is still a mystery. I told this tale to Arie Van De Berg, a Dutch writer and a collector of curious tales concerning animals. He winced. Animal fur will only take a dye if the dye solution is very hot!

Peter Long, father of G. H. Long, bred some of the best fell types at this time – dogs which were both lookers and workers – and he obtained his foundation stock from a stone worker between Egremont and Cockermouth, using the dogs of Jim Dalton for outcross blood from time to time. Peter Long was an inveterate hunter and a great badger digger during his middle years. Come summer time, he walked beagles from the local pack, though their days with Long could scarcely be called a rest period, for Long hunted a wild and rather unruly bobbery pack of beagles, terriers and the occasional foxhound to rabbit, hare, fox, otter and even deer during the summer months. There is a tale, truth or legend (it can be hard to sort out the difference where Peter Long is concerned), that one winter evening, after the beagles had gone back to kennels and were hunting their traditional quarry, the whole pack disappeared into a badger set one morning. 'It's that bloody Peter Long's fault,' cursed a follower.

Yet Long bred and worked some incredible terriers: terriers as good as any found at the Lakeland Hunt Kennels. Long was not enamoured of the Bedlington-cross fell terriers being bred around Egremont at this time, and kept really typey fell terriers with more than a hint of fox terrier about their make-up, and so typey were these terriers that on more than one occasion Peter Long won first, second and third at shows in the Cleator Moor area, a hot-bed of typey terriers in the days before the First World War. Clapham makes no mention of Long in his book *Hunting in the Lakeland Fells*, but Clapham also fails to mention the Pool family of Glenridding, a family producing some of the finest Patterdale types in the Lakes at that time.

In the days immediately prior to the First World War, Kitchen of Egremont, a noted badger digger in the Lake District, produced a rangy type of fell terrier by crossing some of the local terriers with his own strain of Bedlington. G. H. Long says Kitchen's strain of fell terrier had a reputation for bottomless courage, excellent nose and good all-round working ability, hunting the spectrum from rat to badger, but what really distinguished Kitchen's strain of fell was the fact that most of the terriers bred by him were black. These were the first black terriers my researches have revealed, though Buck states his grandfather produced numerous black terriers from his Bedlington/fell strains. There is also fairly well-documented proof that George Chapman (father of the ex-Coniston huntsman) also produced the occasional black terrier using local strains, though I can find no pictorial proof for this statement and Watson, an extremely reliable cynologist of the Lunesdale Foxhounds, believes that Bewley brought the first black fell terrier from Manchester.

The shows changed the appearance of the fell terrier, for the poorer types of terrier, no matter how game they were, had little or no chance of winning in these agricultural shows, and breeders, now thoroughly infected with the

14. Kitchen of Egremont – a noted Bedlington breeder.

58

show bug, sought out good-class fox terriers and possibly small Irish terriers to mate to their rugged fell terriers to breed a superior type of terrier capable of winning at the shows. Long believes that no Welsh terrier blood was introduced at this time, and Frank Buck does not believe Welsh terrier blood was ever introduced into the Lakeland terrier strains, but my own researches lead me to disagree with Frank, for reasons I will explain later.

Certainly a really good terrier fetched a heck of a good price. G. H. Long's father bought a fell type of Irish terrier from a roadworker called Robinson in about 1900 for a song. Yet, that year, he campaigned it around the agricultural shows, transporting it in the pannier of a bicycle and eventually sold the dog for £5. (My grandfather earned 12s. (60p) a week in 1900.)

These agricultural shows certainly put the fell terrier on the map, so to speak, though many, Clapham included, believed that the shows would be the ruination of the fell terrier. Such was the interest in the 'show' type of fell terrier, however, that in 1912 a meeting of fell terrier breeders was called at Keswick and the name Lakeland terrier given to the new improved types of fell terrier being shown in the Lake District. Hitherto these strains had been called simply coloured terriers, although Long recalls that in his youth it was fashionable to call any fell terrier a Patterdale whether or not it came from the Ullswater country. At the time of writing, it is customary to call any black, smooth-coated fell terrier a Patterdale, in spite of the fact that this strain of terriers was bred, maybe even created, by Cyril Breay at Kirkby Lonsdale and Buck at Leyburn in Yorkshire.

The 1912 meeting at Keswick was one of the landmarks in fell terrier history, even though, in the opinion of Braithwaite Wilson of the Ullswater, it marked the end of the line for the genuine fell terrier. Certainly a vastly different type of terrier started appearing in the agricultural shows in the Lake District after that time. After 1912, any typey fell terrier kept as a pet or at hunt kennels was called a Lakeland terrier, while the less typey strains were still referred to as coloured terriers. During the 1950s, however, it became fashionable to call such unregistered strains a Border/Lakeland terrier, even though few had Border terrier blood, in the same way as it is customary (at the time of writing) to call any black fell terrier a Patterdale.

No doubt further infusions of fox terrier and Irish terrier blood were added at this time to improve the type of the fell terriers and create a neat Welsh terrier type of dog that would be acceptable to the Kennel Club, though not everyone found the new type appealing. Geoffrey Sparrow, author of one of the most popular working terrier books ever, *The Terrier's Vocation*, says that he was told by a fell huntsman (Sparrow doesn't specify which, but I would guess it might have been Braithwaite Wilson, who probably knew Sparrow quite well) that he stopped using 'Lakeland' terriers when they became indistinguishable from the Welsh terrier. Then, in 1923, the Lakeland Terrier Association was formed and every effort went into improving the type. Mrs Graham Spence, who owned a large and superbly kept kennel of Lakeland terriers (one of Sid Wilkinson's kin, his brother-in-

15. *Mrs Graham Spence's Egton terriers.*

law Jimmy Overs, helped to build the kennel, which was ranked as a master-piece of workmanship by the pre-war dog breeders), wrote to many doggy and sporting periodicals to beg breeders to stop any further infusion of foreign terrier blood into the already saturated Lakeland terrier bloodlines. Mrs Graham Spence wrote an article on Lakeland terriers for Vesey-FitzGerald, attacking this fox and Welsh terrier cross-breeding – she is the first to mention that the Welsh terrier had been crossed into the fell strains, though I suspect that Welsh terrier blood had been bred in since before 1912. Eddie Pool of Glenridding says that Mrs Graham Spence even bought a working terrier stud dog from his father, John Pool, also of Glenridding, to maintain the racial purity of her terriers, and certainly she sent Jimmy Over's father in pursuit of what she described as 'typical Lakeland terriers'. Curiously, some rather lovely wheaten-coloured terriers were shown at Cruft's in 1935 – possibly these were descended from the dogs sold to Mrs Spence by John Pool, who had an excellent strain of wheaten-coloured fells – but this, again, is mere guesswork and not substantiated by documentary evidence.

The new improved Lakeland terrier was still a worker, however, make no bones about it, for the admixture of other terrier blood did little to harm the Lakeland at this time: Todd's 'Terrier Song', a poem (see page 223) which

16. The 1935 Crufts Lakeland class. Note the Irish terrier-type lakelands.

ridicules the Cruft's-bred Lakeland as being afraid of a mouse, was written a little later than the time when Mrs Spence was putting together her kennels. It must be remembered that when Lucas wrote *Hunt and Working Terriers* in 1930 (it was published in 1931), many hunts were still using pedigree fox terriers. Even Willie Porter of the Eskdale and Ennerdale, who kept the Dobson strain of fell terrier which he considered to be the 'best plucked terriers in England' – terriers which would fight until they died – ran on a few working fox terriers in 1930. (Edmund, his grandson, huntsman for the Eskdale and Ennerdale, still keeps a few very game Jack Russells.) It was this unspoilt fox terrier, not the deformed, elongated-headed dogs of today, that was used to improve the Lakeland terrier, so there was little loss in working ability through the use of such blood. Even Bruce Logan of the Coniston Hunt, the Logan family being a noted hunting family in the Lake District, told Lucas that a few fox terriers worked with the Coniston Hunt. Paisley also ran on and worked an occasional fox terrier or so. Lucas also interviewed Major Sleigh, master of the Bilsdale and the Haydon Foxhounds, who ran on fox terriers with his pack, and he told Lucas that these fox terriers were of the Melbreck Hunt strain, so perhaps fox terriers were also worked by the Melbreck. Curiously, in the literature, the Melbreck seems to have been the poor relation of the other Lakeland packs during Lucas's day. Lucas did not even mention the hunt in *Hunt and Working Terriers*.

Douglas Paisley, one of the foremost Lakeland terrier breeders of his age, kept the new improved type of terrier, and they were certainly excellent workers. Lucas interviewed Paisley when he was honorary whip for the Blencathra, and amazingly seemed unaware that Paisley was using a different type of terrier from the terriers used by such diehards as 'Kitty' Farrer and Braithwaite Wilson. Paisley's dogs looked good, but also worked well, and more than one fell-terrier breeder used Paisley's stud dogs. Mrs Robert Todhunter, mother of Barry Todhunter, the Blencathra whip, once told me that her father, a gamekeeper in the Lakes who bred a very woolly coated Bedlington type of fell terrier, began taking bitches to Paisley's dogs and produced some extremely good workers by using Paisley's new improved Lakeland Terrier Association studs. Furthermore, at a time when show-terrier breeders deliberately excited their dogs to make them seem aggressive in the show ring – Lucas refers to this as the 'no fight, no show' syndrome – Paisley's dogs were extremely quiet and well behaved.

If the meeting at Keswick in 1912 had encouraged fell-terrier breeders to use fox terrier, Welsh terrier and Irish terrier blood, then Clapham's book also had an impact on the working fell terrier strains. *Fox Hunting in the Lakeland Fells* can scarcely be called a well-written book, but it did open up the fells to outsiders by giving accounts of accommodation and railway stations near to the hunt kennels, and during the 1920s scores of field-sports enthusiasts visited the Lakes to hunt with the fell packs. Glenridding experienced a sort of minor tourist boom during this period, for the Ullswater was the fashionable pack for fox hunting during the 1920s, as, indeed, it is today. These tourist field-sport enthusiasts out for a day in the fells irritated some of the diehard fell-pack followers, but provided an entertainment for others, for the sport of tourist baiting also seems to have been very popular at this time.

Buck and two or three other fell-terrier breeders tell an interesting tale from this period. A member of the upper classes, a rather silly young man with much to learn about life, by all accounts, went to the Lakes for a day's hunting and was in turn baited by the locals that evening. An old hunt follower (actually it was Fred Barker, father of Anthony Barker) cornered the idiot in one of the pubs and asked, 'How dost thee tell if thee terriers are game lad?' The young chap, who had hunted with the Quorn or suchlike, no doubt was a little nonplussed by the question, but Fred Barker had a dry wit and a knack of bringing down a cocksure youngster. 'Well sir,' the lad replied, 'we show them a fox and if they bay at it we say they are game.' The old fell man shook his head in disapproval and went on, 'When thee wife goes out to the pictures' – the fool nodded to indicate he understood – 'get thee terriers in house and put poker in fire.' Interest quickened in the sucker. 'Then, when it's red hot, take it out of fire and go *arr, arr* to the terriers. The one who holds on longest is the gamest.' The buffoon wrote this pearl of wisdom down in his notebook and left the next day to tell the followers of the Quorn or suchlike what game and hard terriers there were in the fells. If there is one born every minute, then surely an hour and a half's lapse must have followed this idiot's birth.

Thus tourists came to the fells, but serious hunters, as well as clowns out to see how the other half lived, were among them for the hunting, and many brought useful Jack Russell types of terrier with them, and these too entered into the pedigrees of the working terrier. In 1921, a hunter called Fred Barker came to the fells, bringing with him a red fell terrier that had lost half its face through repeated encounters with fox and was therefore known as Chowt ('chewed' in fell parlance)-faced Rock, and two white terrier bitches bred by the Ilfracombe Badger Digging Club. Barker was an astute terrier man as well as a great wit, for not only was he as tough as whipcord, but he had considerable knowledge of hunting and terrier work, having hunted a pack of Pennine Foxhounds at Ousby (not the same Pennine Hounds that exist today). From this trio of dogs came a game and utterly fearless strain of terrier, for not only had the fell terrier Chowt-faced Rock an impeccable working record, but the white Russell types of terrier were also superbly bred. During the 1920s, several badger-digging clubs were formed in Devonshire and patronized by no less a hunter than Arthur Heinemann, who bred a relatively pure and totally fearless strain of dog descended from those of Jack Russell through Lynton Jack, a wonderfully game badger dog. These badger-digging clubs did much to maintain the working ability of the Jack Russell type of terrier and some outstanding dogs were bred by the clubs. Many of the very valiant terriers bred in South Wales in the days before the Second World War were bred from dogs bred by the Ilfracombe Badger Digging Club. Barker's strain was perpetuated by his son, the dynamic Anthony Barker, by Sid Wilkinson of Glenridding, whose Rock must be one of the most famous studs in fell terrier history, by Middleton of Kendal and Barry Todhunter of the Blencathra Foxhounds. This strain of terrier is still held in high regard in the Lake District.

Another anecdote, and maybe another holy cow about to be destroyed, I'm afraid. Most chocolate fell terriers, and a few appear from time to time, are reputed to be descended from the chocolate Bedlington used by Tommy Dobson to create his strain. However, not all chocolate fell terriers owe their colouring to this cross. In 1928 or thereabouts (Anthony Barker is uncertain precisely when), a red field spaniel misallied to a fell terrier and Tony Pool brought one of these pups to mate to Chowt-faced Rock. Several chocolate fell terriers in Glenridding and neighbouring districts were bred by Rock out of this half-bred spaniel bitch, and none seemed any the worse for their spaniel ancestry. In fact, chocolate 'Patterdale' terriers were rated very highly by many hunters just after the Second World War – though whether or not these terriers came from Patterdale or were a strain of pedigree registered Lakeland terrier (Lakeland terriers were still being called Patterdales by diehard Welsh miners as late as 1948), is impossible to say.

17. *Fred Barker and infant Anthony Barker with Chowt-faced Rock and two Ilfracombe Badger Digging Club terriers.*

18. A chocolate fell terrier.

In 1932 (this date is questioned by some, though both Buck and Richardson agree on the time), a large Irish terrier type of dog was bred by the late Albert Benson, who eventually became joint master of the Windermere Harriers. This terrier, Red Ike, was a hard, game terrier who feared nothing but had a reputation for being uncontrollable. Once, when Albert was a fell pack whip, the hounds flushed a roebuck from a bramble thicket, and though the hounds remained steady, Ike slipped his leash and ploughed into the unfortunate deer, pulling it down in the road. There is no record of Ike's breeding, but he served a considerable number of bitches in the Lake District and played a very important part in the fell terrier bloodlines. Walter Parkin, who hunted the Lunesdale, used the Red Ike bloodline quite a lot, and he mated his bitches to Frank Buck of Leyburn's famous bloodline, thereby producing his equally famous Red and Black Rock strain. Ike's progeny were temperamental, inclined to be slow to enter and bad with children, but they were nailers to work once they started, and renowned stayers – a quality which may have been their undoing, for many had to be dug out of some very bad places in the Lunesdale country. Most terriers in the Lunesdale country before 1950 were bred from Parkin's Black and Red Rock strain, and only when Breay started to hunt with the Lunesdale did this strain lose ground to Breay's slape-coated terrier strain, though Ruby, a chocolate putty-nosed bitch, the mother of Breay's Gem, was of the Red Rock strain.

The wartime years saw most of the fell huntsmen drafted for military service. Wear left the Ullswater in the hands of Anthony Barker, and Johnny Richardson left the Blencathra only to become one of those prisoners no Italian prisoner-of-war camp could hold, for his training in the fells stood him in good stead on the run in Italy. During this time, however, one of the most important fell terriers was born. In 1939–40 (the dates are a bit hazy when one deals with unregistered terriers), Jim Fleming of Grasmere bred a bitch called Myrt (an abbreviation for Myrtle) from mating two very hard-coated local terriers. Lucas, in *Hunt and Working Terriers*, makes mention that when two very hard-coated terriers are mated, the progeny is often nearly smooth coated. Myrt had just such a coat – called 'slape' in fell parlance. Although Myrt was bred at Grasmere in the heart of the Coniston country, she saw service with the Ullswater Hounds, hunted by the then youthful Anthony Barker, son of Fred Barker, now that Wear was in the army. Myrt was a good but not great terrier, according to both Anthony Barker and Tom Robinson, who worked with both Myrt and her sons, her only distinction being that she was in on a dig which yielded one of the first badgers taken in the Ullswater Hunt country. She went into semi-retirement, few fell bitches ever knowing total retirement, and was used as a brood bitch. In this capacity she became one of the most important terriers in fell terrier history.

Joe Wear's Tear 'Em was to be one of her most famous puppies, a puppy bred and owned by Jim Fleming, not Joe Wear, as Eddie Pool, an authority on Wear, told me. Tear 'Em was one of Joe's first terriers when he returned from military service, and he became a famous terrier in the Ullswater country, though he was by no standards a good-looking dog. There is a story about Tear 'Em well worth repeating since not only does it show Wear's patience in handling a terrier – a patience sadly lacking in the flash-in-the-pan terrier addicts of today – but it also indicates that slow developers often make the best terriers if given a chance. Wear used a curious method to enter his young terriers. Few hunt kennels are without rats, and even the Ullswater sported one or two. Wear would watch the antics of the rats for a while before planning a course of action and he would then scrub out the huge boilers used for boiling up portions of fallen cattle for the hounds and once a boiler was scoured would grease the sides, place a piece of meat at the bottom and wait. Rats would then slither into the boiler, and next day Joe would throw a young terrier into the boiler to sort them out.

It was a bit of a kill-or-cure method of entering, and one that certainly would not appeal to many, but Joe started many of his terriers this way. According to story, Joe tried Tear 'Em this way, but perhaps Tear 'Em was a sensitive dog or maybe he was still too young for rats since he yelled his head off and leaped out of the boiler with a rat hanging on him. I asked Eddie Pool, a close friend of Wear's, about the story, but Eddie had never heard Joe mention it though he did confirm that Joe Wear certainly entered his young terriers this way as well as stating that Tear 'Em came to the Ullswater at two years of age after becoming too much for Fleming to handle. Tear 'Em, true to his name, became a very famous fox-hunting terrier in the Ullswater country: a sensible dog that could shift a fox without receiving great damage, and kill one if need be. Seemingly not all fell terrier puppies are precocious workers.

There is certainly some controversy as to whether the Breay/Buck combination used Tear 'Em's line to breed Davy. Maurice Bell, who knew Breay well, says that the sire of Black Davy, a landmark in the smooth-coated black fell terrier, now erroneously referred to as a Patterdale, was sired by a fell terrier owned by James Carr of Askrigg, Yorkshire. Buck assures me, however, that this dog was not the sire of Davy, and Buck should know, for he bred James Carr's dog. Nuttall of Holmes Chapel, an authority on this strain of black fell terrier, says he has documentary proof that one of Joe Wear's dogs sired Davy. Breay, in a letter to Wally Wyld of the Grove and Rufford, enclosed a pedigree – the only written pedigree Breay was ever known to send to anyone – which stated that Davy was bred out of a black bull terrier type of fell bitch called Gem, mated to 'a red dog from the Ullswater'. During the year when Davy was whelped, however, Eddie Pool states that, apart from Anthony Barker's Rock (a dog bred down from Fred Barker's Rock), no red dog was at stud at the Ullswater Hunt Kennels and Tear 'Em was a rather muddy black and tan. Could it be that Breay's impeccable memory was beginning to fail him as he approached his death, or could the red dog be a slip of the pen? My own money would be on a son of Tear 'Em being a sire of Davy. Buck certainly remembers the dog well, as he should since he owned it, and says that he gave it to a man in Leyburn and that it died from bad fox bites, confirming by phone on 29 December 1981 that the sire of Davy was a red dog sired by Tear 'Em.

Hardasty of the Melbreck went in 1946 to the Fleming Myrt bloodline to start up his terriers at Hope Lorton, and by using one or two terriers bred down from Myrt, Sid Hardasty, Harry's brother, bred the incomparable Turk, a superb model of a terrier: a great worker and a wonderful dog to look at, with a perfectly square shape, a good neck and a very fine box-shaped head. Sid Wilkinson of Glenridding, whose superb Rock was frequently beaten by Turk at showing, describes this terrier as the best-looking fell terrier ever to come out of 'the Lakes'. Hardasty says that Turk worked for five seasons with the Melbreck, and that during this time he bred most of Tyson's winning line of terrier. Tyson was seemingly unbeatable at the shows in this period. Winch's Chanter and a great many top-class red terriers now winning in the Durham area (Graham Ward's strain dates back to Turk through many bloodlines, though with a liberal admixture of Jack Russell and Border terrier blood).

A son of Tyson's Rock, whose father was probably Hardasty's Turk, mated to Frank Buck's incomparable Viper, an iron-hard worker from the Black Davy line, produced Maurice Bell's (Wensleydale Foxhounds) superb worker Britt, described by many hunters in the North Yorkshire area as one of the hardest terriers ever bred in the region. Again he was a dog of incredibly docile

19. Frank Buck with Black Davy.

disposition (ironically being killed by hounds in kennels), and yet was capable of dealing death and destruction to any fox unfortunate enough not to be able to bolt. Britt was not only a great killer of foxes (as, it seems, are all his progeny), but also a wonderful finder. On hunting days, Bell has seen other terriers flash down every earth, whining in anticipation, while Britt sat quietly at the mouth. Then Bell knew that there was nothing at home. When Britt showed interest, however, he entered quietly and seriously, slaying his fox quickly and with little fuss by means of a dextrous throat bite. Britt died at a ripe old age in a kennel fight, after Bell had introduced two new rowdy hounds to the kennels, but had by then been sire to some of the best fell terriers bred in Scotland. Proof of Britt's worth was that only days before his death Bell was offered a good sum for his old dog. He refused, of course.

The Second World War altered the conformation of the show Lakeland considerably. At first, with the possibility of invasion from Germany or a famine through submarine siege, many breeders sold their stock for ridiculously low prices to get rid of them. Miss Irene Morris of Kelda Kennels, Stroud, bought a ticket-winning male from Tom Megeen, who had bought up and bred dogs to produce the finest kennel of Lakelands in the world at that time, for £5. But the panic selling lasted only a short time, in spite of the fact that many dog breeders had to keep their dogs alive on bone broth, potato peelings and nettles. There were no shows at the time, so breeders experimented, and Miss Morris recalls dozens of crossbred fox terrier/Welsh terrier hybrids being produced to improve Welsh terrier type. Most of these crosses had a mark or a distinct bar above the eyes, and one Welsh breeder, who must for discretion's sake be nameless, told Miss Morris he had sold fifty of these hybrids to Cumberland in 1941–2. What became of them is a mystery, yet, sufficient to say, towards the end of the war many Lakeland terrier puppies were bred with this self-same mark of Cain, as Miss Morris called it.

The cessation of war saw Wear and Richardson return to the Lakes, and while Wear began keeping terriers from the Fleming stock, Richardson kept the old Blencathra bloodline, bred down from the dogs of Jim Dalton. Richardson returned from his hectic wartime experiences in 1946. A matter of a week or so after he took up his duties at the hunt, a Blencathra terrier bitch, Spider, whelped a litter of puppies to Dobbin, a dog owned by Porter of Borrowdale, reputed to be one of the wettest places in Britain. (Natives of Borrowdale had a reputation for being addled-brained according to the population of Keswick, who referred to them as 'Borrowdale Gowks' (cuckoos).) Dobbin and Spider had all the qualities Richardson admired in a dog. Both were game and capable of staying with the fox, both were excellent finders, even in a difficult place. Dobbin was also free from 'pedigree' Lakeland blood (and some bloodlines were heavily soused with registered Lakeland blood even in 1946). Dobbin was, in fact, everything Richardson desired in a terrier, and he came out of most of his forays at fox relatively unmarked, for he had the sense to stay back and avoid the jaw-to-jaw collisions so beloved by writers of terrier books who do not comprehend the damage which such encounters can inflict on a dog. Furthermore, Dobbin was totally steady with all stock, sheep, cattle, chickens or whatever, a nonfighter and easily kennelled. He also proved an excellent stud, for the mating 'twixt Spider and Dobbin produced Tarzan, a dog that made a considerable contribution to the blood of the working fell terrier in the Lake District, if not outside the Lakes.

Tarzan was a smallish red dog, lacking the class of Hardasty's Turk or Wilkinson's Rock, perhaps, but he became a renowned worker in the Blencathra country, and such was his worth that when Hardasty retired from hunt service at the Melbreck, his successor and son-in-law, Richard 'Pritch' Bland, started up his own team of terriers, using a grandson of Richardson's Tarzan instead of continuing with Hardasty's illustrious Turk bloodline. Likewise, one of Ogilvie's dogs at the Coniston can trace its bloodline to Tarzan, and Jock, the noted stud dog bred by Sid Wilkinson of Glenridding, now a veteran at stud with Bill Brightmore, could be traced back to Tarzan, though most of the bloodline of this dog was descended from the Chowt-faced Rock line.

Tarzan – a curious name (but appropriate, perhaps, for Greystoke is a few miles from Threlkeld, and Edgar Rice Burroughs's hero was really Lord Greystoke) – was another of those sane workers so admired by Richardson and rarely let himself be bitten up and knocked about. He was an ideal hunt terrier, and his worth seems to have been more appreciated by fell huntsmen than by lay hunters outside the Lakes where his bloodline seems to have had little impact.

In 1948, however, a terrier destined never to see a fox was to become a potent sire in the Lake District. In that year Alf Johnston, who worked as kennelman for Tom Megeen of the Cumberland Bus Company, bred a black-and-tan pedigree-registered Lakeland terrier, Oregill Copper Coin. Coin became a champion, though he was not everyone's idea of an outstanding Lakeland terrier. Miss Irene Morris judged the dog and gave it its first ticket, but there was much disapproval from the ringside spectators, who considered the dog to be, and I quote Miss Morris, 'too much of an Irish terrier in type'. Coin made little impact on the pedigree Lakeland terrier scene since, despite the fact that he had presence (the reason why Miss Morris helped him to become a champion), he did not have a particularly appealing type to make registered Lakeland terrier breeders use him on their bitches.

Copper Coin, or Jack as he was known to Alf Johnston, was a tiger, and that seems to be an understatement. As a young dog he not only showed himself fearlessly in the ring, bristling with fury and indignation if another male or female approached him, but would fly at any dog he met when out at exercise, regardless of the size of the dog or how bad a drubbing Jack took from his reluctant opponent. Legend has it that, while at stud with Alf Johnston, he would kill any cat which walked across his yard, flying straight into their claws and teeth, regardless of the punishment he took and oblivious to pain. Alan Johnston, grandson of Alf, now the owner of the Oregill prefix, remembers Jack slightly. Alf warned Alan repeatedly about going down the yard when Jack was loose as Jack was a bit protective about his

20. Oregill Copper Coin.

territory. Joe Mawson, a great raconteur concerning the early Lakeland terriers in Egremont – and at one time Central Avenue, Egremont (Alf's home) boasted six top-class Lakeland terrier breeders – told me that Copper Coin was a demon of a dog, fearing neither man nor beast.

This period was the heyday of the Lake-based Lakeland terrier breeders, and many are the tales of how the type of dog was improved. It would be madness to quote names of breeders, but certainly Irish terrier blood was used to improve the type still further in the postwar years, as was fox terrier blood. Mawson remembers breeders who regularly produced fox terrier coloured puppies in their litters, and quite a few who went to a breeder who owned what they knew to be a half-bred Irish Lakeland terrier stud dog. Racial purity – a tongue-in-cheek word by now – suffered greatly perhaps, but type improved dramatically.

To return to Copper Coin. While the show-breeding fraternity did not make much use of this dog, the hunters certainly did, and not only did Jack mate quite a few hunt terriers to improve type and coat, but Willie Irving actually kept pedigree dogs bred from Copper Coin at his kennels as well as working them. Turk, his famous terrier, was of registered stock, and a gamer terrier could be hard to find (many of Irving's terriers were called Turk). It was true that Turk could be hard to a point which might be considered suicidal, but no one could question his courage. Lakelanders still disagree about the manner of his demise. Richardson believes he picked up some poison – maybe strychnine, for mole catchers used the poison at one time and once Walter Parkin nearly died trying to give mouth-to-mouth resuscitation to a dog that had strychnine poisoning. Others say Turk was killed in a kennel fight. Arthur Irving, however (the brother of Willie Irving and hunts-man for the Eskdale and Ennerdale), used this bloodline to work with the hounds and found its courage and constitution unquestionable. Robin, Arthur's famous stud – a stud used by many fell-terrier breeders, including the 'Wilkinson' group – was bred down from Coin, and Cowen used this blood to improve his Hardasty-bred stock at his kennels at Embleton. It is my belief that many of the good showy black-and-tan unregistered fell terriers winning at the shows today can be traced back to Irving's Copper Coin-bred stud dogs. Willie Irving, however, in a letter to George Newcombe, a great authority on the Lakeland terrier of the late 1940s, says that he had seen several litters by Copper Coin, yet was unimpressed by them, possibly because Coin bred an Irish-terrier type. Miss Morris of Kelda Kennels says Coin made little impact on the show-bred Kennel Club Lakeland pedigrees, but he certainly altered the general appearance of many strains of working fell terrier.

Whether or not the infusion of Copper Coin blood into the Lake District fell terriers did harm will no doubt be argued for years to come. Cowen of Embleton told me that the only objection he could find to using pedigree Lakeland blood on his strain was that the puppies were usually fiendish fighters, while Winch quotes cases of pedigree Lakeland terriers from the Johnston kennels at Egremont that were nailers to work. Other breeders, such as Richardson and Bland and Barry Todhunter, try to avoid registered Lakeland terrier fell dogs, since they are a nuisance in kennels and none too constitutionally sound after hard work on cold days in the fells.

In the 1950s, an apparently entirely new breed of fell terrier began to appear at the hunt shows in the Lake District, and in the 1960s in the Midlands. These dogs – slape- or smooth-coated dogs, black or red tan and a trifle large for some breeders – were erroneously known as Patterdales, though they originated at Kirkby Lonsdale and Leyburn and had only tenuous connections with the Ullswater Hunt country, for they were the product of the Breay/Buck breeding programme. It is commonly stated that Breay created these terriers, but this is not only unfair but also untrue, for the Buck/Breay bloodline was the same and the pair swopped dogs, bred dogs for each other and approved of one another's breeding schemes. George New-combe, writing in the *Shooting Times* in 1981, states that the name Patterdale terrier should be dropped and the term Breay terrier used, but Buck con-tributed just as much to the creation of this new type as did Breay; and Leyburn, as much as Kirkby Lonsdale, must be regarded as its original home.

No two more unlikely friends could have been imagined. Breay was an intellectual, a brilliant graduate of Corpus Christi, Oxford, and curiously enough an expert on Western stories – Zane Grey for preference, but even cheap trash when nothing else was available. In his middle years he gave up his teaching post and earned his living by juggling stocks and shares, spending his time hunting during the winter and fly fishing during the summer. He was a quiet, reserved sort of chap, but I have yet to meet someone who was as respected by his fellow men. Terry Breay, his son, says that he only knew one man who addressed his father as Cyril, and even today those who knew him – even Buck, who was a close friend – still refer to him as Mr Breay. Nuttall, Wyld and Maurice Bell continue to revere the memory of this tall gentleman, who, as Winch once joked, 'came to the Lakes to teach them how to catch foxes'.

Originally Breay bred Sealyham terriers of the type worked and bred by Jocelyn Lucas of the Ilmer Kennels, but soon his interest turned to the fell type of terrier, and no better strain of dog than the Buck/Breay terrier ever came out of the north. His stuff looked good, won well at shows. In fact Bramham Moor Hunt Terrier Show, at one time the place where the best terriers in Britain congregated, was for a while called Breay's show by some terrier men, so frequently did Breay win the 'Best in Show'. I met Breay at Bramham Moor, the year Brockley's Driver was Reserve Champion to his dog Rusty, and determined to write an article on this gentle legend of a man. I approached him cautiously since he was surrounded by a crowd of admirers. 'I'd like to do an article about you, Mr Breay, if you don't mind,' I interposed a bit timidly. He glanced down at me, for Breay was an imposing man, eyeing the somewhat cocksure but unconfident and scruffy would-be writer. 'Why?' he asked, gently taking the wind from my sails.

I never wrote that article and I doubt if he would have assisted me, for Breay valued his privacy and was reluctant to disclose any data about himself. As it is, it has taken me four years to learn what I do know about him, and I feel I have as yet only scratched the surface. He was already a diabetic when I met him and repeated asthma attacks were taking their toll of him, but he hunted with the Lunedale Hunt whenever he could, and walked those rugged fells until a short time before his final illness.

He was a superb hunter and a keen dog breeder, but entering a terrier was his forte and he took infinite pains over starting a dog to fox. He never used force and rarely spoke to a dog in anything other than his normal voice, but Wyld of the Grove and Rufford said Breay could get a terrier to do 'damn' nigh anything for him'.

Perhaps he actively encouraged the mystery surrounding the origin of his terriers, or maybe he was reluctant to discuss his breeding programme with anyone. Maurice Bell first saw one of these powerful-headed dogs while Breay was out with the Lunesdale. His attempt to extract some information by casual conversation failed, this anecdote being told more fully later (page 106). The bitch was probably Gem (see page 105), a small but good strong animal which gave rise to Davy, Topsy and eventually Bingo and Rusty. Breay could trace the ancestry of this family back to 1920, yet he was reluctant to divulge information concerning his stock. John Conners went to Kirkby Lonsdale to buy a puppy sired by Bingo (bred in fact by Frank Buck rather than Breay). Breay showed him the litter which he had for sale at a ridiculously low price, for Breay made little money out of his terriers. But when John asked for the breeding of the animal, Breay replied, 'I believe he is out of my own strain,' and would add no more. He confided in few people except Frank Buck, and to my knowledge he gave only one person, Wally Wyld, a written pedigree of his dogs dating back to 1920.

Frank Buck is a different kettle of fish: an ebullient lorry driver from Leyburn, with a great sense of humour and an outgoing disposition. He comes from a long line of terrier men. His grandfather and probably his father before him were breeders of a type of Bedlington-like fell terrier, and thus he was born to the sport, so to speak. His association with Breay dated from 1929, and he states he kennelled Breay's terriers between this time and 1936 while Breay had domestic problems. Frank kept a few terriers, and at that time he worked his terriers with several packs, and even kept his own team of hounds. In his youth and middle years, Buck was a peerless terrier man and a passionate fox hunter. His most famous dog was Tex, a border type of fell terrier, quiet, docile yet a tiger to fox, and this became a base of the Breay/Buck bloodline. Buck had an uncanny knack with trapped terriers, and once excavated one of Parkin's dogs from thirty feet below a rock, clay and fox bench, and eight times he was called by fell packs to dynamite out terriers trapped in bad places. It is said he dynamited Barker, one of Breay's first terriers, a white undocked dog, out of a tight spot, and that this cemented the Buck and Breay relationship. Certainly they continued their curious breeding partnership right up until Breay died. I say curious, because it was difficult to fathom out which breeder bred certain dogs in the pedigree. Take, for instance, the pedigree of Rusty, one of Breay's best and most prolific sires. Breay owned Gem, and bred Davy, who went to Buck. Buck bred Topsy and Bingo. Breay owned Tig and was given Bingo. Yet Monty, the sire of Gem, was bred out of Blitz, who came from Buck's line. Newcombe calls the present bull-terrier-headed terriers Breay terriers. Personally I should refer to them as the Breay/Buck terriers. One thing certain is that they are not Patterdales.

What Breay and Buck didn't do, however, was to add bull-terrier blood to a fell-terrier strain and produce the smooth-coated fell terriers so popular today. What they did was to use the best-quality fell terriers with ultra-hard

Bloodlines of Breay's Rusty:

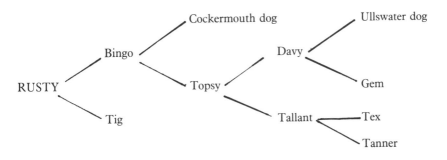

21. Breay showing Skiffle, daughter of Black Davy.

coats and produce a slape-coated strain. Keith Clement of Kendal, former secretary of the Lunesdale Foxhounds, believes that the bull-terrier type heads first appeared in the progeny of Blitz, a dog bred by Buck, a dog with a decided trace of Border terrier in his ancestry. Certainly terriers, both rough-coated and smooth-coated with bull-terrier types of head, began to appear in

22. *Frank Buck emerging from rock pile with rescued terrier.*

the fells after the use of Blitz as a stud. Quite recently, Bill Galpin of the *Shooting Times* has been plagued with letters asking for and suggesting the different classes of those smooth-coated bull-terrier-headed dogs. It is true that they are becoming a distinct type, but they remain, quite simply, smooth-coated types of fell terrier.

Both Breay and Buck (Buck quite vociferously) denied that they used bull terrier blood in the creation of their strains, although way back into the pedigree of most terriers, some bull terrier blood is usually present, even in fell terriers. In the modern strains there has been much admixture of other blood by breeders out to cash in on the reputation of Breay and Buck's strain. Jack Russells, and often poor-grade Jack Russells, have been mixed in with this peerless strain, and I've seen many advertisements for Staffordshire bull terrier 'Patterdale' hybrids. Thus the working abilities of these reputedly pure Patterdales have suffered. Many now lack the common sense of the original strain – a common sense that made Wally Wyld, terrier man for the Grove and Rufford Foxhounds, say that his first Breay terrier, Kipper, entered *him*, Wally, to the skill of fox digging. Many of these new Patterdale crosses are now huge dogs bigger than the original dogs of Breay and Buck, and of such a size that they cannot possibly work in normal earths. I saw one such monster at the Game Fair: a huge, nearly pure bull terrier with a docked tail, aggressive to all dogs, hard as iron and as useless as a broken anvil. 'Thirty-three pounds of unworkable terrier,' I wrote in my diary.

Westmorland of Troutbeck, an expert on the Breay/Buck strain, a good terrier man and an authority on fell terriers says that the breeder of today's slape-coated fell terriers (I remain reluctant to use the word Patterdale) has lost sight of the type of dog bred by Breay and Buck, and now nearly all these terriers are too big to work to fox.

Buck still keeps a strain of small, rough-coated black terrier, and uses them with local hunts. They are bred down from the Davy line, and Buck is careful about the dogs he uses to mate his bitches. I own a few such terriers myself – neat, narrow terriers and a far cry from the muscular, broad-chested bull-headed terriers to be found in today's working terrier shows.

A few other breeders still try to breed a relatively pure strain of the Buck/Breay bloodline. Nuttall of Holmes Chapel is one such. His dogs are bred down from puppies from Breay and other stock from Buck. Nuttall worked this strain with the Cheshire Hunt, and now works as terrier man for a mink hound pack. Like Wally Wyld, he cannot speak too highly of the original strain and is trying to keep his strain relatively pure. Most of Nuttall's dogs are black or black and tan, and though he produces a bull-terrier-headed puppy now and again, he will not countenance bull-terrier-bred stock, since not only is such stock lacking in brain and hunting instinct, but, Nuttall believes, bull terriers are not so game as those smooth-coated fell terriers. Phelan, a professional terrier man late of the Fernie Foxhounds and now at the Hereford Foxhounds, is another breeder of these black terriers. His stud dog, Poker, is one of Nuttall's strain, and Phelan, too, has endeavoured to keep the strain pure.

Amazingly high (and, I happen to think, ridiculously high) prices are often paid for proven workers of this strain. A few weeks ago I heard of a pair of bull-headed blacks being sold for £500 as the pair, while individual trained dogs are often sold for as much as £350. Personally I am baffled at such prices. I can remember Breay selling a useful work dog for £15 and even throwing in a puppy for that price. Even allowing for inflation, £350 is a heck of a lot to pay for a working terrier.

Hinchcliffe of the Pennine Hunt is another who has tried to keep the strain pure. His stock dates from a terrier bred by Nuttall, a powerful male called Flint admixed with dogs he obtained from Breay. Hinchcliffe cites a case of how the huge show-bred fell terriers came to grief in an earth near Holmfirth after a smaller Bray/Buck type of terrier had worked the place without trouble. He is convinced that this strain is the best for working the hills in the Pennine Hunt country, a country that has seen much glaciation, limestone erosion and quarrying. Hinchcliffe is a systematic breeder, and like Nuttall a good, practical geneticist, so perhaps the relatively pure strain will be saved from extinction by the few such sensible breeders. Like Nuttall, Hinchcliffe likes blacks, but I have a red specimen bred from Hinchcliffe's stock which exactly resembles Breay's Rusty. John Parkes of Kirkby Overblow keeps this strain alive by careful line breeding using only a tiny dash of Hardasty's Turk in the mix.

Lastly, I, too, am indebted to the work of Breay and Buck. My own Jack Russell bloodline is roughly one quarter Breay and Buck bred, and though the colour has now been bred out, the excellent working ability and the good strong heads and straight fronts still remain.

Many strains of fell terrier are descended from dogs bred from Border

23. One of Graham Ward's good-quality fells with slight border terrier influence.

terriers. Border terriers are probably closely related to the fell or Lakeland terrier, and may well in fact constitute an intermediate type between fell terriers and Dandie Dinmont and Bedlington terriers. In 1920 it was even suggested by Lord Lonsdale that a breed of terrier similar in most respects to the Border terrier had been bred and worked near Lowther since 1732, but these terriers were not only blue, pale tan and dark bundled, but also white. Lord Lonsdale refers to these terriers as Ullswater terriers.

Bowman is reputed to have owned and worked Borders. Indeed, his bitch Wasp (Ullswater Jack mated to Ullswater Nettle) is one of the ancestors of the Border terrier North Tyne Gyp. Anne Roslin Williams, in her book *The Border Terrier*, states that Bowman owned red Lakelands which she describes as the 'ancestors of the present-day Patterdale terrier' (a somewhat baffling statement, I feel), but no one could remember Bowman ever keeping a Border terrier in his kennel. Bowman, however, owned an enormous number of terriers in his lifetime, ranging from the amazing-looking Bedlington terrier types of fell in his famous Mardale photograph, to Lil, a Jack Russell type of terrier which he gave to Sid Wilkinson in 1924. Hence Bowman may have owned and worked a Border terrier or so during his long and eventful life.

What is more than likely, however, is that fell and Border terriers are descended from the same root stock, and Bowman's Wasp was one of those terriers which gave rise to both fell terriers and Border terriers. It is also more than likely that fell blood mingled quite freely with the type which gave rise to the Border terrier during the early part of the twentieth century. However, after the formation of the Border Terrier Club in 1920 and the production of a standard for the breed, it seems unlikely that further infusions of fell-terrier blood entered into the pedigrees of Border terriers.

Border terrier blood is, on the other hand, often added to fell strains. Many of Buck's early terriers, Tex, Blitz and so on, looked decidedly 'Borderish'. I asked Frank about this, and he told me that Blitz was in fact one quarter Border terrier. For about four years prior to Blitz's birth, Buck had had a very useful fell-terrier bitch called Tiger – a black with slight brindling (hence the name Tiger) – and after watching Tiger work, Major Burdon of the Bedale Foxhounds had been so impressed that he asked Buck to mate this fell terrier to a Border terrier crossed with a fell which he owned, a terrier bred from a registered Border terrier that had seen service at the Percy Foxhounds. Thus a tiny infusion of Border-terrier blood entered into the famous Buck/Breay pedigree, but it took years for Buck to breed away from this Border type. Tex, his greatest dog, a brilliant hunter and a great stayer to fox, would have passed as an early Border terrier of the 1890s.

Few fell terrier breeders seem averse to mating their dogs to bitches with a dash of Border terrier in their pedigree, though some, including Maurice Bell, are opposed to such a mating. Nuttall, who follows a fairly tight and clearly scientific breeding programme – a programme he uses to keep alive the Breay/Buck strain – once showed me a young stud fee puppy he was

24. Fell-type border terriers bred by Bradley, whose strain was continued by Buck and Breay.

25. Note the border-type head of Breay's Blitz – third right.

running on. The pup, a black, smooth-coated dog of the type liked by Breay, with a magnificent bull-terrier type of head, a straight front and a good general type, had been bred from a half-bred Nuttall-strain/Border-terrier bitch mated to a Nuttall-strain dog. Nuttall intended to try this infant to test him to the utmost, and if he proved game, to breed him into his own strain of terrier. He did not believe that an infusion of Border terrier blood did any damage to the working qualities of his fell terrier strain.

Richard 'Prich' Bland of the Melbreck Hunt used Border terrier blood from Otterburn in the creation of his own strain of fell terrier, mating it to Johnny Richardson's strain of Blencathra terriers and producing some curious-looking but very useful, sane and sensible workers. Bland, too, believes that such a cross prevents a fell strain from getting too hard, for Border terrier blood tends to encourage a terrier to stand back and respect his fox a little. Some of Bland's hybrid terriers have a reputation for being not only excellent bolting terriers but also for being great finders in deep earths.

In Durham, Graham Ward has produced a very useful strain of terrier by mating his Hardasty-bred terriers with a stray Border terrier – a terrier without a pedigree, perhaps, but an exceedingly good worker. I trained one of Ward's terriers three years ago, and it had a strong Border type of head, but most of Ward's dogs are very classy dogs of the Hardasty type.

Richardson similarly has no inhibitions about adding a dash of Border-terrier blood to his strain of fell terrier, though he admits he has never owned or wanted to own a pure Border terrier. Yet he bred Tinker, a good if rather strange terrier, by mating Tarzan to a half-bred Border/fell-terrier bitch.

There has been in fact, a marked tendency in recent years for fell terrier breeders to cross their fell terriers with Border terriers to produce a sensible, sound worker which is not too hard and which will give tongue freely. Hard terriers, however, are becoming more common each year – terriers which quickly throttle a fox, terriers which close with their quarry and take a bad mauling as a result of the encounter, terriers which tackle badgers in catch-as-catch-can duels and get torn to pieces. Richardson and Bland believe that these terriers are the result of mating pedigree Lakeland terriers to the sane and sensible fell strains, and many huntsmen are now seeking other blood to ameliorate these strains. Several now use Border terriers on their fell bitches. Mrs Lesley Gosling told me at the Lowther Show (1981) that a local hunt terrier man had mated his fell terrier to her Border as the local strains of fell terrier were too 'madheaded' and took unnecessary punishment from fox and badger.

Of the strains referred to collectively as Border/Lakeland terriers, normally rough-coated, small types of terrier without any of the classic lines of some of the showable fell terriers, there are obviously no recorded data. Most have little registered Lakeland blood in their veins and precious little Border-terrier blood. Many are simply the old, unadulterated fell terrier strains, and excellent workers they prove to be. Laurie Dent, who keepers an estate near Pennhill, once used good-class showy fell terriers bred down from Maurice Bell's illustrious Britt, but found them too hard and often too stupid for his job. He has now reverted to a shaggy, rather unsightly strain of so-called Border/Lakeland terrier, and they are excellent workers. I watched one work out fox in a bad place in Pennhill and was most impressed.

The future of the fell terrier looks good. Show entries are increasing each year. Huge classes are now found in the Home County shows. The standards of the exhibits also improves each year. Few of the exhibits resemble the real old fell terrier, however, and some are nearly pure-bred Lakeland terriers. Further addition of registered Lakeland terrier blood is not desirable. Furthermore, the breeders of those huge dogs of fifteen inches and above at the shoulder that are winning all the Midlands and south of England shows would do well to remember that they would never be suitable to work in the Lake District (or anywhere else, for that matter). I consulted Bland of the Melbreck, Olgivie of the Coniston, Richardson at the Blencathra, Nicholson at the Lunesdale, Bell at the Wensleydale and Barrow at the Ullswater. Not one of these huntsmen favoured a terrier of above thirteen inches at the shoulder. Show judges to the south should remember this when they casually put up elegant but gigantic fell terriers at hunt terrier shows.

PART FOUR: THE TERRIER MEN

Joe Armstrong

(Interviewed at Dalston, Cumbria, in August 1982)

Joe Armstrong is the last of a famous troop of hunters who hunted the Melbreck during the heyday of Willie Irving – hunters like 'Mowdie' (a mole catcher, moles being called mowdies in the Lakes) Robinson, who was as good a terrier man as the Lakes ever knew, and one who Buck described as a marvel with a spade. Sadly, Armstrong is the last of this colourful band.

Armstrong was born at Great Orton, a spit away from Dalston, from a family of gamekeepers, not terrier keepers, though the family had strong connections with the local hunts. Joe Armstrong described himself as a hunting fanatic, for he truanted from school to follow the hunt, and considered subsequent thrashings from teachers as fair payment for the pleasure he obtained from hunting. He left school and took a job with the local bus company, a job which not only allowed him to see the Lake District but also allowed him time to hunt during his night-shift rest period. At one time he worked his terriers with seven packs: the Cumberland Farmers, the Blencathra, the Bewcastle (he knew and respected the late Eddie Proud), the Dumfriesshire, the College Valley, the Ullswater and the Melbreck.

Joe considers Ben Goddard of the Cumberland Farmers to be the best huntsman the north has seen, and from Goddard he obtained his first terrier, a blue bitch with an open coat, the typical fell-terrier/Bedlington hybrid that was common in Cumberland some sixty years ago. This bitch started his interest in working terriers (Armstrong, not a show enthusiast, remarked dryly, 'I breed onions for show,' and waxed a little scathing about the dogs winning at working terrier shows today), and with the Cumberland Farmers-bred bitch worked the spectrum, through rat, fox, badger and otter, before she died of old age some fifteen years after he bought her.

83

26. Joe Armstrong, 1982.

His next terrier of note was Mac, bred by Billy Irving. Armstrong remarks that Irving kept two strains of terrier at his kennels at Hope Lorton: a fell type, which did service with the Melbreck, and a classy, showy type, with which Billy won many shows. However, unlike many others, Armstrong does not decry Irving's show-bred terriers and remarks that he saw several go to ground and work like Trojans, taking fearful punishment and not giving an inch. Mac was of Irving hunt strain, and was sold as a pet to Great Orton. A fell terrier denied a chance to hunt soon becomes an absolute liability, however, and Mac rampaged in the village, becoming a great cat killer, and an even bigger liability as time went on. Eventually, after a particularly bad incident, his owner literally asked Armstrong to take him off his hands. The early socializing Mac had had as a pup soon paid off, and after Armstrong had broken the dog of his habits, he settled down and became one of the best workers imaginable, with an almost human intelligence. When Armstrong hunted rabbit, the dog ignored foxes. When Armstrong followed the hunt, Mac became indifferent to rabbit. Mac, too, lived to a ripe old age, dying a fireside death at the age of fourteen. Throughout his working life to fox, badger and otter, he was utterly biddable, and Armstrong could call him out of the most furious subterranean fracas. As a ferreting dog, he left little to be desired, and travelled to nearby warrens on the bars of Armstrong's bike.

Bess, another Bedlington type of fell terrier, bought from Faulder of Buttermere, was his next terrier of note, and this bitch also became a noted terrier among the huntsmen of the Lakes. Bess was unsightly, with an open coat, yet, according to Joe, she never suffered from the freezing fell weather. Armstrong valued this bitch highly, as her nose was unerring, and many times, after a fox was given up as lost in a borran earth, or a badger had dug in, she managed to 'find'. This ability to find is rated highly among the older fell men, far above the quality of being able to finish a fox. In fact, Todd, author of 'Terrier Song', once told Eddie Pool while out hunting with the Ullswater that he only rarely found terriers which were good at fox killing were also able to find in very bad places. Richardson also deems the ability to find as more important than the ability to finish a fox.

Later, Armstrong bought a red-and-black bitch from Billy Irving, a dog bred from some of Irving's best workers, and this bitch, Dart, became not only a good strong fox-bolter, working badger and otter equally well, but was also an important brood bitch, for, mated to Ronnie Porter's dog Mike, a fell/Border first cross, a good finder, a sensible dog and a renowned stayer, Armstrong bred from her Rock, his most famous terrier.

Rock kicked off to an inauspicious start, for after Dart whelped she became ill and her milk-flow ceased. Hence Armstrong's wife reared the entire litter on Ostermilk, feeding them every two hours, day and night. Rock justified her efforts, however, for he developed sterling qualities. He had a wonderful nose and was a devil for deer, once running a roe for nearly a day and returning four miles across busy roads to make it home to Armstrong's house. He, like his sire, was a renowned stayer, and stopped thirty hours in a freezing drainage pipe at a badger, his fur crackling to the touch when Armstrong finally dug him out. He, too, passed on his great versatility, since he bred Gyp, a good all-round terrier, as good at retrieving as at earth work and capable of fetching shot duck off water.

27. Joe Armstrong's elderly fell/borders.

His final purchase was a Johnny Richardson-bred dog called Major, a rough-coated black-and-tan fell, bred down from Jim Dalton's famous lines. (Dalton worked with the Blencathra during the times when Skelton was writing up notes for his *Reminiscences of Joe Bowman,* and Farrer of the Ullswater often went to Dalton to obtain 'the very best fell terriers'). Major was a sensible dog, for Richardson is a very selective terrier breeder and will not countenance the unruly, the headstrong or the excessively hard. He stayed back, giving tongue freely, an ideal dog by any standards, and rarely became a problem underground. Yet badger sets proved his undoing, for in 1950 Armstrong was employed by British Rail to clear badger from railway embankments. This interest in badger hunting finished Major, for he suffocated in sand, his mouth so full that he could not draw breath. Armstrong later trapped ten badgers from this bank since the place was too dangerous to dig.

Major once took part in a curious hunt that caused Armstrong some grief and not a little embarrassment. He was hunting the river Lyne when he found a drainpipe nearly filled by the tidal waters and only a two-inch air space. Major began snorting and snuffing in the pipe and baying frantically. After checking exits and entrances, Armstrong let Major go. He swam up the pipe and a battle royal took place, Major splashing, barking and screaming with rage. Armstrong went to the end of the pipe and waited. Slowly a tail appeared at the end of the pipe, and a twenty-four-pound dog otter inched out, spitting defiance and yickering at Major. Armstrong crouched and, knee-deep in water, tailed the otter, swinging it clear of the pipe and dodging Major's lunging attack. However, in the process of tailing the otter Armstrong succeeded in swinging too far, and the upset beast latched on to Armstrong's buttocks, biting like a fiend and holding on like a bulldog. It took Armstrong a considerable time to get the otter to release its grip and to tie up Major, and his backside bears the scars to this day.

Another embarrassing incident occurred when Armstrong owned a fell-terrier bitched called Millie. At that time, Armstrong and Ronnie Porter had been given the task of shifting foxes to release them out of sheep-rearing country. Porter bagged two and set off on his motorbike, Armstrong riding pillion and carrying the sack containing the foxes over his shoulder. Every person they passed stared in amazement, which baffled Joe, until he saw their reflection in a shop window and realized that both foxes had their heads out of the bag.

Armstrong is quite fond of Borders, and states that the old type of Border was as good as a fell terrier, his present terriers being fell/Border hybrids. Sadly, the strains of Border known to Armstrong are no longer available, and the Border terrier's working ability has suffered considerably in the last fifteen years.

Joe is also a keen naturalist, with an eye for the beasts he has hunted. Some twenty-five years ago he reared a badger cub from a few days old. Eventually it became so tame it would follow him to the local pub and leap up on the seat with him, sitting there until closing time. As Joe mentioned, no one ever took his seat! Each evening it strolled abroad with the terriers, feeding on slugs, worms and sundries, but when Joe eventually released it, the mating urge got the better of it and it forsook Joe's house for a set in the nearby woods.

When we left Joe's house and set off home, David remarked, 'When his generation dies, will it be replaced with another generation of fell men of Armstrong's ilk?' I reflected on the comment, considering some of the young rabble we had met at a show in the Midlands. 'No,' I answered, 'Armstrong's generation will go the way of the dinosaur. Armstrong's type of man is a one-off job, never to be repeated.'

Postscript: In the winter of 1982 Armstrong died of a heart attack.

2. Anthony Barker

(Interviewed at Patterdale, Cumbria)

Anthony Barker lives on the outskirts of the village of Patterdale – a district famed for its Lakeland terriers. Indeed, the first registered Lakeland terriers were often referred to as Patterdales.

His father, Fred Barker, once hunted the now extinct Pennine Foxhounds (not to be confused with the present day Pennine Foxhounds) at Ousby from 1914 to 1918, but moved to the Lakes while Anthony was a child. In addition to the family, Fred brought with him three terriers. Two of them were white, rather ugly terriers bred by the Ilfracombe Badger Digging Club: straight-legged, loose-coated dogs similar to the dogs run by Major Doig in Africa, and in all probability bred down from the Jack Russells of Arthur Heinemann, for the club certainly made use of Heinemann's stud dogs. The third was a red typey fell terrier, one which had seen considerable work at fox, for his jaw was shredded and hinged badly, and this peculiarity gave rise to the dog's nickname Chowt ('chewed')-faced Rock. In spite of his physical peculiarities and his unknown breeding, however, he was to make a great impact on the breed of fell terriers in and around the Ullswater Hunt country.

Anthony remembers a peculiar-looking chocolate bitch, the property of Tony Poole, being brought to this stud dog – a game but ugly hybrid, a misalliance 'twixt a small chocolate or liver spaniel and a fell terrier. This bitch mated to Chowt-faced Rock gave rise to a great number of chocolate fell terriers around Patterdale, the most famous of which was Snip, a game and fiery terrier, the property of Miss Belk of Grasmere. There is no doubt that Rock also carried this chocolate colour in his genetic make-up as the first litter from Rock and the spaniel-terrier cross had a few chocolate-coloured puppies.

During Anthony Barker's early years war broke out, and Joe Wear, who hunted the Ullswater Hounds at that time, was drafted for military service. Barker took over the hounds, hunting them with some considerable success considering that he was barely in his early twenties at the time between 1940 and 1946. During this period a bitch bred by Jim Fleming of Grasmere was put to work at the kennels. This bitch, Myrt (short for Myrtle, for Sid Hardasty refers to the bitch by this name), was a not particularly attractive slape-coated, black-and-tan terrier, but she was an excellent worker to both fox and badger. Her impact on the breed was in fact tremendous. She became the dam of Joe Wear's Tear 'Em, one of Joe's most useful terriers, and the granddam of Hardasty's illustrious Turk. Tear 'Em's sister Judy was kept by Anthony Barker, and, mated to a brown and white dog from the old blood (Chowt-faced Rock x Ilfracombe Badger Club's bitch), she bred a bitch that was given to Anthony's cousin. This bitch was in turn mated to Jimmy Burcott's dog (Anthony cannot remember the dog's name) and bred Anthony Barker's most famous stud dog, Rock; a dog which, when mated to Sid

28. *Anthony Barker at Patterdale, 1981.*

29. Anthony Barker's Rock (right) and a son of Rock.

Wilkinson's bitch, bred Wilkinson's Rock, a dog that fathered a dynasty of both fell and Russell types of offspring. See interview with Gary Middleton.

Anthony Barker's Rock was a superb worker and quite a looker, as the photograph clearly shows. Once, while hunting with the Ullswater Hounds, he was put to ground in a bad place and killed two adult foxes. He was frightfully lacerated and Anthony 'lifted' him. Later that day Wear put in another fox in an equally bad place and two terriers were entered. It was a difficult uphill earth, the sort of earth where a fox can keep a terrier at bay, and the fox 'dusted' both terriers badly, finally getting the better of both. Joe Wear then asked Anthony to try the now badly swollen-faced Rock, who entered quietly, took hold of his fox after a few lunges and killed it. Rock's dauntless courage was passed on to his offspring, and despite the quality of any bitch brought to him, he never sired a quitter.

Like many fell men Barker rarely worked badger with his dogs and was strictly a fox-hunting man. His own dogs were kept out of earths known to house badger (it should be added that Myrt, the ancestor of Rock, was a useful badger dog, and Anthony Chapman and Eddie Poole's grandfather dug many badger using this bitch). Rock was far too hard for badger, however, and to use him at Brock would certainly have resulted in tragedy. Rock seems to be Anthony Barker's ideal terrier: a chunky dog of maybe seventeen pounds in weight, having a strong head and a good harsh Irish terrier type of coat. He no longer keeps this family of terriers, and his last Rock descendant died a few years ago, but the dynasty lives on through the terriers sired by Sid Wilkinson's Rock and the terriers of Gary Middleton.

3. Dennis Barrow

Dennis Barrow, huntsman for the Ullswater Hunt, is from a family of quarrymen, but quarrymen with a passionate interest in hunting. Even as a schoolboy Dennis hunted, following hounds at every opportunity. In 1960 he became a professional whip for the Coniston, taking up his present post as huntsman for the Ullswater, certainly one of the more fashionable fell packs, in 1971.

Barrow describes himself as a houndsman more than a terrier enthusiast, for he came by his first terrier when he became a whip in 1960. He obtained his first fell terrier, a chocolate bitch, from Bob Crawford, but the terrier was bred by John Capstick of Kendal. As Barrow laughingly stated, it was the only terrier he ever bought, for he bred or 'came by' the others. Bracken, however, was seemingly a worthy purchase, for she worked well throughout her life, dying at eighteen years of age (she was a two-year-old bitch when Barrow bought her).

The bitch became a prolific dam. She was mated to Edmund Porter's stud

30. Dennis Barrow, 1982.

dog, Turk, and produced a useful litter of puppies, some of which were sent to hunts in America. Later she produced another useful litter to Eddie Pool's useful and dead-game terrier, Trim, and she also bred a third litter to Frank Buck's dog, Badger, a dog from the Davey–Topsy line.

Bracken II, the result of the first mating from Bracken, worked some three seasons for Barrow and died in a most peculiar manner. He had mated her to Tear 'Em, Edward Tyson's useful stud dog, and her puppies were six weeks old at the time of the tragedy. One day Bracken II got out and followed the hounds. A fox was driven to ground in a difficult borran, so Barrow allowed the eager bitch to enter to it. She went in, killed her fox and disappeared. And though Barrow dug for her, finding his fox, there was no trace of the bitch. Joe Wear came that night and, on hearing the puppies howling, told Dennis they could hear their mother barking – a comment that Dennis considered absurd at the time. Three weeks later he found the cadaver of the bitch lying against a wall only a few hundred yards from home.

He kept a dog puppy from this bitch: a rather long-backed black and tan called Rebel. Rebel was a good all-round terrier, not too hard and with some sense, but after six seasons he fell out of a crag while flushing a fox and severely injured himself, so Dennis retired him.

About that time Sid Wilkinson, one of Ullswater's most famous terrier breeders, gave Barrow a terrier called Tim. The dog came to him when it was eighteen months of age – a rather gaunt, scruffy blue dog, the result of a Bedlington terrier/fell-terrier cross perhaps, or at least a dog with a strong trace of Bedlington in its pedigree. It was a controversial dog, and though Barrow didn't rate the dog highly among his terriers, Eddie Pool, who worked with the dog many times, said it was one of the best hunt terriers Barrow owned. It went out for its first time shortly after Barrow had him and worked to a lamb-killing fox that had gone to ground in a borran. He went like a lion, but after Dennis had begun to shift the earth to dig to the dog, Tim went mute, offering no indication of where he was. Barrow entered another terrier and dug three cubs and an old vixen with the dog. Dennis then reached down into a rock crevice and felt teeth close on his hand, piercing the flesh until the fangs met. Below him was Tim with a dead cub, reluctant to give up ownership of his victim.

Tim never lived to fulfil his early expectations, in spite of what Eddie Pool, a reliable terrier man, believes, for he was a sickly dog, a dog which in livestock breeding circles is called a 'poor doer'. He refused to flesh out and looked poor, and at the age of three he died of kidney failure. Seemingly courage alone is not enough. For a terrier to work in this sort of country it must be constitutionally sound as well as game.

Barrow rates constitutional strength as being very important in a terrier required to work on the fells, hunting from ten to twenty-five miles, three and frequently four times a day. Fell terriers, and fell terriers without pedigree-registered Lakeland blood, are his ideal workers. He admits that he has never owned a pedigree Lakeland, but he has seen dogs of this type suffer on bad days. Border terriers are also not up to Barrow's standard for the same reason, and he avoids Russell types of dog (he makes a distinction between Jack Russell terriers and white throwbacks bred out of fell parents – dogs which he calls white Lakelands, incidentally) since they are a 'bit fragile' for

31. Dennis Barrow's fell terriers at Ullswater.

the work he requires of a terrier.

Barrow is patient concerning the entering of a terrier, and consequently he has never owned a failure, a dog that wouldn't eventually 'go' to fox. When a puppy is a year old he takes it out with the hounds, and when it is ready it usually goes. He quotes the case of a dog of his called Jack, a dog which showed no interest in fox or going to ground. Barrow took him out time and time again with no success. Then, one day, he found hounds marking in a borran and Jack baiting his fox below ground.

4. Maurice Bell

(Interviewed at Hawes, North Yorkshire, on 31 October 1980)

Hawes is a small town in Wensleydale, and it was to here that I journeyed to meet Maurice Bell, an enigmatic man whom Winch had once described as a

32. *Maurice Bell, master of the Wensleydale Foxhounds, Hawes.*

dodo – not a derogatory term, for Bell is regarded by many as the last of the dyed-in-the-wool fell hunters. As Winch predicted, Bell eats, sleeps and lives fell hunting, and after learning his trade with the Lunesdale Foxhounds, set up his own pack at Hawes, starting with a few trail hounds and a small team of draft hounds from Scotland. With seven trail hounds broken of their bent for aniseed trailing and four bitches from Scottish packs, he set about hunting the bleak fells around Wensleydale and took eighteen foxes above ground during his first season. Now with eleven couple of hounds, no passengers, he hunts Saturdays and Sundays over some of the worst country in the southern fells. His hounds, described unkindly by some of the other fell packs as a pirate pack, are not what they seem, and Bell insists that he deserves recognition as an official fell pack since the Wensleydale Foxhounds existed at the turn of the century and he has merely revived the pack, not created a new one.

Bell, a robust giant of a man in his mid forties, has been an active breeder of fell terriers for twenty-five years and rejects the name Lakeland for his terriers as he considers such a name more appropriate for the Kennel Club registered breed. His disdain for such stock, now commonly mated on to rugged fell stock to produced dogs capable of winning at the hunt shows, was apparent within moments of meeting him. Bell hunts icy-cold country with no crags to harbour foxes, so the earths are in shakeholes, peat and sodden earths along side gills (steep-sided flood brooks), hence the long woolly coat of the pure-bred Lakeland would be regarded as anathema by hunters of Bell's ilk. Such coats, while they are excellent blankets, suitable for trimming and shaping a show dog, are death-traps in the frozen fells where winter temperatures are invariably low and drop suddenly as evening falls. Bell tells of an open-coated dog, perhaps show blooded, perhaps not, which worked an

33. *Maurice Bell hunt terriers.*

earth in Wensleydale and emerged sodden and badly bitten after an hour or so underground. The temperature outside the earth was below zero and the heated, badly bitten terrier died before its owner could carry the dog half a mile to the nearest farm. Smooth-coated dogs are also out of favour with Bell particularly as he hunts in places where the wind is strong enough 'to blow your 'ed off'. He tells a tale of Cyril Breay whose dogs showed the height of courage and soon cleaned themselves when they came out of a peat earth, but looked decidedly unhappy when they had to stand for hours in sub-zero temperatures in a howling gale. Bell breeds some open-coated and smooth puppies from time to time, but gives them away as soon as their characteristics become obvious.

He keeps four to six terriers, most of which he can trace back six generations to his original stock. Most of his dogs date back to the formidable and important stud, Harry Hardasty's Turk, a neat red dog with no trace of Kennel Club blood in his pedigree. Hardasty's Turk must be regarded as one of the most important studs in the working Lakeland/fell terrier lines, and both Winch and Buck believe that this dog carried a strong dash of Irish-terrier blood in his veins. Certainly some of Bell's terriers have coats that exactly resemble those of a good old type of Irish terrier. Bell came by this line through Buster to Tyson's Rock, which sired one of Bell's most famous dogs, Twist. Twist, in turn, was mated to Viper, one of Buck's bitches, for Buck's stock at that time, to quote Maurice Bell, was 'some of the gamest in the world and had no peer in the fells or the Lakes'. Twist in turn bred Britt, a dog famed throughout North Yorkshire. Twist died before he could be established as a top breeder and the manner of his death was both curious and macabre. Twist had gone to ground in a gill earth in Wharfedale, and after a titanic struggle emerged in a very sorry state with bad face and throat lacerations. Within hours the dog had choked to death, and autopsy revealed a huge blood clot in the throat and upper reaches of the respiratory tract. Damage to tissue, shock and icy gill water see off many valiant fell terriers!

Britt proved a famous sire and bred good lookers as well as workers. He was, to quote Bell, 'the hardest terrier I have ever seen', and could fence with a fox until he had a throat or jaw hold and quickly finished the foe. His progeny were also a bunch of brawlers, and I can do no better than quote Joe Landerly on the subject. 'We had many dogs from Bell up here [the Highlands of Scotland], and many of the keepers would go nowhere else for terriers. We don't want or need baying, yapping dogs, but big powerful game dogs that will finish a cat [the Scottish wild cat] or a fox. Bell's stuff was ideal. I had a puppy bred from a red dog and a black bitch both bred by Bell and down from his bitch Brick, and this dog would draw any wild cat or fox.'

Bell hunts his terriers over formidable country, country which takes a savage toll on his dogs. The earths are some of the most difficult in a country where shake holes (swallow-holes) abound, some supposedly being bottomless pits. The eroded sides of gills prove difficult and dangerous places to hunt, but Bell puts terriers to ground in earths which would be considered

34. Maurice Bell's Britt.

impossible to work down south. He was born and bred in this area and has farmed this bleak fell, so there are few earths he does not know. His advice on working such earths is wisdom indeed. 'I will put a dog into an earth where water is coming out, but I will never put a dog into a lair where water is running in.'

It is common practice down south to breed huge fell terriers quite unsuitable for southern earths, and their breeders often state that such dogs are needed on the fells. Indeed, I have seen a sixteen-inch dog win at the MWTC show in Northamptonshire, and not for a moment did any spectators question the judge's decision. Bell considers such a type of dog to be useless. 'Too leggy to get,' was his statement on the subject of size. Thirteen inches is about right in Bell's opinion, and bitches should be a shade smaller. Any terrier not spannable is useless, Bell believes, and up to sixteen pounds but no more seems to be the correct weight for a terrier required to work the rugged Wensleydale earths.

Bell's method of entering a terrier to produce a baying dog suitable for working with his hounds is considered irregular by many, but Bell produces few failures using his training programme. He enters his terriers at between a year and two years of age to badgers, and works to them badger regularly until they learn caution. Only then does he try them to the leggy hill foxes that live in the country he hunts. He has bred many hard terriers, terriers that, according to one Scottish gamekeeper, will 'bite a hole in an iron bar', but now prefers a dog that will bay and fix the fox so that it can be dug.

Bell looks after his terriers, and some of his best live in. He requires them to work hard, and that is an understatement, but when they are damaged, torn badly or simply knocked about in a skirmish underground, he treats for shock immediately, dipping and cleaning them in hot water and keeping them under heat lamps until they are right. His dogs look right, battle-scarred but fit and well, and as Winch predicted, Bell is the beau idéal of the fell huntsman. It is to be hoped that Winch's other statement, that Bell is a dodo, the last of a breed, is by contrast incorrect.

5. Richard Bland

(Interviewed in Cumbria, on 18 October 1981)

I interviewed Richard Bland, otherwise known as 'Prich' Bland, outside his house at the Melbreck Kennels. Bland is from farming stock, and joined the Melbreck in 1966, whipping in for seven seasons to Harry Hardasty, finally becoming huntsman to the pack in 1973. He is also Harry Hardasty's son-in-law, for he married Harry's daughter.

Bland has owned terriers since he was a boy, but his first useful workers were Tarzan, a grandson of Johnny Richardson's illustrious dog, and Tess, a cross-bred Jack Russell terrier. In spite of his relationship to Hardasty, Bland does not keep any of Hardasty's terriers and prefers the terriers bred from the Blencathra bloodlines. For outcross blood, he used the Border terriers of

John Dickson of Otterburn, who keeps, breeds and works a very useful strain.

'Prich' does not favour pedigree Lakelands, not because they are not game, nor because they are constitutionally not up to the vigorous life on the fells, but simply because they are invariably fighters; and since the terriers are kennelled with hounds, an aggressive terrier can be a cause of great upset and often get killed by hounds.

His best terriers are pictures of docility and most reluctant to fight. Judy, his former brood bitch, the result of crossing a fell terrier from Tarzan II line with an Otterburn Border terrier, was a nailer to fox, an excellent finder and a great bolting dog, yet the bitch rarely if ever displayed aggression to other dogs. She died in 1980, aged thirteen years, having been born and buried at the Melbreck. Gyp, another dog with Border-terrier blood mated back to the Tarzan line, is another quiet terrier. He finds well and stays, yet is not in the least quarrelsome. In fact Bland refuses to keep a fiery-tempered terrier, no matter how well it works, for it disrupts the harmony of the hunt kennels. His dogs which show obvious Border-terrier ancestry all kennel with hounds until they retire.

He likes a smallish terrier; one, in fact, under twelve inches tall, since he believes these are the most suitable to work the earths in the Melbreck country, which range between enlarged rabbit warrens and the deepest of borrans. He likes narrow-chested dogs, preferably with a wire coat, though he does not stress the importance of a hard, wiry jacket as much as do most terrier men who work the fells. In fact, Bland has known smooth-coated dogs which have worked well in very inclement weather. His dogs are all related to Richardson's, and Bland seems unwilling to go for out-cross blood when the dogs of the Tarzan family produce such consistent workers. His dogs find well and bring readily, but most will kill a fox if they need to. He keeps about six terriers in all, and they must earn their keep hunting three days a week in a country only slightly smaller than the Blencathra country.

6. Joe Bowman

(Based on the recollection of those who knew him)

No book on any aspect of hunting in the Lakes could be complete without a mention of the late Joe Bowman of the Ullswater Hunt, the almost legendary hunter of the Lake district and an equally legendary raconteur of hunting yarns.

Bowman's contribution to the creation of the fell terrier is doubtful, however, and there are many conflicting views concerning his methods of

506. A. & P., KENDAL.   JOE BOWMAN
WITH HIS FAVOURITE HOUNDS

entering and of his breeding of fell terriers. John Farley believes that Bowman kept a strain of red terriers, bred as selectively and carefully as Bowman bred his hounds, but there is great doubt as to whether this is fact or simply one of the legends. There is even a suggestion that Bowman's dogs were used in the creation of the Border terrier. North Tyne Gyp (1917) was sired by a dog called Griff, reputedly out of Bowman's Wasp, who in turn was bred out of two red-tan Lakelands, Ullswater Jack out of Ullswater Nellie. Certainly Border-terrier blood did enter into the pedigree of the modern working fell terrier, however, for Yaks Bob, a registered Border terrier, appears in quite a few working Lakeland pedigrees. Might it not therefore also be likely that some Lakeland or rather fell terrier blood was included in the making of the Border terrier? To make any claims regarding

101

the racial purity of any northern working terrier is not only presumptive but also very unscientific. What is certain is that no relative of Joe Bowman – and I have interviewed some eleven of Bowman's kin – can remember Border terriers at the Ullswater kennels.

John Farley believes that Bowman kept a strain of red Irish-terrier types similar to Anthony Chapman's Red Ike in colour and shape though harder coated, and it is easy to see why such terriers undocked (and some say Bowman rarely if ever docked his terriers) could be confused with a Border terrier, for the Border terrier Fury, bred in 1895, had a decidedly Lakeland type of head. Ann Roslin Williams in her book *The Border Terrier* mentions a Mr Basley of Carlisle who had a dog from the Lowther Castle strain in 1920 with a strong short muzzle and small dark ears which may have been a Border terrier, but also mentions a terrier judge called James Garrow, a man well acquainted with terriers, who visited Lowther and went to the Ullswater Kennels. He reported having seen dense-coated blue and white dogs, but he made no mention of seeing Border terriers (and as a terrier judge he would certainly have recognized Border terriers) at the Ullswater kennels in Glenridding.

Walter Parkin, former huntsman of the Lunesdale, cousin of Bowman and a reliable witness of the hero's latter days, states that Joe kept no real strain of terrier and often relied on borrowed or begged dogs to flush, bolt or kill foxes. Parkin recalls that Bowman's terriers were often a motley crowd, kept for their useful qualities rather than their type, and that Russell-type terriers were as common as fell terriers in Bowman's kennels. Certainly such was Bowman's esteem in the Lakes – and his funeral saw literally hundreds of mourners – (Parkin says 'everyone went to Bowman's funeral'), that he would have had no difficulty in acquiring terriers on loan from the Lakeland farmers, and good terriers were certainly kept by sheep farmers in the Lakes. Joe Wear, huntsman for the Ullswater, often relied on terriers from sporting farmers and miners in the Lakes.

Frank Buck recalls a time some fifty years ago when Bowman hunted the fells near Hawes. The schoolboy Buck, aged ten, watched Bowman arrive with the hounds, and the temptation proved too great for him, for he truanted from school and went with the hunt. Buck, with an eye for terriers, remarked that Bowman's dogs were the long, open-coated type bred and kept by Tommy Dobson with obvious Bedlington ancestry, dogs without class but obviously efficient and good enough to satisfy the most famous huntsman in the Lakes. Buck, ever the raconteur, finished his tale by saying that when he absconded from school to hunt alongside Bowman, he then found to his dismay that his father was also out with Bowman that day. But such was Bowman's charisma that no action was taken against the boy, though Bowman asked Buck Senior to keep Frank close to him, for the fells around Hawes were mist covered and a ten-year-old lost on such fells could easily die of exposure.

7. Cyril Breay

(Based on the recollections of those who knew him)

No more baffling or enigmatic character flits across the fell-terrier scene than Cyril Breay. I met him once in 1964 at Bramham Moor Show after his dog had yet again won Best in Show. He was a very tall man, above six feet, gaunt through illness and with his skin paper-thin, but possessing enormous

36. *Cyril Breay (right) with Rusty, Wally Wyld with Kipper.*

presence and dignity. Few people referred to him as Cyril, most called him Mr Breay, and no one ever referred to him by his surname alone – a curious compliment in the bickering world of terrier breeders.

Cyril Breay was a retired school teacher, but he had little of the pompous, rather pretentious air one associates with school teachers. His knowledge of the fells, its fauna, its hunting and its people was incredible, and his views, ameliorated by a first-class education, were free from ignorance and not coloured by the curious superstitious that pervades the working terrier world. Few people, Buck aside, could match his knowledge of terrier work, and fewer still could equal his knowledge of the deadly fell earths that were in reach of his home at Kirkby Lonsdale, earths which claimed above eight terriers bred by Breay throughout his lifetime. Buck, an expert at the recovery of terriers trapped in rock earths, recalls rescuing by dint of crowbar, pick and even dynamite many of Breay's terriers in the Lunesdale country, and Breay listed in his letters to friends at least eight terriers who came to grief in these death-traps.

In Breay's youth he was an athletic man, much involved in the arduous and tiring sport of fell walking. Even after he became ill he could scale some of the scarp-edged hill sides like a chamois. During later life he became seriously ill with asthma, and this condition was further complicated with diabetes, two ailments which prevented him from driving any distance and a condition that had a curious effect on his breeding programme, as I shall explain later.

Breay's strain played a very important part in the creation of the modern working fell terrier. Middleton of Kendal, a thinking man by anyone's standards, once stated that the public should cease to use the title Patterdale terrier for the smooth- or broken-coated fell terriers that seem to abound in North Yorkshire and Lancashire and call the strain the Breay terrier, such was Breay's influence on the creation of the strain. Yet the Buck terrier might be an equally appropriate name, for Breay's and Buck's dogs were often traded between the two and Buck often worked Breay's dogs. Buck did, in fact, kennel Breay's dogs during the years between Breay's first and second marriages, years which made the kennelling of terriers impracticable. Subsequently, as I shall show in the pedigree that is to follow, it is impossible to separate the two families of terrier.

Breay kept a strain of strong bull-terrier-headed terriers – often very typey terriers which had a reputation for never quitting. In 1970, I saw an advert in *Exchange and Mart* for a litter of these terriers from Breay's strain, the appraisal of these dogs reading 'will not give an inch'. Such qualities are commendable and often desirable, but this blind courage often brought about injury and death for many of the progeny of Breay's dogs.

Late in the 1960s, Brockley of Etwall bought an entire litter of Breay-type terriers bred by Colin McDermot and sired by Breay's incredibly good-looking dog, Rusty. Brockley kept a male from this strain, also called Rusty, who displayed no fear of any quarry and somehow never learned discretion

37. Cyril Breay with Gem and Skiffle.

when badgering. By the age of two and a half he had lost most of his lips, quite a few teeth, and his face had taken on a curious twisted mean look as a result of his injuries. At fox he was very hard, closing with his quarry, taking any grip anywhere and mauling his foe to death. I once saw this dog work a fox in an artificial earth in Brockley's farm and commit mayhem on a fully grown dog fox in a matter of minutes, the whole art performed in near silence except for roars of anger when Rusty's victim retaliated. Brockley eventually sold this dog to some diggers in the north of Cheshire and he was never seen again. One can only guess at his fate.

Wally Wyld, of the Grove and Rufford Hunt, Nottingham, tells a similar story of a bitch sired by Rusty's brother, a black terrier called Kipper. Stuff from Kipper tended to enter to quarry quite late, often being still infantile at the age of two years. One bitch from Breay's strain eventually entered to fox and became a demon below ground, closing with her fox, refusing to allow it to bolt and killing there. She lost an eye through such tactics and became of no use to the Grove and Rufford Hunt because of her refusal to give ground to quarry. Wyld eventually gave her away, but kept the breeding rights in the strain.

Buck and Breay were a curious pair of friends, very dissimilar in appearance and ways. Buck is outgoing and talkative, whereas Breay was taciturn and inclined to be a little remote with people who were strangers. Both in their day were the top fell-terrier breeders in the north (a title that, funnily enough, Breay often gave to Harry Hardasty of the Melbreck hunt), but one thing serves as a common bond between Buck and Breay, and that is the difficulty one has unravelling the pedigrees of the dogs these breeders kept. Buck kept no written records and Breay, a meticulous man regarding the breeding of his dogs, was reluctant to discuss his breeding programme with anyone.

To give an instance of his taciturn nature, Maurice Bell first saw one of Breay's bull-terrier-headed animals while out hunting with the Lunesdale. He approached Breay and said, 'Useful sort of bitch, Mr Breay. Bull-terrier bred, is she?' Brey stiffened slightly, for he was touchy about this comment often levelled at his dogs by fell terrier men. 'I don't think so Maurice,' he replied. 'I believe the strain originated in Wales.' Later he confided to Wally Wyld, 'There is not a drop of bull-terrier blood in the entire strain.'

I am in fact indebted to Wally Wyld for the pedigree of Breay's dog Rusty, taken from a letter from Breay written in the spidery hand-writing of a man who knew the sweet scent of mortality. Some of the origins of the strain may seem a little curious to the reader, but Breay was a very truthful man and had no reasons to lie about the genealogy of his dogs. The reader may also care to note the number of dogs either bred or hunted by Buck that appear in the pedigree as well as the incidence of chocolate-coloured stock often attributed by some to the inclusion of dogs bred from the Bedlington x fell cross used by Tommy Dobson. Yet there is little proof of Dobson's very diluted strain being used by Breay, though many of the fell packs, Coniston, Ullswater and

106

Bloodlines of Breay/Buck terriers:

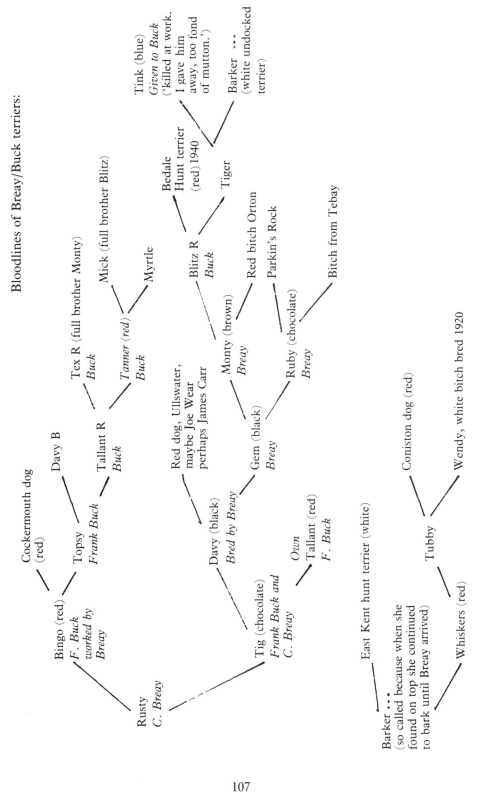

Cockermouth dog
(red)

Davy B

Tex R (full brother Monty)
Buck

Mick (full brother Blitz)

Myrtle

Tink (blue)
Given to Buck
('killed at work.
I gave him
away, too fond
of mutton.')

Barker ...
(white undocked
terrier)

Bedale
Hunt terrier
(red) 1940

Tiger

Tanner (*red*)
Buck

Blitz R
Buck

Red bitch Orton

Parkin's Rock

Bingo (red)
*F. Buck
worked by
Breay*

Topsy
Frank Buck

Tallant R
Buck

Red dog, Ullswater,
maybe Joe Wear
perhaps James Carr

Monty (brown)
Breay

Ruby (chocolate)
Breay

Bitch from Tebay

Davy (black)
Bred by Breay

Gem (black)
Breay

Coniston dog (red)

Rusty
C. Breay

Tig (chocolate)
*Frank Buck and
C. Breay*

Own
Tallant (red)
F. Buck

East Kent hunt terrier (white)

Tubby

Wendy, white bitch bred 1920

Barker ...
(so called because when she
found on top she continued
to bark until Breay arrived)

Whiskers (red)

to a certain extent the Melbreck, may have used dogs from Dobson's strain at some time or other. Thus the suggestion that Breay merely continued the Dobson strain, simply ameliorating the bloodline with bull-terrier blood, should be totally disregarded. Many Breay-bred strains of today do, it is true, still occasionally produce woolly coated dogs with a decided Dandie Dinmont appearance (Nuttall of Holmes Chapel showed me such a dog which carried numerous lines to Breay's dogs), but this does not necessarily indicate that Breay's bloodlines were simply an extension of Tommy Dobson's dogs. Breay, I am sure, would have been very quick to assert otherwise.

Thus, the reader will see, it is impossible to separate the dogs of Breay from those of Buck, and thus it would be unreasonable and incorrect to refer to the smooth- or slape-coated fell terrier as the Breay terrier.

8. Frank Buck

(Interviewed at Leyburn, North Yorkshire)

To write a book on the fell terrier without including a chapter on Frank Buck would be not only a serious omission but an impossibility, for few lines in Britain today do not include the dogs of Frank Buck in their pedigrees. Wyld of the Grove and Rufford, Jack Smith of Midhope Stones, John Parkes of Harrogate, Nuttall of Homes Chapel, Westmorland of Troutbeck, Maurice Bell of Hawes, and a hundred other noted breeders, all have strains of terrier that owe at least some of their pedigrees to the dogs bred by this genial Leyburn lorry driver.

Buck, together with Cyril Breay, must be regarded as one of the creators of a strain of black-and-red, smooth- or harsh-coated fell terrier, erroneously known as the Patterdale. The Bucks have long been noted for their interest in livestock, however, and there are records of a family of this name dealing in horses in Durham as early as 1630. Frank's grandfather was quite a noted terrier man in the North of England, and bred Bedlington-type, shaggy-coated terriers, which he used for badger digging, fox hunting and ratting. Many of these terriers were probably similar to the short-legged terriers kept by Davidson of Hindlee, the sporting squire, on whom Walter Scott modelled Dandie Dinmont. With such an ancestry, it does not seem surprising that Frank Buck was destined to become one of the greatest terrier men in English history.

Greatest terrier man ever is a more accurate way of describing Frank Buck during his youth and middle years. Winch described him as an authority on the fell terrier, and Maurice Bell referred to him as one of the greatest hunters Yorkshire had ever produced. At the time of writing, Buck is an old man,

38. Frank Buck with Topsy.

well into his seventies, who is prone to comment on approaching death all too frequently, but he still hunts most days of the week, and is terrier man for the Bedale Hunt.

Buck's first terriers were of his grandfather's and father's strain: rough-coated, blue-and-wheaten terriers of no particular type, and certainly without the class one finds at Buck's Kennels in Leyburn. But, by the age of twenty, Buck had established himself as one of the best terrier men in the Wensleydale area, able to talk as an equal to such notables as Joe Bowman and Braithwaite Wilson. We have already told the story of Frank playing truant from school at Hawes, when Bowman hunted the Ullswater Hounds on the surrounding fells, only to find to his horror his father out with the field. Frank's father shrugged his shoulders and allowed his ten-year-old son to remain with the field, possibly sensing that the fells were more beneficial, and certainly more educating, than the classroom at Hawes.

Frank's connection with Cyril Breay is of interest to all fell-terrier breeders. During the 1930s, Frank became a great friend of the refined, reticent, yet eloquent Breay, a friendship that was probably reinforced when Breay gave Frank a terrier from a white undocked terrier called Barker (Breay's eldest daughter denies that Barker was docked), descended from a Sealyham-type terrier Breay mated to a blue fell terrier called Tink he had bought from Robinson of Maryport (a sheep worrier which Breay described as being 'too fond of mutton' and later gave to Frank Buck). Buck's puppy from the pair was called Tiger, an ugly, Bedlington-headed much-photographed dog, and an incredible worker. Buck worked this bitch with the Bedale hunt one day, and succeeded in bolting a fox which all other hunt terriers had failed to shift. Major Burdon, out hunting with Bedale, was greatly impressed by Buck's Tiger, and requested that Frank mate the bitch to an outstanding redcoated, half-bred Border/fell male. Buck obliged, and the result of the mating was Blitz, one of the most important stud dogs in the history of the fell terrier. Blitz was the first of the fell terriers to produce the gigantic bull-terrier-headed terriers, associated with so-called Patterdale terriers, and Keith Clement of Kendal, former secretary of the Lunesdale Hunt, is convinced that there was something in the genetic make-up of Blitz which produced this massive skull and masseter muscle. Buck is convinced that this head type is the result of an injury to one of the bitches, which produced an enormous swollen head, and this acquired characteristic was transmitted to the puppies. I am inclined to agree with Clement, who made a careful and exact study of the Buck/Breay pedigree, at a time before Blitz was a popular stud dog in Consett, County Durham. Bradley (grandfather of John Winch) bought a Border type of terrier called Rip from the Newcastle Dog Market for 5s (25p), a ferocious, utterly game terrier with no pedigree but an incredible nose, and sense underground. This terrier was mated to numerous hunt terriers in the north repeatedly, including one of the Percy Hunt terriers, bred by George Sordy, who bred many of the best working Borders in the north. It is my opinion that this terrier is responsible for the massive heads found in the modern strains of fell terrier.

To return to the terrier breeding policies of Frank Buck, however, Blitz was a superlative stud dog, and bred many outstanding workers. One bitch which came to him, a red bitch from Orton, of unknown breeding, proved a

110

39. Buck's Tiger, one of the most important dams in fell terrier history.

remarkable dam. She was mated to Blitz a few times, and produced Monty, owned and worked by Breay, and Tex, owned and worked by Buck. Monty became an incredible worker, and soon many bitches in the Lunesdale Hunt country were brought to him to serve. Tex, a shy, retiring fell, with a decidedly Border-terrier appearance, became Buck's most famous worker, a dog which took over a hundred foxes from Penhill in one season. Tex was not only an outstanding finder, even in places like Penhill, or the difficult limestone earths in the Wensleydale area, but also a dog which Buck could control to almost gun-dog efficiency. Many fell hunters have remarked that Buck could call out this dog from a jaw-to-jaw encounter with a fox. Tex died old, senile, blind and deaf from a collision with a car that tipped the pavement while Frank was out exercising him.

Breay's Monty became the sire of Gem, when mated to a chocolate bitch called Ruby bred from Parkin's Red Rock strain (the first of the many chocolates produced by the strain of fell terrier – and a great number of bull-terrier-headed chocolate fell terriers are seen at the shows today). Tex sired Tallant out of a bitch called Tanner, bred out of a brother of Blitz, a dog called Mick, a little-used dog, who made little impact on the fell-terrier

111

40. *Bradley's Rip (foreground), a border (?) terrier with an enormous head. It is believed that this dog, purchased for 5/- (25p) from Newcastle dog market, was the ancestor of the Breay/Buck strain of terrier.*

41. Buck with Tex, his most famous terrier, after his successful season on Pennhill.

bloodlines, since most terrier bitches were brought to his more famous brother Blitz. Breay now mated Gem to a dog bred out of a bitch from Joe Wear's Tear 'Em, a red dog of good type owned and bred by Buck, and from this union came Davy, perhaps the most important stud in fell-terrier history. Breay did not like Davy, however, and gave him to Frank Buck, who was then involved with the Wensleydale Harriers, a pack of hounds he had inherited from Sinclair, a vet in the Wensleydale area – a vet, in fact, that James Herriot used as the model for Siegfried Farnon in his book *All Creatures Great and Small*. Buck, however, valued Davy highly, and kept him until he died of old age. Davy won Rydal Hound Show terrier class three years running (Frank points out that the show was then open to all terriers, not simply to terriers in service in the fell packs) and became an incredibly good fox dog, able to find in any earth, from rock to peat hole. Davy served dozens of bitches, one of which was Tallant, a daughter of Tex, a bitch that Frank says died in a rock hole in Wales.

From the Tallant x Davy mating, Buck bred Topsy, a black smooth-coated, strong-headed bitch with one cocked ear – a characteristic still passed on in many 'Patterdale' terriers of today. Topsy was no looker, though she was straight-legged and of good conformation. She worked well for Frank, however, but died when a fox bit her through the jugular vein, and she bled to death in moments before Buck could save her. Topsy bred few puppies, but was mated to Robinson's dog at Cockermouth, a sire that Buck particularly liked, and his choice did not prove wrong. Bingo, a sharp-witted dog with a strong frame and powerful head, came from this mating, and Frank gave Bingo to Breay. Bingo was a superb finder, and could finish most foxes (though in the end one fox killed him). Breay once told John Parkes that he would not keep a male which could not kill a fox in a tussle. Bingo killed many before he met his death in a quarry in the Lunesdale country. (See interview with Roger Westmorland.)

Bingo mated Tig, another puppy from the Davy x Tallant mating, and bred Rusty, perhaps the most used stud in the north, during his time. Buck found Rusty irritating, and when Breay, ailing rapidly with diabetes, offered Rusty to him, Buck refused, as the dog was fiery, keen to latch on to a hound that upset him and hysterically keen to get to ground. He was utterly fearless, however, and would face fox or badger. Breay found him hard to handle as he became sick and prone to the bouts of lassitude that are typical of the late stages of diabetes although Breay's eldest daughter attributes this to asthma augmented by the shock of the death of Breay's wife. Rusty, however, was not only a confirmed cat killer, but had developed an almost insane hatred of Bingo, his sire. (Buck called Bingo 'Bing', and corrected me every time I referred to the Wally Wyld pedigree.) Eventually, Breay gave Rusty to a man in Lancashire as a pet, but no dog bred from such an illustrious pedigree and worked as this dog had been could be expected to adapt to such an existence, and thus Rusty was returned to Breay, and ultimately Roger Westmorland at Troutbeck, in whose kennels he eventually died.

114

42. *Some of Black Davy's offspring.*

Breay died in the mid 1970s, but Buck continued to breed this strain of terrier. At one time, he introduced pedigree Lakeland blood, but the results were not good, so Buck scrapped the project and returned to his old programme. He now breeds a neat, cobby strain of fell terrier, primarily black-, rough- or broken-coated dogs, with short, strong muzzles. Buck breeds twelve-inch terrier types, for he has no use for terriers which are large and can only be worked in certain earths. Neither does he favour long-headed terriers, as he believes such jaws lack power. In fact, so distinctive is the type bred by Buck that it is possible to pick out Buck bloodlines at any show.

To enumerate the talents of Buck as a terrier man would be difficult if not impossible. He is a skilful breeder, a good man at starting a terrier, a wonder (in his heyday) with a spade, and a first-rate shot with a gun. He is, perhaps, the most knowledgeable terrier man concerning North Yorkshire earths and sets, and a fount of information about which sets to avoid. His skill as a dynamiter and excavator of trapped terriers prompted the late Josie Akerigg to say that Buck was a one-man fell and moorland rescue system, long before that club was formed. He has hunted with most northern packs, both mounted and foot packs, and he knew other all-time greats as personal friends – Wear, Wilson, Fred Barker, both Willie and Jack Porter, the Chapman's, father and son, and above all, Cyril Breay. His anecdotes of their lives would fill a fascinating and informative book.

Frank's wins in the show ring are numerous, and his rosettes would fill a heavy chest. There are few shows which he has not won with his fell terriers, and he has won the coveted Great Yorkshire Terrier Club cup three times. Certainly, few winners of the last few years could fail to trace their ancestry to the dogs of Frank Buck of Leyburn – a terrier man extraordinary.

9. Anthony Chapman

(Interviewed at Ambleside, Cumbria)

Anthony Chapman still lives at Ambleside close to the hunt kennels where he, and his father before him, spent most of his working life. Anthony is one of four generations of huntsmen, and his grandson has taken up service with the Mendip Farmers. Few people can claim to know the Coniston Hunt country as well as Anthony Chapman, for he hunted the Coniston from 1944 until he retired in about 1980, shepherding during the summer months and running hounds over some of the most picturesque country in the Lake District.

Chapman's father, who took over the post of huntsman to the Coniston in 1908, was an enthusiastic terrier breeder and once kept a rather leggy strain of black, rough-coated fell terriers. Indeed, Anthony Chapman believes this strain of terrier originated in the Lakes rather than in North Yorkshire as is popularly supposed. Certainly Cyril Lewis, who hunted the Snowdonia region, obtained a black terrier from the Coniston Hunt kennels in the summer of 1920, and no one considered the dog to be anything unusual.

43. *Anthony Chapman, 1981.*

Anthony, however, was a hound man, and though he kept many useful hard-working terriers he does not consider himself to be a serious terrier breeder. He obtained his first terriers from the Coniston Hunt kennels, but his best ever terrier was a typey black-and-tan male, Riff, bred by Ernie

Towers at Grasmere. Riff was a phlegmatic dog with a stoical indifferent to pain, quiet and reserved in kennels (he lived for thirteen seasons with hounds), but a really useful dog to work. Anthony described him as a quiet terrier, not a yapper, but when he gave tongue below ground he was true. His son Rock, bred from a Coniston Hunt terrier of no particular breeding, was a replica of his sire in appearance, but was a more excitable, less biddable dog. However, Rock appears in quite a few Lakeland/fell pedigrees, so perhaps Anthony Chapman did not value the dog as much as some of the hunt followers.

Riff's other son was Crab, an untypey dog, small, rather light-muzzled, but utterly game and capable of working anywhere from a deep borran to an excavated rabbit burrow earth. In spite of his small size and rather weedy type, Crab could bay well to shift his fox; but should the fox refuse to bolt, Crab was capable of killing his fox in double-quick time. Crab worked several seasons for Anthony, finally dying of senility during the summer off season. Crab appears in the pedigrees of many families of fell terriers.

Later, after the cessation of the Second World War, the Coniston Hunt kennels had an influx of Buck-bred terriers given by Frank to Logan, the Master of the Coniston. Anthony speaks highly of these black terriers. Skiffle, Breay's terrier, was *en route* to the Logans when Breay gave Buck a replacement animal instead. Of puppies sired by Benson Red Ike, Chapman was curiously unenthusiastic and described the one Red Ike puppy working with the Coniston during the days preceeding the outbreak of the Second World War as being only an average worker and nothing sensational. Walter Parkin of the Lunesdale Hunt, however, swore by these Red Ike strain puppies at this time, but seemingly Anthony Chapman liked a less fiery, more phlegmatic type of dog.

Stan Mattinson's dogs were also used by the Coniston after the Second World War, the best of which was probably Badger, a small, tiny would be more accurate, nine-inch terrier who could follow a fox anywhere and bolt or worry any fox.

Chapman hunted some incredibly difficult borran-filled spots in an area that can take a heavy toll on any team of terriers. At Buck Barrow in 1934, a fox was driven to ground in a huge borran and four terriers were entered to it, Nip, Tats, Set and Turk. For a while baying was heard, but the earth was impossible to excavate and all Chapman could do was to wait. Ernie Parker, the huntsman for the Coniston at that time, sent the youthful Anthony back to wait by the earth to recover the terriers, and for seven days Anthony sat by the borran. On the fourth day, Turk crawled out, bitten, exhausted and near dead from exposure, but the other terriers were never seen again.

Anthony likes small terriers of quiet disposition – fell ameliorated with Border blood is rated very highly by Anthony, who has never seen a large terrier to be of any use in the Coniston district. Coats are important to him, however, and whereas he admits he has seen good smooth- or slape-coated terriers, the best are invariably hard, wiry-coated terriers who could clean

44. *Anthony Chapman with Coniston hunt terriers.*

the water from their coats with a quick shake. Soft coats are considered a bit
of a liability by Anthony, as this type of jacket absorbs rather than sheds
water, and more than once has he had to take home a soft-coated dog near
dead with hypothermia. 'Whisky and lying in front of a fire usually revives
such dogs, but a hard-coated dog suffers far less.'

Entering was, according to Anthony Chapman, easy if one had the right
type of terrier. He simply took the dogs out, encouraged them in rat and
rabbit a little, and they soon got used to the job. Hounds marking to ground,
baying enthusiastically at a fox, gee up terriers quite a bit, and Anthony used
this built-up excitement as an aid to slip his youthful terrier.

119

10. Keith Clement

(Interviewed at Heron Hill, Cumbria, on 22 February 1982)

Keith is a reserved, well-spoken man with a history of keeping working terriers dating back to his childhood. His first dog was a smooth-haired fox terrier of the old type (the type bred by terrier keepers before the craze to exaggerate the length of head became the rage). Clement hunted his dog to

45. Keith Clement with Tarquin and Coniston Riff.

rat along the river banks around Kendal, and as might be expected in such a district, bolted numerous otter with this fox terrier. To supplement his team, he also used to borrow Ullswater black-and-tan terriers (of the sort bred by Braithwaite Wilson which were still common around Ullswater during the wartime years).

During this time he received some tuition concerning the training and entering of working terriers from Major Roslin Williams (the father of Anne Roslin Williams, the photographer and author of *The Border Terrier*). Clement considers Roslin Williams to be an authority on the entering of terriers, and states that he learned much from this man. Later Roslin Williams was to introduce Clement to Breay of Kirkby Lonsdale.

In 1951, Clement returned from military service and spent some time looking around for new blood to start out his own strain of terrier. He eventually saw what he wanted in the back garden of Harry Smith, who hunted the Kendal and District Otterhounds. These terriers had been bred by Major Roche of the Ynysfor Foxhounds and were reputedly sired by a Coniston-bred dog, but the Ynysfor Hunt at this time still had their own strain of terrier, a black-and-tan, strong-headed terrier that perhaps resembled an early type of fell terrier. This blood, not a whit inferior to the fell strains, was the foundation of Clement's initial stock. One of these puppies, Dot, was purchased by Clement for £5, and though she proved an excellent hunter of rat and rabbits, she refused to go to ground until she was four years of age (curiously, many of the Ynysfor terriers were late enterers, though many proved rock steady in very bad places). Lucas once told me that several were given away as failures only to become excellent workers when they were good and ready for the job. Likewise Dot. At four years of age she entered to fox and became a useful dog to otter, though it was at badger she really excelled.

At this time Clement had little to do with the official Lakeland hunts and went south into Lancashire to do his digging, but towards the end of the 1950s he joined the Lunesdale Foxhounds and eventually became their secretary. In spite of the fact that he had access at the time to the stud dogs of Walter Parkin's Black Rock strain, he chose a somewhat more unlikely line. Todd of Darlington (a name that appears in many Lakeland hunting stories) owned two useful terriers at that time: a black-and-tan Lakeland dog bred by Arthur Irving, supposedly dating back to Willie Irving's Turk and eventually to Alf Johnson's controversial registered Lakeland Oregill Copper Coin, though some dispute Turk's pedigree, and a small white terrier called Dusty, an iron-hard fox killer which got stuck into its fox quickly, efficiently and with great fervour. By mating these together, Todd of Darlington produced a good-looking litter and Breay bought one of the puppies. However, the puppy from Todd grew undershot and Breay, whose strain was, according to Clement, plagued with undershot terriers at this time, passed the dog on to Josie Akerigg, who in turn gave Breay a useful terrier called Flint. The undershot puppy Rip grew into an outstanding worker, and in spite of his obvious defect, Clement used him to mate to Dot. From this union came

Tarquin, Clement's favourite dog, a black-and-grizzle-tan male who made quite a name for himself around Kendal. Tarquin was an early starter, and at twelve weeks of age killed a fully grown rat – no mean feat for a puppy. He followed this by killing a fox when he was six months old, and grew into Clement's idea of the near-perfect dog. However, Tarquin had one serious fault. He refused to give tongue even when in difficulties, taking grim punishment without a whimper. Clement had to learn to dig to the furious subterannean bangings and bumpings to locate his dog. It came about at the start of his sixth season that the Lunesdale marked to ground in a bad place and Keith was invited to try Tarquin. He entered furiously, but transferred his attentions to a large badger. He attacked his badger with gusto, not giving an inch, but his entire nose was sheared off as a result of the encounter. After this he gave tongue readily and loudly when at either fox or badger. Curiously, many fell hunters start their dogs by allowing sapling terriers to be dusted by badgers to teach a dog discretion. It took Tarquin six years to learn such discretion, but Parkes of Kirkby Overblow believed that no tougher terrier ever drew breath.

Tarquin was a game dog, a quick starter and an excellent dog to ground. As might be expected, he therefore had many bitches brought to him, including many really game bitches that had proved themselves working some of the most difficult land in Britain. However, as a stud he proved somewhat less than satisfactory. He bred bold-looking puppies, puppies of excellent type and good bone, but none which proved any good as hunters. They were slow to start and were, to quote Clement, 'uninterested in going to ground'. It was not an auspicious start to a dynasty, but Clement, an intelligent man with a good knowledge of genetics, was determined to perpetuate Tarquin's line through the right bitch.

The right bitch eventually came along – one bred from a Breay line spiced with the 'swop dog' Breay obtained from Akerigg. Clement believes that the best of Breay's line was not Rusty or his sire Bingo, but the result of mating Blitz with a black bitch at Crosby Ravensworth, a line that produced Foxy, Tickle and eventually Jess. Jess proved just the right bitch to mate to Tarquin, and though Jess died at Petts Quarry, Ambleside – a bad spot for a dog to go in – she succeeded in producing at least two useful litters, one to Tarquin and another to a dog belonging to Tony Pool, a dog which Clement believes could be traced back to Oregill Copper Coin of Egremont, a prodigious sire of workers.

The result of mating Tarquin to Jess produced Riff, a terrier that won at Rydal – not a great distinction at this time since the show was restricted to dogs working at hunt kennels. But he worked well for George Lothian (the father-in-law of John Nicholson at the Lunesdale), and also for Nicholson when Lothian died. Riff, in turn, was mated to pedigree Lakeland terrier, while Mist, the result of mating Jess to Tony Pool's dog, was in turn mated to Frank Buck's famous Davy and produced Sherry, a very game bitch with a tremendous bite. She killed three foxes for Clement and each fox had its bottom jaw smashed. Sherry met her death when she upset two Labradors and they set about worrying her to death, but she it was who was the grandmother of Clement's present stock.

11. Tommy Coulson

Coulson was present during my interview with Ralph Hodgson, when he described himself as not having kept terriers long enough to merit inclusion in a section concerning fell-terrier breeders, but such a statement was not borne out by the interview Coulson gave me later that evening.

Coulson is a builder by trade and works for his father's company. There is no family connection with terriers, but Coulson followed the Braes of Derwent Hunt when still at school. He obtained his first terriers from John Cowan of Embleton, who was at that time keeping a fairly pure Melbreck strain of terrier derived from the terriers of Sid and Harry Hardasty suffused with a dash of Irving's strain which carried many bloodlines to Copper Coin. Tarka, Coulson's first fell terrier, proved a little too big for use in the rabbit-warren earths of the Braes country, but Coulson worked him with ferrets, ratted him and dug badger and fox using this dog. Tarka died quite suddenly of a heart attack when he was eight years of age.

His next bitch was from the George Newcombe Rillington strain, a small neat bitch who was a bad fighter in kennels which was why Coulson was able to buy her cheaply. Lindy was a black-and-tan registered Lakeland bitch, quick-tempered and quick to enter to fox. However, one day while Coulson was trying to extract a live fox from a net, Lindy ran in and received a savage bite for her trouble. After that she refused to look at a fox again. However, Lindy became an important bitch in the Durham fell-terrier strains. Coulson mated her to Alan Johnston's pedigree registered Lakeland terrier, Oregill Henchman, and bred Vic, a black-and-tan registered terrier who not only obtained a working certificate from the Braes of Derwent but worked seven consecutive days with seven different packs (Blencathra, Ullswater, West Percy, College Valley, North Tyne Border, the Wensleydale and the Bewcastle) and drew foxes on five of those hunts. Vic is, according to Winch's description, well marked. Lindy also bred Winch's bitch Spider, and mated to David Bewley's Mel (Hardasty's line), she bred the dam of Ward's Dandy.

Coulson's next purchase was Judy, a red fell terrier bred from a Gary Middleton bitch (Sid Wilkinson's Rock strain) mated to a dog from David Windle. Coulson was on holiday at the time of the purchase, but the chance of a good-class fell bitch which had worked with the Ullswater for a season for £5 was too much of a temptation. Judy is very game and steady to badger.

His next purchase was a puppy from Longstaff's Sting, sired by Winch's Chanter: a bitch called Mischief, a diminutive mite ten pounds in weight, small for a Hardasty strain bitch, which suffocated in a rabbit earth while working a vixen with cubs.

Coulson hunts every Saturday with the Border Hunt or the Braes, but prefers working with the footpacks since he considers this real hunting. He has also worked his dogs with the Dumfriesshire Mink Hounds.

12. John Cowen

(Interviewed at Embleton, Cumbria, on 29 December 1980)

I was particularly anxious to visit John Cowen of Bully House Farm, Embleton, since he is a well-respected fell terrier breeder who keeps accurate records and breeds useful, typey dogs, terriers that he has bred for twenty-eight years. His original stock came from Willie Irving of the Melbreck Hunt, dogs that were the foundation stock of the modern Kennel Club registered Lakeland. Later he added dogs from a bitch bred by Hardasty's Turk mated to Walter Parkin's Riff, a red, smoothish-coated dog bred down from the formidable Red Ike blood. Further additions of new blood came by mating a Kirkstile bitch (bred by Irving) to a dog bred by Jock Lennox – a gutsy, fiery, typey dog who left his stamp on many terriers around the Lakes.

Cowen uses a dash of Kennel Club registered stock from time to time to improve type, but chooses his outcross blood with care. Oregill Copper Coin (bred by Alf Johnston) was used on one of Cowen's bitches and produced some good lookers and also excellent workers. Likewise, a dog called Netherfield Newsboy was used on some of the Hardasty blood when Cowen considered his dogs were getting coarse in type. Cowen finds such dogs work just as well as the unregistered fell terriers, but unlike the fell terriers, which are quite placid, show-bred stock is far more fiery, and for a while Cowen had bad fights between his terriers.

It is a sad reflection on the terrier world that, as soon as Cowen made his name as a breeder of working terriers, he was visited by thieves who stole two of his best workers: Rock, a dog bred by mating Hardasty's Turk to a bitch from Johnston – a looker as well as a worker – and also Grip, a superb dog bred from Grip, a blue dog from Ridley and a bitch sired by Hardasty's Turk. Ill luck usually attends such thieves, and tale has it both dogs died of distemper shortly after being stolen. Sadly, no similar infection saw off the thieves.

Cowen likes twelve- to fourteen-inch terriers, narrow of chest with a good jacket. Broken coats are preferred, and he has preference for red or black-

and-tan terriers. His terriers are usually worked regularly, and during Hardasty's stay at the Melbreck, Harry kept several of Cowen's terriers in kennel.

Cowen's stock influenced much of the terrier blood around the Lake District, but it is in the Midlands and the south that his stock played a more important part. During the 1970s, many of his dogs took every Lakeland class in hunt shows in the south of England, and at one show all four places were won by Cowen dogs. At another show, three working certificated Lakeland types of terrier were the only entries in the Working Certificated class. All were sired by Cowen's dogs out of bitches bred by him. His terriers are very narrow chested, a little fine in the head perhaps, but still capable of killing foxes and holding their own with badger. Some of the top-winning Jack Russell terriers in the Midlands also owe their fine type to a dash of Cowen's spirited fell terriers.

13. Bill Crisp

(Interviewed at Askham, Cumbria)

Bill Crisp of Askham does not describe himself as a terrier breeder, for he keeps one, or at the most two, terriers which he works with the Ullswater Foxhounds. His claim to fame is that he is a Lakeland poet and author of many hunting songs, such as 'The Red Rover', that are sung in pubs throughout the Ullswater Hunt country.

Crisp's father was a chauffeur for the Lowther family, a family which has a considerable history with the Ullswater pack. In fact Lady Jane Benson is joint master of the pack at the time of writing. Crisp's mother was the daughter of a gamekeeper, and Crisp believes that his enthusiasm for terriers came from this side of the family.

Bill's first terriers were Jack Russells, or maybe white throw-ups in Lakeland or fell-type litters. Some twenty-five years ago, however, he bought a fell terrier from Johnny Richardson's strain of fell, bred down from Johnny's famous Tarzan. Mischief, Bill's terrier, was a box-headed, red dog with a coat like coconut matting and resembling a very tiny Irish terrier. In fact, one day at an Ullswater meet, an Irish gentleman approached Crisp and asked if the dog was one of the unregistered strains of Irish terrier that are still worked in some parts of Kerry. Mischief became a cracking worker and an all-round terrier of the sort that would have delighted any Irish crofter of a hundred years ago. He not only worked fox, badger, otter, rat and rabbit, but was shot over and retrieved duck, pheasant and partridge. His most famous party piece was salmon catching, however, and during the salmon run he

46. Bill Crisp's Mischief (far right).

would wait along the banks of the becks and snatch up salmon, pulling them to the bank. This story threw me a little, I must admit, and Crisp, seeing the disbelieving look on my face, asked Pat O'Malley and Eddie Pool to corroborate the tale, which they did.

Some twenty years ago, Mischief achieved the unique distinction of having a feature spot on Tyne Tees TV. Crisp had been out after eels with his children and had taken the terrier with him. Crisp saw the dog slide into the water, but thought no more of it for the stream was no great size. An hour or so later he missed the dog and saw an otter bolt out of a hole in the bank. Far below, Mischief had entered the hole and tried to climb towards the otter, but had jammed in rails not far above the water level. It was a difficult spot to work and it took a gargantuan effort to extract the terrier. Tyne Tees did a feature about the dog's rescue.

Mischief entered to the first fox he ever saw and bolted it from Black Crag. Thereafter he worked fox regularly with the Ullswater Foxhounds, killing more than he bolted. He entered to badger of his own volition in a difficult place, and was so game that he took terrible maulings rather than give ground. Crisp despaired during badger digs with Mischief, for the terrier refused to give ground and always had to be dug out. One terrible beating he took in the Ullswater country (where badgers are now common, though they were a rarity in there before 1940) tore out his throat and nearly killed him, but he never learned to stand back and bay at badgers.

126

Mischief was mated to Gyp, bred by Arthur Robinson, the rabbit catcher from Lowther – a slape-coated black bitch bred down from Buck's Adder and Viper (few terriers in the Lakes are not descended from Frank Buck's dogs) who bred one litter of puppies before she was killed in a three-way kennel fight. Three puppies came from the mating. Nettle, a black-and-tan bitch, went to a gamekeeper near Crisp's home and died after an encounter with a fox – in fact, a dig found her dead across the body of the fox. Rip, a big strong husky dog, joined his mother in the killed-in-kennels statistics. But the third pup, a runty undersized bitch with a slape red coat, went to Barrow at the Ullswater Kennels. She was an unsightly animal: a weakling, thin coated and puny with a poor head and a frail body – so puny, in fact, that Barrow called her Pet. At fox she was a demon, however, and set about her work with gusto, finding quickly and seizing her fox. Barrow rated this bitch highly, though one day she simply upped and disappeared.

Pet continued the line when she was mated to Turk, a dog bred by David Windle, a good sound animal that Eddie Pool persuaded Windle to sell to Dennis Barrow. Bonny, the only traceable puppy from this union, was lost in a bad place at Heron Pike.

Crisp, sadly, did not keep the line alive, and his present dogs are now bred down from Sid Wilkinson's Rock, as are most of the terriers in the Ullswater Hunt country.

14. Tommy Dobson

(Based on the legends told)

No more colourful character than Tommy Dobson ever hunted a pack of hounds and his eccentricities and curious jerky speech would have put southern hunters such as Froude and Russell in the shade.

Tommy was born in 1827, and was apprenticed as a bobbin turner in Bootle. His apprenticeship indentures are still to be found in the archives of the Ennerdale and Eskdale hunt, the hunt that Tommy helped to form through the coalescence of the Ennerdale and Eskdale packs. The combined packs will always be associated with the Porter family – Willie, Jack and Edmund – but Willie received his tuition in fell hunting from the pack's first master, Tommy Dobson.

Dobson was a diminutive elfin-like man, agile even into senility, who spoke in such a curious jerky manner that few could immediately understand his almost private dialect, and though he eventually became master of one of the fell packs – an elevated and respected position in the fells – he remained no respecter of persons and treated rich and poor alike, doffing his cap to no

"Tommy Dobson" & Jack

one. Even though Tommy was under five feet tall and had an almost ethereal build, he was game for anything and as pugnacious as his terriers. Arthur Irving related a tale told to him by Willie Irving of the days before Tommy became 'respectable'. He had been poaching with his brother at dead of night, using a long net and lurcher to catch ground game. In the blackest time of night he was approached from behind by a 'gamekeeper', so Tommy upped his long net stakes and 'skinned' the keeper's face, felling him like a poled ox. At home Tommy related the tale, until his brother arrived at the cottage, his eyes blackened and his face 'skinned'.

Tommy's contribution to the genealogy of the fell terrier is, however, rather questionable. Certainly he was a bit unhappy about the typey, improved fell type of terrier that were appearing at the shows, terriers which clearly had fox-terrier blood.

In 1888, though a host of other dates are offered, Dobson mated a chocolate Bedlington terrier, a renowned worker, to his own strain of fell terrier. Cumberland has long been famed for its top-quality, hard-working Bedlingtons. In fact, many of the Welsh terrier men who swore by the bottomless courage of a Bedlington terrier obtained their dogs direct from

48. *Arthur Irving at Tommy Dobson's grave in Boot churchyard.*

Kitchen, a Bedlington-terrier breeder from Egremont – dogs reputed to be utterly game and capable of tackling any quarry. Dobson's hybrids were useful, no doubt, but ugly, as the photograph of Tommy with a team of these near-pink chocolate Bedlington/fell crosses indicates, and such blood was fairly rapidly absorbed by the other fell-terrier strains around Eskdale and Ennerdale. Dobbie, Dobson's all-time favourite terrier, a dog capable of killing any fox, Dobson once boasted, had slight traces of Bedlington terrier blood, while Jack, another favourite terrier, had even less. Most of Dobson's dogs were silky coated terriers, and a great many were chocolate in colour, but there is no real evidence to suggest that the spate of chocolate Lakelands and fell terriers seen at the shows in recent years are in any way descended from Dobson's dogs. Bedlington blood was frequently used to give fell blood and Russell-type blood as well as a bit of extra courage, and chocolate Bedlingtons were fairly common in the Lakes during the years preceding the First World War. Yet when a chocolate Lakeland is born to a registered pair, most breeders still refer to it as one of 'Tommy Dobson's chocolates'.

Certainly farmers kept dogs reputedly bred from Tommy's strain, and dogs of the type bred from the first-cross Bedlington to Lakeland hybrids are still found at the Ennerdale and Eskdale hunts. Dobson's contribution to the fell terrier must be considered limited to say the least. Even so, he was a fascinating character whose biography would be well worth a book. He died as a result of a chill contracted hunting the fells and is buried in Boot churchyard. Here friends contributed to erect an elaborate gravestone with hunting motifs, and from the stone is sculpted the saturnine face of Tommy Dobson, the diminutive fell hunter.

15. Eric Dodson, with David Reed

(Interviewed at Egremont, Cumbria, on 16 May 1981)

On 16 May 1981, Alan Johnston and I visited the home of Eric Dodson of Egremont to see the N'Beck strain of working Lakeland, a strain that not only wins at the top-class hunt shows, but works well to fox and badger. The terriers were strong, powerful, straight-fronted animals with enormously strong biting heads capable of giving a good account of themselves against any large quarry in Britain. Indeed, many of these terriers bred at their kennels have seen considerable work at hunts throughout the length and breadth of the country.

A puppy from Cyril Tyson, a bitch called Magda bred out of Tyson's Mantle and Cowen's hard-bitten stud dog Rock (another descendant of Hardasty's Turk), began this strain, though Dodson had had many terriers

49. *Eric Dodson with N'Beck terriers.*

before this purchase – primarily dogs bred by Edmund Porter of the Eskdale and Ennerdale Hunt. This bitch was mated to Oregill Henchman and Oregill Hacksaw, and infusions of the blood from Brian Graham, who died in the North Sea oil rig disaster (stuff again bred from Harry Hardasty's Turk), contributed to the bloodlines. By judicious additions of Kennel Club type Lakelands, Dodson and Reed have bred an excellent homogeneous strain of Lakeland which has both the nose and courage of some of the original fell terriers.

Dodson, a devoted hunt follower, enters his puppies to rat at six months old and graduates a dog to fox when it is eighteen months – though many of his terriers enter sooner.

16. Monty Fairish

Monty Fairish breeds, according to Eddie Proud of the Bewcastle Foxhounds, some of the hardest, gamest terriers in the north, and when one examines his terriers' bloodlines, one can understand why.

Fairish is an outgoing, friendly sort of fellow who is surviving the economic depression by rabbit catching, mole clearance and general agricultural work. His father was a gamekeeper – indeed, Monty tried a spell of gamekeeping before being made redundant – but there is no history of terrier breeding in the Fairish family.

Monty's first terrier came by a peculiar quirk of fate – or was it? His school friend owned a hard-bitten, rabbiting, ratting and fox-killing Border/Lakeland type of terrier of unknown breeding, and Fairish was obviously impressed by the animal. In the village lived a woman who owned a similar type, scruffy, of pedigree unknown, but a devil to cats. Fairish, aged fourteen, selected this bitch as the dam for the puppies and engineered (Fairish was reluctant to explain this expression) the mating. Monty bought an undocked male puppy from the unlikely, unpromising union. Unpromising the union may have been, but Champ, the puppy bought by Fairish, became one of the most reliable terriers in the north.

Fairish has always been a keen Bewcastle supporter and went with the Prouds from the time he was eight years old. He received much training from them and had considerable opportunity to work his first terrier. Champ grew into a first-rate terrier, utterly game, sensible with a great nose and sense enough to come out of a furious tangle below ground relatively unharmed by the battle. He was a nailer to badger and learned how to stay back from his foe. Fairish no longer hunts badger and deliberately discourages his dogs from entering to them. Badgers that are a nuisance (and despite the opinions of professional naturalists, Fairish believes rogue badgers do take lambs) should be gassed rather than dug with dogs, so Monty advocates.

To continue Champ's line, Fairish bought Bess, a blue Lakeland terrier from the Tear 'Em line. She became a useful working terrier to fox, but died of jaundice, a particularly unpleasant death, after a ratting session, so Fairish was forced to look further for a suitable dam to continue Champ's family.

His next bitch, Pat, a slape- or nearly smooth-coated fell terrier, was obtained from Willie Gray, a Safety Officer for the Ministry of Agriculture and a man who has a name for having quite a few useful terriers on his premises. Pat, however, was not of Gray's breeding, but had come from the Scarteen Hunt Kennels in Ireland. Ireland produces some very useful fell types of terrier, though whether the Scarteen strain is bred from fells that were imported to Ireland – and Watson, Willie Porter and Ernie Parker sent quite a few useful terriers to the Irish hunts – or simply a bred-down type of Irish terrier will always be debated. Certainly Colonel David Hancock in a letter in the *Shooting Times* (February 1981) mentions that, during a visit to

Ireland, he met a man with a few useful fell types of terrier who indignantly protested that they were not Lakeland bred but simply an old unregistered type bred from Irish blue-and-tan strains.

These Scarteen terriers have a reputation for being terrific hunters and great nailers to fox below ground. Fairish, who does not favour rough-coated terriers since he saw a sodden rough-coated terrier work a freezing peat hole with the Bewcastle and go into near coma with shock, liked this bitch and bred two litters from her before selling her to a hunter in Scotland. Both litters were quite exceptional at work, and Fairish went into Scotland to mate this bitch to Scamp and breed a third litter. After several hundred miles of travelling, the bitch produced a litter, but Fairish found they were useless. From this he surmised (inaccurately, I believe) that when a dog and a bitch become geriatric, the quality of their puppies suffers considerably from the waning strength and constitution of their parents – an interesting theory I have heard a hundred times or more, but one that is not scientifically proven.

Later that year the elderly but still working Champ was mated to Scamp, a game fell bitch with maybe some Border-terrier blood, the property of Bob Proud at the Bewcastle Foxhound Kennels. Fairish was enthusiastic about the outcome of the litter as he rated Scamp as perhaps the best of Proud's terriers at finding, bolting and killing if need be. The outcome of the litter was Dot, a small, hard-coated dog who proved a good worker, but did not live long enough to become the great worker Monty believed she could have become. In her third year she was bowled by a car and never really 'put things together' again. She would appear to be on top form one day and well below par the next. Fairish worked her in a peat earth, a deceptively large earth he now realizes, and after finding her fox she became silent. Fairish dug up an enormous amount of hillside – 'half the fell' as Monty described it – but when he broke through to the bitch she was dead, lying on her side near some water. Shock or maybe a heart attack had finished her, for she was unmarked, but Fairish has a sneaking suspicion that the motor accident contributed to her demise.

His next bitch, a bitch that shaped his breeding policies, was bought as a puppy from a woman advertising in the local papers. Monty saw the adver- tisement saying 'Bull terrier x Lakeland puppies' in a local paper, and as he had problems about bone and jaw strength in his puppies, he went and tried to buy a puppy. In spite of the fact that he went immediately, the litter had been sold, but such was the demand for the puppies that the lady who bred them had several extra orders and decided to breed another litter. Six months later she contacted Fairish and Monty bought a small, slape, hard, strong- jawed bitch called Jill. She was dead game and gave tongue well, which is rare in a first-cross bull terrier x Lakeland, and once a fox dragged the bitch in and out of an earth, but Jill refused to release her throat-hold. Some bull- terrier blood has obviously been used on the creation of many fell strains, as a glance at the head on some of the dogs shown at Lakeland/Border/fell classes in hunt shows often indicates. Sparrow in his book *A Terrier's Vocation* advocates the use of a bull-terrier cross every ten generations, since many strains of terrier become rather snippy jawed if inbred.

In due course Monty mated Jill, the half-bred bull terrier, to the now very ancient Champ, and bred Dick, a hard-coated dog that curiously, in a roundabout way, brought about the end of his dam. Dick was sold to a keeper in Scotland, a keeper who tried him and found him useless. Fairish, not to disappoint the keeper, sent Jill as a replacement. She was sent by rail but never reached her destination since she was stolen *en route*. Later Dick, her supposed 'failure' of a son, was kept a short while by Monty, properly entered, and sold to Alan Andrews in Yorkshire. Dick found success with Andrews and became one of the best terriers Andrews had ever worked.

By this time Champ had become very old and incapable of siring further litters, so Fairish was in need of a stud dog to continue the line. He went to the inevitable Willie Gray at Dalston and bought a young male, bred from a half-bred Border x Lakeland or unregistered fell type of terrier mated to a pedigree Border terrier male, Raisgill, bred by Jack Morgan of Whaddon Chase. Like the Prouds, Fairish finds that Border-terrier blood ameliorates or cools down the fiery Lakeland-terrier disposition. The sire was anything but a softy, for it had been given to Gray when six years old and battered. His offspring, the result of his mating to the fell terrier, Fairish called Mick, and he scarcely qualified for the term ameliorated fell terrier, for he was a tiger by nature. At twelve weeks old he saw a fully grown rat with a leg trapped in a fen trap (Fairish was a keeper at this time), and went berserk as soon as the rat nipped him, shaking the rat long after it was dead.

To ground he was a demon and certainly wouldn't have suited some of the southern hunts, for he seldom bolted his fox, but closed with it instantly, literally biting it to pieces. He let Monty down once perhaps when the Bewcastle were on a hunt for a lamb worrier. The fox was to ground in a badger set and the Prouds wanted the fox dead and not bolted for hounds. Hence the other terriers were put up and Fairish's terrier entered, for Mick was certain death to any fox. Surprisingly, he held off the fox, baying and teasing, and the fox bolted.

Mick mated the quarter-bred bull-terrier/fell hybrids, and Fairish's strain are descended from this mating. His terriers are not typey and would certainly do badly at shows, but all have reputations for being good workers. Most have excellent noses and are utterly fearless. From time to time puppies with enormous bull-terrier heads appear in Fairish's litters. Most would be unsuitable for the 'nip and tuck' work of a terrier working with hounds in the shires, but as terriers to work with fell packs or terriers for fox hunting, they certainly take some beating.

17. *Willy Gray*

(Interviewed at Dalston, Cumbria)

Willy Gray is a soft-spoken Cumbrian, and a man whose dogs have made considerable impact on the working fell-terrier scene. Willy's father was a pilot, who was killed during a bombing raid over France. Hence Willy became heavily influenced by his uncle, the local vet, who was not only secretary of the local hunt but tended to the damaged hunt terriers. Thus began Willy's interest in working terriers.

His first terriers were not fell bred, however, for Willy obtained his first Border terriers from his cousin, Robert Cubby. In 1961, he bought Corrie, a Border terrier male, from John Coates of Locherbie, a male sired by Tarka, a renowned Dumfriesshire Otterhound Hunt terrier whose courage was bottomless and whose nose and common sense made him a legend. Tarka was, in turn, a son of Maxton Matchless, who threw many peerless workers. Corrie was a superb dog, and because of him Gray began keeping an accurate diary of his hunts and dogs. Later still, Gray obtained a dog from John Morgan of the Whaddon Chase Hunt, an excellent terrier man, and an expert at entering sensitive Border terriers. Morgan's dogs were Raisgill bred, and had a terrific reputation for work, partly because of their excellent breeding, but also because Morgan was a wonderful terrier man with this strain of terrier. Gray, too, had great success with his Borders, for, once entered, they were not only game but sensible enough to stay out of trouble below ground. Gray values this sense to stay back very highly, and for this reason he will not use a show-bred fell terrier or a dog with pedigree Lakeland terrier ancestry.

Early in the 1970s, the Border terrier began to develop a more squat pug face, a face which took punishment along the eyes rather than the muzzle, and this, together with the fact that fewer and fewer breeders had an interest in working their dogs, turned Gray away from pedigree Borders.

A fairly distinctive type of fell terrier was being bred in Dalston in the 1970s: a strong-boned, square-headed type of black-and-tan terrier, with powerful jaws and enormous teeth. These terriers, bred relatively true to type, had an excellent reputation for courage and determination. Most were brave to the point of recklessness, and there are some fairly hair-raising stories concerning their adventures when they went to ground on badgers. Gray infused these strains with the blood of the Border terriers he obtained from John Morgan, and produced not only game dogs but also sane and sensible dogs, capable of killing a fox but also having enough sense to survive a hard, gruelling dig to badger.

Later, Gray made the acquaintance of P. J. Shanahan of Tipperary, a colourful and likeable character by all accounts, who presented Gray with what Shanahan described as a Scarteen terrier – a black-and-tan terrier with a wirey to slape coat. I became interested in this strain of terrier in 1982, and wrote to the *Shooting Times* for data concerning it. My letter was answered by

50. Willie Gray.

Colonel Hancock, who stated that the Scarteen terrier was a strain bred by the Scarteen Hunt to match the black-and-tan hounds. (I later inquired about these hunt terriers during a conversation with two Irish workers in Leicestershire, one of whom had followed the Scarteen, and was told the Scarteen Hunt

136

now used white-bodied terriers.) Gray is convinced that the dog brought from Shanahan was simply a good-class Cumberland-bred hunt terrier, which had been bred in Ireland for a few generations. Whatever the breeding of the bitch, Gray could not speak too highly of it, since not only was the terrier game, but its nose was almost as good as that of a beagle. Gray stated the dog ran everything from deer to pheasant.

At this time Willy was working in Scotland and returning home only at week-ends, for Gray is by trade an agricultural officer. Thus Gray gave his Scarteen terrier to Monty Fairish, who found it such a problem with pheasants that he put the bitch out on breeding terms to a gamekeeper in Scotland while it was in whelp to his own dog Champ – a Border/Lakeland type of fell (see section on Monty Fairish). One of the puppies from this mating later became the property of Eddie Pool of Glenridding, and was used as an outcross for his own strain of terrier.

Gray's present terriers are tallish fourteen-inch terriers from his Border x Dalston fell hybrids, and though he has sought for outcross blood from P. J. Shanahan, he has had little success with the other dogs purporting to be Scarteen terriers – one of which, according to Gray, resembled a Dandie Dinmont. His own strain of Border x Lakeland, however, bred from Morgan's Pickle mated to Dalston-bred fell terriers, seem more than adequate since Gray has worked rat, rabbit, fox, otter, badger and wildcat with them. Gray keeps absolutely accurate and exact results of both his breeding programme and his hunts, and must be considered a credit to the working-terrier world.

51. Willie Gray's so-called Scarteen terrier.

18. Harry and Sid Hardasty
(Interviewed at Ennerdale, Cumbria, in October 1981)

My interview with Harry Hardasty was, to say the least, a trifle bizarre. I had gone to the Melbreck Kennels on the morning of 15 October 1981 to interview Richard Bland, and Bland's wife had arranged for her father, Harry Hardasty, also to be interviewed there. Hardasty could not attend, however, as he had to collect some sheep from a near-by fell. Subsequently I conducted a fleeting interview with Harry Hardasty, one of the more important names in fell-terrier breeding, in a thirty hundredweight van full of sheep and a sheepdog who seemed baffled by the whole business.

Harry Hardasty, like many of the professional huntsmen of the Lakes, comes from farming stock, his father having specialized in shepherding. All of the family were very fond of hunting, however. Harry became the hunts-man for the Melbreck during the 1946–7 season, a post he held until ill health forced him to retire in 1973 when he relinquished control of the pack to Richard Bland, his son-in-law.

Hardasty's first terriers were obtained in 1946 when he visited the kennels of Jim Fleming of Grasmere, and though Hardasty is very hazy about the breeding of his terriers, he is certain that they all date back to Fleming's dogs (see Tyson's pedigree of Turk in interview with John Winch).

Turk was Hardasty's most famous dog, a dog on which a whole dynasty of terriers was founded. Turk was a red, rough-coated male with a strong head and a box-like shape. Winch described the dog as a miniature Irish terrier. He was, to quote Hardasty, 'a beautiful animal on the lead or off, the sort of dog that always showed himself well'. Hardasty won well with Turk when he showed him, but Harry is a dour man and the social life of the showing did not appeal to him. Hence Turk was rarely seen in the show ring. His contribution to the working terrier scene is nevertheless tremendous. Graham Ward of Durham, Winch of Consett, Maurice Bell of Hawes all based bloodlines on this dog, largely through the use of one of Turk's sons (though there are doubts in certain areas, I should add), Cyril Tyson's Rocky. Winch described the puppies of Rocky's getting as being like peas in a pod, all typey, all game, all perfect miniature Irish terriers.

However, Harry Hardasty did not breed Turk – in spite of the fact that this famous stud dog is always referred to as Harry Hardasty's Turk. Turk was, in fact, bred by Sid Hardasty, Harry's brother, who lives at Hows Hall, Ennerdale. I visited him shortly after my interview with Harry, but even Sid seemed doubtful about the breeding of Turk, save that he was bred from a bitch given to him by Harry – a bitch Harry bred from the original Jim Fleming bloodline. Sid confessed to being more interested in hounds than in terriers. I left him my phone number and address and he promised to inquire into the ancestry of this illustrious stud dog. Alas, Sid Hardasty has never phoned to confirm Turk's pedigree. With the breeding of fell terriers, it seems, fact and legend must often remain hopelessly intertwined.

138

19. Nigel Hinchcliffe

(Based on correspondence)

Nigel Hinchcliffe is an articulate, hyperactive terrier man from Holmfirth, and though in a letter to me, dated 15 June 1982, he describes himself as being out of terriers, continuing to keep only one dog at home and not having bred a litter for two years, he is still held in high regard as a terrier man thoughout the country.

Curiously, although I have spoken to Hinchcliffe over the phone, exchanged Christmas cards with him, and even once bought a puppy from his strain to mate into my own family of Jack Russells – Pagan is sired by one of Hinchcliffe's dogs – I have never met him in person.

Hinchcliffe was once chairman of the Pennine Foxhounds – not the pack kept at Ousby in 1920 by Fred Barker, but a pack which works some equally difficult country, a country with earths ranging from excavated rabbit warrens to borran areas which equal the worst places in the Lake District.

During Hinchcliffe's term of office with the Pennine Foxhounds, he kept a kennel of six or eight terriers at his kennels at Holmfirth , Yorkshire. In fact he deplores the number of dog dealers who are trading in vast numbers of fell terriers.

After buying various types of terrier, Hinchcliffe finally decided on the Buck/Breay strain of terrier as the most suitable type for his hunt country – terriers strong enough to cope with fox, yet small enough and nimble enough to negotiate the rock piles of the Pennine Chain. He stressed the importance of keeping a small, agile terrier, during a telephone conversation at Christmas 1979, and cited a case where a large terrier would have no chance of working those earths.

During Hinchcliffe's early days as terrier man for the hunt, when he was building up his strain with stock direct from Breay, fortified with Breay/Buck stock from Nuttall, he would be plagued by macho terrier men, eager to match their large, powerful Lakeland-bred fell terriers (the type supposedly worked by the Lakeland packs, but, in reality, a million miles from the type kept by huntsmen in the Lakes) against Hinchcliffe's smaller, black terriers. After Hinchcliffe had taken much baiting from one idiot, and such clowns can be the most irritating types of people ever, he finally agreed to match his terrier against the bigger Lakeland in a fox-bolting contest in one of the more difficult rock piles, an angled rock which sloped down to a deep and difficult earth. Hinchcliffe allowed the challenger the first try, but the bigger, less agile dog could not manage to negotiate the slope, let alone bolt the fox. Hinchcliffe's dog, by contrast, being slightly built and more agile, slid easily down the slope, clambered over the rocks in the earth, bolted the fox, and scaled the slippery rock back to Hinchcliffe. The humiliation of an annoying, pestering macho is, to me, the happiest of endings, for I know what it is to be constantly plagued by such 'expert' human oddities.

52. A Breay-type terrier from Hinchcliffe's strain.

One of Hinchcliffe's foundation stock came from Nuttall, a dog called Flint, a game, useful dog which Nuttall had originally sold to Wales but which returned to the north to end its days. Flint proved a real stamper of type, for most of his stock were black with white chests, though a percentage did carry one ear cocked, as did Buck's Topsy, a bitch from which Flint descended. At many shows one sees this Topsy type of ear on many of the black, bull-terrier-headed stock, erroneously called Patterdales by their owners.

Hinchcliffe has a theory concerning the type of terrier – a theory questioned by many, though, like all Hinchcliffe's notions, it is well thought out and carefully expressed. He believes that bull-terrier blood, mingled with the blood of an unregistered herding dog called the Lancashire Heeler, gave this type of fell terrier its characteristic type marking and head. The theory was hotly disputed by Breay and Buck, but is possibly not without foundation. During 1982 I visited Harold Watson of the Lunesdale Hunt – an authority on fell men and their terriers. Watson recalled that the first black fell terrier he ever saw was a curious-looking dog of corgi or similar type which Jimmy

Bewley brought back from Manchester in about 1912. (Even Watson, a man with a remarkable memory, is a little hazy about the exact date.) Perhaps Hinchcliffe's theory therefore does have a foundation in hard fact.

Hinchcliffe likes medium-sized, smooth or broken-coated black terriers, with good strong heads and moderately narrow fronts. Just now and again pale fawn and red puppies are thrown up in his litters, and Hinchcliffe refers to these as 'rat coloured', but the majority of his dogs are very typey.

It is saddening to think that such an intelligent, articulate and thinking terrier man is no longer in the business of perpetuating a strain.

20. Ralph Hodgson

(Interviewed at Rowlands Gill, Cumbria)

Ralph Hodgson is eighty-three at the time of writing, deaf and with failing eyesight. During his youth, however, he was considered to be one of the great northern terrier men. He worked as a pit official during his working life, and his expertise with a shovel and his knowledge of how to prop roofs has saved numerous terriers during Fell and Moorland Working Terrier Club rescues.

Ralph has spent a lifetime with working terriers, and his interest in terriers was kindled by the fabulous Tom Easy (an associate or rather an acquaintance of Jocelyn Lucas, so Winch assures me). Easy was a gentleman farmer, a keen horseman who supplied terriers for the various local foxhound packs. Easy bred a curious type of terrier, the result of fox-terrier/Bedlington-terrier crosses, which looked rather strange but were totally fearless. Ralph says that these dogs were excellent as fox killers, but such was their disposition that when they came upon a badger they tangled with brock and would be literally torn to pieces. Many of the Easy hybrids went to America, South Africa and Australia, and quite a few American hunt terriers can be traced back to them. Some of these hybrids were blue, but many were black, and Buck mentions that, during his father's youth, there were many shaggy black Bedlington-type fells in the Durham area.

Ralph kept these Easy hybrids for a while and bred Jack, a rather woolly Jack Russell type from them. Jack was game, too game, and inevitably came unstuck at badger one day.

Hodgson was a fanatical terrier man during his heyday, and between 1925 and 1975 he rarely missed a week-end out digging, but fell terriers did not become a passion with him until the later 1960s. His interest came about after a fruitless exploration of an earth some miles south of Rowlands Gill. Three lads materialized and asked to try their terriers which were red, black and black, and tan slape coated. Ralph was impressed by one black bitch and

53. *Ralph Hodgson.*

booked a puppy from her. The young man offered Ralph a puppy at £5, money back if it didn't work, and he took the chap up on the offer.

The young man was Brian Nuttall of Holmes Chappell, and thus began Ralph's autumnal interest in fell terriers. His puppy from Nuttall, a result of breeding from the Buck/Breay strain, was called Shandy, and she was undershot (bad mouths were becoming far too common in the Breay line at that time, as Breay explained to Clement of Kendal), but Shandy was dead game, sensible and steady. She worked fox and badger all her life and died, aged eleven, at Ralph's home in Rowlands Gill.

His next terrier was a John Cowen-bred terrier bred down from Hardastys Turk, a quiet sensible dog called Mel (a common name in Durham, derived from Melbreck, the hunt for which Hardasty worked). Mel saw the declining years of Ralph Hodgson, though the dog saw much work at both fox and badger.

Hodgson has worked most types of terrier, but finds fells most suitable for the difficult earths around Durham. He dislikes Borders, since even during the golden years of the Border he found them to be capricious and unreliable until they settled down at four or five years old.

Postscript: Ralph Hodgson died in 1982.

21. The Irving Family

(Based on an interview with Arthur Irving in Cumbria, on 26 May 1981)

It would be impossible to write a dissertation on the Lakeland terrier without reference to the illustrious Irving family. The Irving brothers were as native to the Lakes as the granite, and their mother's maiden name was Tyson, another famous hunting family in the Lakes. They were originally sheep farmers by trade, but they had a more than ordinary interest in hunting. The eldest brother, John Tyson Irving, had a casual interest in fox hunting, but chose to follow the family tradition of sheep farming rather than take up professional hunt service.

Hunt service during the early days of the present century was very different from hunt service in the shires. During summertimes, most of the hounds were farmed out to neighbouring farmers and the whips either went home to their parents' farms or worked on others near by. When autumn came, both hounds and hunt servants returned to kennels for the winter hunting. This system, curious by today's standards, could only have existed in the Lake District where most families were related and communities very tightly knit as a result of their consanguinity. Many hunting families intermarried. Walter Parkin was a cousin of Joe Bowman and the Irvings had family connections with both the Bowmans and, through Arthur's wife, the Dobsons.

Willie Irving, the second brother, took up service with the Porter family at the Ennerdale and Eskdale, whipping in during the winter and farming during the summer months before becoming full-time huntsman for the Melbreck Hunt. Much has been written about Willie and his terriers, but there is little concrete evidence for many of the stories. Certainly Willie improved the working Lakeland type and produced stylish dogs rather than the rough rag-tag terriers found at the Melbreck before his arrival. Willie has also been criticized for ruining the Lakeland hunt terrier temperament – a statement that does not bear careful examination.

Certainly he bred some stylish terriers, and these he produced by taking certain bitches to Alf Johnston's Copper Coin – a stud dog that was to alter the shape and temperament of the breed. Contrary to legend, Arthur Irving states that at no time did Willie introduce fox-terrier-blooded terriers into his hunt terriers, though H. G. Long, Alan Johnston and Joe Mawson were all of the opinion that Copper Coin owed his type to a liberal addition of fox-terrier blood. Turk, one of Irving's top stud dogs, a renowned worker and a great fighter, had several lines to this dog. (There are two Turks bred by Irving, incidentally. This one was bred in 1950, after Willie had left the Melbreck.)

Another story concerning Willie Irving is that he introduced Irish-terrier blood into his fell terriers. Winch tells of men who actually saw small Irish

54. Willie Irving during the war; even then the Melbreck had classy terriers.

terriers kennelled at the Melbreck; but Arthur Irving denies this. Joe Mawson, however, says that Willie did actually use a local stud dog which Joe knew to be a half-bred Irish terrier, but which was nevertheless an excellent worker and a top-class looker. Certainly Willie's kennel did not suffer in working qualities through this mixture of alien blood. Arthur says, 'All were shown, but all were worked. All went – there were no failures. I've never heard of one of Willie's who wouldn't go. Certainly I've never owned a quitter from Willie's kennels.' Furthermore, Arthur states that, during the time Willie bred his Melbreck strain of Lakeland terrier, no white puppy was born in the litters. (White throwbacks were common during the early days, Alan Johnstone believes, and many breeders would show visitors their litters of terriers with any white puppy concealed in their pockets. H. G. Long states that at this time, the 1920s and 1930s, as many as a quarter of some Lakeland terrier litters were white fox-terrier types.) The fact that Willie produced no white puppies is perhaps (and only perhaps) an indication that he used sires with Irish-terrier ancestry rather than fox-terrier blood – though again Arthur states he has no knowledge of such sires being used.

Whatever the blood that went into Irving's dogs, a vastly superior type of Lakeland terrier was then being bred at the Melbreck Kennels, most of them resembling small Welsh terriers. Arthur states that Willie bred black-and-tan terriers, but Long says that early Lakeland terriers were a rather dingy tan grizzle rather than the rich tan found in Welsh terriers. Willie did not favour reds, though he bred several and there were red terriers at the Melbreck at the time of Willie's retirement. Indeed, there is some belief though little actual factual evidence for Tyson's famous winning reds being descended from the dogs of Willie Irving through Hardasty, who took over the post of huntsman of the Melbreck. Hardasty in fact bred his stock from Fleming's Myrt and did not use Irving's dog.

The third Irving brother was not a professional hunt servant, though he was sometimes secretary of the Eskdale and Ennerdale Hunt. Although he obtained his terriers from Willie Irving, he worked them privately as often as with the hunt, using his dogs on hunt days only by invitation of the huntsman. Although his dogs were stylish and descended from the illustrious Copper Coin, their progeny never quite made the grade as show animals. Harry used a dog belonging to Bob Gibbons – a registered dog of good type, but one not suited to the Copper Coin family. The progeny were woolly coated Bedlington types (not an uncommon occurrence in early pre-registered Lakelands, since Bedlington blood was often used by some breeders to fortify certain strains of fell terrier), but while these were excellent workers, they were unsuitable as show specimens. Arthur Irving believes that this line passed into extinction and had no influence on future fell-terrier families.

The fourth son of the Irving family was Arthur Irving, the last surviving of the Irving brothers, and Winch expressed an urgency about my interviewing Arthur, lest the data of the contribution the family made to the fell terrier should be lost for ever. Arthur obtained his first terriers from Willie when he

55. *Arthur Irving with lakeland terriers.*

left school at the age of fourteen. At eighteen he obtained a post as full-time whip to Willie Porter, working on neighbouring farms during the summer. After a spell with the Eskdale and Ennerdale, he whipped in for the Blencathra, but after two seasons with this hunt returned to be huntsman for the Eskdale and Ennerdale.

At this time the Eskdale and Ennerdale terriers were a nondescript bunch, game but not particularly typey. Willie Porter bred small terriers and kept particularly small ones to work in deep earths. Porter's original strain, willed by Tommy Dobson, were some of the hardest terriers in the Lakes at that time and killed underground at the first possible chance. This fact was confirmed by the N'Beck terrier men, who stated that dogs from the strain were the hardest terriers they ever saw.

Arthur, however, brought his own typey terriers with him to the Eskdale and Ennerdale and worked them on fox throughout his time with the hunt. His dogs, too, were descended from Alf Johnston's Copper Coin, though Arthur never registered a dog in his life. His terriers were not as hard as the Eskdale and Ennerdale terriers, and he generally favoured a dog that would bolt rather than kill a fox below ground. Curiously, in spite of the awesome terrain hunted by the Eskdale and Ennerdale, Arthur lost very few terriers during his time with the hunt. His terriers were not only renowned workers but also good workers, a statement that can be backed by the number of times Arthur won at Rydal Hound Show.

Now in retirement, Arthur keeps two or three terriers and breeds only for himself. He still goes out with the Eskdale and Ennerdale and, when opportunity arises, still works his terriers.

22. Alan Johnston

(Interviewed at Egremont, Cumbria, on 16 May 1981)

When I travelled to Egremont to interview Alan Johnston, it was at least in part to research his grandfather, Alf Johnston, one of the founder members of the Lakeland Terrier Association. The late Alf Johnston became interested in the fell type of terrier at the turn of the century, when what we refer to today as the Lakeland terrier was called the coloured working terrier. He developed his interest in these dogs by his association with the Kitchens of Egremont, a sporting family who had bred fell terriers and Bedlingtons for several generations (see photograph of the Salters Hall Wood badger dig). His interest, however, was interrupted by the First World War when Alf served in France and also in Bagdhad, and in the latter theatre of war received a serious shrapnel wound.

Egremont was at that time the breeding centre of the dog later known as the Lakeland terrier, and the town boasted up to fifty breeders of these dogs during the early 1920s. Alf's injury prevented his taking part in fox digging, but many of his dogs found use at local hunts. In the late 1920s, Johnston was employed as a kennel man by Tom Megeen, a curious perfectionist who spent a small fortune collecting a kennel of some of the finest Lakeland terriers in the Lake district. Alf Johnston managed these kennels and bred, shipped and showed Megeen's dogs. Few of the dogs were worked after Megeen bought them, though quite a few had seen hunt service prior to being purchased, and the highlight of his career was his judging engagement at Cruft's in 1935. Alf was undoubtedly responsible for a great deal of the improvement in Lakeland type in the late 1920s and early 1930s, and his grandson Alan states that there is little doubt that Alf used terriers with Welsh, Irish and fox-terrier blood to bring about this transformation. Whether or not such blood had a deleterious effect on the working qualities of this breed is a moot point, but Irving used many of Alf's dogs with hounds, and High Lee Laddie (bought by George Long), a dog who bred many excellent workers, came from Alf's improved

56. Alf Johnston (seated), of Oregill fame.

strain. Alan recalls a tale told by his father of a lady in the south of England who advertised a tiny Irish terrier, too small for show, but 'suitable for a pet'. This dog was purchased by an Egremont breeder and used to breed many top-class Lakeland terriers not a whit inferior in pluck for their mixed ancestry. Several fox terriers were bred at Egremont at this time, and Alan believes that these too entered into the Lakeland terrier pedigree, refining type and breeding out the old Bedlington style so beloved by Tommy Dobson who used a chocolate Bedlington on many of his bitches (chocolate-coloured Lakeland terriers still appear today). However, the new improved type of dog ameliorated the rough, uneven appearance and much of the credit for the improvement must go to Alf Johnston.

His grandson, Alan Johnston, a man in his early thirties, is an avid Lakeland enthusiast whose house is filled with interesting fell paintings, ornaments and photographs. Alan breeds the famous Oregill strain of Lakeland terrier, a strain that not only wins well at Kennel Club Shows but also works quite well (see interview with Tommy Coulson). Alan, however, believes it is impossible both to show at Kennel Club Shows and work his terriers, for the furnishings of such dogs are severely damaged by going to ground. Winch assures me that one of Alan's pedigree Lakeland terriers (owned by Coulson) worked with seven hunts in one week and slew seven foxes. Furthermore, many fell breeders, men who work their dogs regularly, have used Oregill dogs to improve their strains of terrier. Dodson and Reed, who breed the N'Beck strain of working Lakeland, used Oregill dogs to polish up their own strains of terrier. One of the Oregill dogs, an unworked six-year-old bitch, went to Davey Hope, a Scottish gamekeeper, and within a month the bitch had not only entered to fox but had killed a fully grown vixen.

23. George Henry Long

(Interviewed at Clophill, Beds., on 10 May 1981)

On the advice of John Winch, who had met this gentleman at Cruft's, I visited the house of George Henry Long to have a talk, for George was born at the turn of the century and lived through an age that saw Bowman at his greatest and Irving at his best. Originally a native of Egremont, he came from a family of fell-terrier breeders, though he does incidentally refrain from using the expression fell terrier, preferring to call the motley collection of terriers working in the fells at the turn of the century coloured working terriers. His father, Peter Long, and his grandfather were well known at the early terrier shows in the Lake District.

57. G. H. Long as a young man.

Blues, reds, grey grizzle and just now and again black-and-tan terriers were popular in those days, and dogs resembling Farrer's Gyp (hunt working terriers) were fairly typical. Occasionally, then as now, an odd white terrier was thrown up in the litters of coloured puppies, and while such dogs were not liked by some, George said they found a ready market among rabbit hunters, who for some reason seemed to prefer an all-white terrier to a coloured.

The shows of George's youth, the agricultural shows where non-Kennel Club stock could be shown, were, by today's standards, ill-run, badly organized affairs, yet they were taken seriously. Terriers of all sorts – white-bodied fell terriers, Border terriers – were humped together in one class with no distinctions of age or sex. George still has his cups, rosettes and plaques won at these shows. One of his most famous terriers, an unregistered dog of doubtful origin, was whelped around 1906. His father acquired this dog, Scamp, from an itinerant stone chipper called Robertson, who was road repairing near Ennerdale. He bought the dog from Robertson when he cycled past the stone chipper on his way to an agricultural show, paying 18s (90p) for the animal, which was a great sum for an unregistered dog. Yet he won every agricultural and hunt show with it over the next two years. He finally sold Scamp, who was a doughty worker and lethal with foxes, for £1, but retained all stud rights on the dog. Scamp was a chunky strong dog of early Irish terrier type (see photograph in Salter's Hall Wood badger dig). He was eventually mated to Floss, a home-bred bitch, also a great winner, and George believes that much of the original foundation stock for the Lakeland Terrier Association descended from this union. This theory was confirmed by Walter Parkin, ex-huntsman of the Lunesdale Hunt, who remembers Alf Johnston, grandfather of Lakeland terrier breeder Alan Johnston, talk of this pair of terriers.

When the Lakeland Terrier Association was formed in 1921, however, red dogs of miniature Irish-terrier type were not all that popular, and Alf Johnston parted with one of his red dogs, a strong powerful male called High Lee Laddie, to Long. This dog was not only faulted because of its red colour, but also because of its white toes, for white-toed dogs were very unfashionable at all hunt shows in the north and George had to dye in the foot to get the dog to win even at agricultural shows. High Lee Laddie was, however, a very game dog with an excellent nose, who was only a bad fighter when not gainfully employed. George hunted this dog regularly to fox, and also often ran him in a summer bobbery pack of beagles, curs and terriers

58. *High Lee Laddie.*

after the winter beagling ceased. Also living at George's kennels at this time was an unregistered working fell bitch called Spiffy, related to the line bred down from the Floss and Scamp mating. Spiffy bred a litter to High Lee Laddie, and the puppies were registered with Bruce of Harrington, who kept a fell register of hounds, trail hounds and terriers. From this mating came Tinker's Retreat, a dog with which George won at Cruft's in 1935.

Colour in Lakeland terriers during those early days was poor. Most were blue rather than black and the tan markings were invariably a muddy grizzle. As a practical joke, a mill-owner from Cleaton Moor, an Irishman with an interest in the recently exploited aniline dyes, asked to borrow two of Peter Long's terriers, a pair of blue and muddy tan males, only to return them coloured jet black and rich tan. At the agricultural shows that year, 1924, various members of the doubting public tried to remove the dye with paraffin, petrol and other solvents, but failed to budge the dye. What chemical was used is a mystery to this day.

Gradually the motley collection of coloured fell terriers refined into the modern Lakeland terrier following judicious infusions of Irish-terrier and good-class fox-terrier blood. George does not agree with the theory that Welsh terrier blood was used to breed the modern Lakeland. Nor does he believe that the original hybrids were a whit inferior as workers to the fell type of Lakeland. He cites Irving's famous Turk (not the Turk sired by Johnston's Copper Coin) as an example of a looker and worker, for Turk was one of the hardest, gamest terriers that ever worked in the fells, and Turk, who was eventually killed in kennels, stamped his type on most of the Lakeland terriers in the early 1930s. Likewise, Douglas Paisley owned some very typey dogs with fox-terrier or Irish-terrier ancestry, and these dogs, who worked many seasons with the Blencathra, were incredibly game. It must be remembered that many of the founder members of the Lakeland Terrier Association were in fact working huntsmen, and men such as Mills or Bill Tomlinson, or Glaister who worked terriers with the otterhounds at Carlisle, were unlikely to appreciate a non-worker terrier, no matter how close it was to Kennel Club standard. Many of the top Lakelands of the time were bought by Tom Megeen, managing director of the Cumberland Bus Company, and Megeen was understandably reluctant to see his wards knocked about, and so he worked them sparingly, if at all.

George still likes a good working Lakeland. He recently buried Candy, a daughter of Wilkinson's Rock and a good working bitch from Hardasty's old line. He enters his pups to rat at six months or younger, for he believes any fell puppy to be ready for rat at that age (though personally the writer disagrees) and starts his babes to fox at nine months old, getting them 'made' dogs at a year.

Badgers are left strictly alone by George. He has always respected the battling power of this beast, and believes it is grossly overmatching a seventeen-pound terrier with a disposition to close with quarry against the badger, for he has seen many badger-digging Lakelands come very unstuck

59. *George Long's Candy at the Anglia Championships.*

against brock. George's account of the Salters Hall Wood dig is fascinating.

George Long represents an interesting hybrid of a dog breeder, a man who actually saw and helped in the transition of the rugged fell type of terrier into the classy box-shaped Lakeland we know today. Few men have his incredible memory for detail, and a book could be written on the times of George Henry Long.

24. Joe Mawson

(Interviewed at Egremont, Cumbria, on 16 May 1981)

On the same day that I spoke to Alan Johnston, I also visited the home of Joseph Mawson at Egremont. Mr Mawson, now aged seventy-two, is no longer able to breed terriers since he is an invalid, but he is one of the oldest and most experienced breeders of Lakeland terriers in Britain today. Joe is the third generation of breeders of a fell type of terrier, for both his father and grandfather bred these dogs and showed them in agricultural shows in the

Lakes when the breed type was referred to as simply a coloured working terrier.

Joe literally grew up with terriers, for his father showed fell-type terriers before Joe was born. Indeed, Joe has in his possession a medallion for best-coloured working terrier that his father won at Grasmere some three months before Joe's birth, and which is inscribed 'J. Mawson', for his father was determined to call his future child Joseph or Josephine – a curious and unique gift to an unborn child. Joe Walton, Ted Keardon, Ned Barget and Willie Irving influenced Joe's views on the Lakeland type of terrier. At the age of three, however, Joe developed polio, a disease that rendered him a cripple, but while his disabilities prevented Joe developing an interest in fox digging and fell hunting, he still maintained the family interest in breeding terriers of the fell type.

His accounts of early shows were passed on to him by his father. In 1859, a sporting-gun maker called W. R. Pape organized the first dog show in Newcastle upon Tyne, giving shotguns as prizes to the best exhibits, and although the show was limited to pointers and setters, it was not long before the craze spread to the Lakes and embraced terriers in its classes. According to Joe's father, and Joe's father was a noted exhibitor of fell-type terriers, the original exhibits were hard-bitten but unsightly dogs with long couples, tiny apple heads and protruding eyes resembling poor-grade Border terriers rather than the type we now consider typical fell terriers. But even before the turn of the century, breeders were introducing fox-terrier blood into fell types of dog to improve type. Curiously, this blood probably did not have any deleterious effect on the working qualities of the fell terrier. In those days, many of the fox terriers were excellent and game workers, and indeed, many of the old prefixes, Belvoir, Grove and so on, indicated that they were bred at 'hunt' kennels. Thus the addition of fox-terrier blood did little to harm the ancient fell breed of terrier, but it certainly improved the type. Joe recalls a pair of dogs from the same litter winning best fox terrier and best coloured terrier at a show in Grasmere, while G. H. Long, a contemporary of Joe, states that white terriers born to early Lakeland terrier litters found a ready market among rabbit hunters. Thus it seems likely that classy terriers were not uncommon before the formation of the Lakeland Terrier Association in 1921, and that much of this neat appearance could have been a result of the introduction of fox-terrier blood. I have seen a photograph of a 1909 Agricultural Show winning fell type of terrier: a black and grizzle tan whose fine front and elegant head would not have been out of place on one of the fox terriers of John Russell.

Joe saw the boom time for Lakeland terriers, a time that left the mongrelly type 'twixt Bedlington and Lakeland far behind. Egremont became a boom town for breeders of terriers. In 1930, Central Avenue, Egremont, boasted

60. *Opposite: Joe Mawson's father's terrier Jo, after whom Joe Mawson was named.*

six noted Lakeland terrier breeders. Today it is hotly denied by many modern Kennel Club registered breeders that the new improved shape of the Lakeland terrier following the founding of the Lakeland Terrier Association was the result of including other terrier blood. Joe, who bred several champions, quite openly admits, however, that he crossed wire-haired fox-terrier-blooded dogs with his Lakelands to produce better fronts and type, and states that another breeder used a stud dog bred by mating a small neat Irish terrier dog and a Lakeland terrier to produce his winners. Later on, even Welsh terrier blood was added to the brew by another Egremont breeder who specialized in producing black-and-tan terriers with good red tan colouring (obtained by the inclusion of Welsh terrier blood). This hybridizing to produce type did little to ruin the working qualities. Arthur Irving used Joe's stud, Rendale Roundup, to produce his hunt terriers, and most fell packs had a 'pedigree' terrier or so running with hounds from time to time.

61. *Gary Middleton (centre) with his winning fell terrier.*

25. Gary Middleton

(Interviewed at the Wensleydale Foxhound Show, Hawes, Cumbria, on 31 August 1981)

Middleton breeds a rugged, masculine type of fell terrier, some of which are red but the majority black and tan. They are a somewhat stronger, cobbier type of terrier than either Tyson's or John Cowen's, and even the bitches have strong, box-shaped heads, broad skulls and powerful masseter muscles. Middleton favours a very wiry coat, a coat more akin to an early twentieth-century Irish terrier than to the modern show-bred Lakeland.

Gary started keeping terriers at the age of fifteen (he is now forty), and his first terriers he obtained from his grandfather, who farmed around Dent. Gary's first terrier, Judy, was the product of the union of two farm-bred terriers kept for keeping down rats, rabbits and bolting the occasional fox (most Lakeland farmers keep such terriers). She was a mousey-headed, open-coated fell terrier that displayed decided Bedlington ancestry – as, indeed, did most terriers around Dent, where Bedlington blood was frequently used on fell types of terrier during the halcyon days of Bedlington-terrier breeding when it was said that no gamer breed ever existed.

Middleton was not particularly happy with the type he was breeding, however, and sought out new and better bloodlines to improve not only the physical type of his terriers but also the hunting instinct of his strain. After some trial-and-error matings, Gary eventually met up with Sid Wilkinson of Patterdale, who bred a powerful cobby strain of fell terrier and whose stud dog, Rock, a son of Anthony Barker's Rock, was a strong, utterly game red dog that displayed, as Gary believes, a decided hint of Irish terrier in its ancestry. Middleton in fact considers that Wilkinson's Rock played one of the most important parts in the creation of the modern fell terrier.

As a fount of courage, Barker's Rock was peerless. Middleton told a tale of how, during a Lakeland hunt, a large fox was driven to ground in a difficult borran earth, the sort of earth where terriers need to attack their quarry head-on to shift it or kill it. Five terriers were tried, all game Lakeland types, and all five came away badly bitten and skinned by the fox which had found itself a vantage point beneath a heavy, unmovable slab of granite. In disgust, Barker stated that he would go and fetch a terrier capable of finishing the fox and 'showing the hunters what a real terrier was about'. He returned with the senile Rock, a 'dotage' terrier complete with decayed teeth, near-blind eyes and the hideous double rupture that seems to go hand in hand with many senile Lakeland types of terrier. Rock entered slowly, took a bad initial bite, but closed with the fox, killing it deftly, neatly and quickly. This convinced Middleton that this was the strain to bring into his own terriers, and henceforth he has used only dogs descended from Wilkinson's Rock or his sire, Barker's Rock.

The ancestry of Barker's Rock is interesting, for not only is the strain bred down from unquestionably game dogs from the Lakes, but it also carries blood from some tan-and-white Russell-type terriers from outside the fells. Some fifty years ago, during the early 1920s, Fred Barker introduced terrier blood from the Ilfracombe Badger Digging Club: thirteen-inch, leggy terriers similar to the dogs bred by Heinemann. Lucas, author of *Hunt and Working Terriers*, once said that though badger digging was already falling into disfavour during the days preceding the Second World War, some of the gamest dogs were produced by members of these clubs, who not only bred a neat, elegant type of terrier (such strains were as often as not called fox terriers by the clubs), but also produced dogs whose raw courage and working ability was hard to better. Tom Evans of Blaengarw took terriers from the Ilfracombe club to South Wales, and many tales are still told of the prowess of these dogs to fox and badger.

There is a commonly held opinion, not supported by fact but perpetuated in a great many books, that most of the early breeders of fell-type terriers held white-bodied working terriers of the Jack Russell type in disdain, but this is far from the truth. Various strains of very game fell terriers still produce white puppies in their litters – proof of the inclusion of Russell or fox-terrier ancestry in the strains. Middleton still occasionally produces a white puppy or so in his litters, and one of them became a Great Yorkshire Show winner. Some excellent Russell-type terriers have appeared in litters of fell terriers over the years. Derek Hume's strain of workers, which are hard to beat at working terrier shows, are all descended from dogs with apparently pure fell-terrier parents who carried the recessive genes of good-quality game Jack Russell or fox-terrier ancestors. Likewise, Maurice Bell's present Jack Russells are simply white-bodied terriers that have appeared in fell-terrier litters. It is speculation perhaps, but educated guesswork nevertheless, to venture an opinion that many of these fell-bred Russell types of terrier are descended from the dogs of those Devonshire badger-digging clubs that played an important though vastly underrated part in the creation of the modern working Lakeland terrier.

At this point it is expedient perhaps to digress a little and include some of Middleton's own ideas on fell terriers. Middleton is very much against calling the black bull-headed fell type of terrier a Patterdale and suggests Breay terriers (after Cyril Breay of Kirkby Lonsdale) as an alternative and far more accurate title for the breed. To Middleton, the Patterdale terrier is a synonym for the rough-coated, true working Lakeland terrier, and he recites a story of how Breay, who must with Buck of Leyburn certainly be considered the creator of this strain of smooth-coated fell terrier, showed a bitch called Skiffle, a powerful, smooth-coated bull terrier-headed specimen, at a show in Patterdale.

'What do you call that, Cyril?' the huntsman judging the show asked Breay, for such a terrier was obviously unknown in the Patterdale area before the 1960s. 'A black fell terrier,' Breay replied. Winch also confirms this story, as does Maurice Bell, who was present when Breay made his show début with these terriers. Brockley of Etwall also tells a tale regarding the attitude of Lakeland judges to the labelling of smooth-coated bull-terrier-headed dogs as Patterdales. Brockley bought a litter of puppies out of one of Breay's bitches mated to Breay's dog Rusty, and kept back a pair of smooth-coated puppies to work and to show. At the Midland Working Terrier Show in 1967 or 1968 (Brockley is uncertain as to which), he showed a male from this breeding, a rugged, bull terrier type of red dog, also called Rusty, under a judge from the Patterdale district. The judge informed Brockley that such a dog was in no way a Patterdale terrier, and walked across the ring to a heavy but hard-coated Lakeland terrier to indicate to Brockley what a real Patterdale terrier should look like. Breay, however, called his dogs simply working terriers, but even during Cyril's lifetime, the strains derived from Breay's Skiffle, Rusty and Bing were being referred to as Patterdales.

To return to the terriers of Middleton. By dint of crossing back to the original Barker strain Middleton has succeeded in producing a very typey terrier. Some red but mostly black and tan though never black was how he described dogs of his breeding. Certainly, to judge from his progeny, Wilkinson's Rock proved a homogeneous stud, for most of his puppies, regardless of the type of bitch mated to him, resembled the sire. Middleton's own breeding programme, using only stock from Barker's and Wilkinson's studs, has refined the type still further. Gary uses certain curious rules of thumb in the breeding of his dogs, however. First, he is reluctant to breed from a baiting type of male – which in fell terriers means a dog which stands off its quarry and bays to direct the digger to the spot – but prefers to use a dog who will go in and mix it with a fox. His reasons for this are twofold. For one thing, he is a traditionalist who believes that the original Lakeland type of terrier was bred to kill rather than bolt foxes, and for another, he considers that the male, because of its greater fecundity (one male can easily produce over a thousand puppies, whereas even an overbred bitch can never produce a hundred or so offspring), is of greater importance to the breed than a bitch, and therefore only the very toughest, gamest males should stand at stud. (Tommy Dobson once told Farnell that he would only consider keeping an iron-hard male to perpetuate the line – hence his frequent matings to an ultra-game chocolate Bedlington male.) Bitches, even the 'doggy' bitches of Middleton's strain, are, because of their more fragile make-up, not required to be so hard, for Middleton will use bitches who 'bait' their fox. Similarly, Breay told John Parkes never to breed from a dog which was not capable of killing a fox.

Middleton enters his dogs at rat at six months, though is not dismayed if his puppies take considerable time to generate interest in quarry of this type. Funnily enough, impetuosity is a characteristic of southern terrier owners rather than of breeders north of the fells, who are usually prepared to give a dog a fair chance before dubbing it useless and disposing of it. If Middleton's dogs display no early interest in rats, he will leave them until they do – an admirable approach I believe, in a world of 'can you sell me something ready

159

for starting?' terrier men.

At a year or so old, terriers are taken and tried at bigger quarry. Badgers are usually their first heavy game, for not only does a brush with a badger teach all but the most foolhardy terrier some discretion, but badgers are always available to ground. Foxes spend possibly five months above ground, living in corn, kale and so on, but badgers are always at home. Middleton is reluctant to allow puppies to get hurt during their early encounters with fox or badger, for a beating not only tends to make some of the dogs too hard, but can also daunt a rather sensitive animal to a degree where it will refuse to go to ground again. Cobby, of the South-West Wiltshire Hunt, a hard and severe man with 'quitters', was also very keen to prevent early damage to starters and withdrew his puppies as soon as their enthusiasm for the dig began to wane. Such discretion in the entering of a terrier is to be commended.

After several apprentice runs entering a terrier at the end of a dig, Middleton allows his sapling puppies a try at finding in the earths to encourage the use of their noses. (Lucas followed similar steps during the days when he dug badger with his team of Ilmer Sealyhams.) Finally, when the dogs are well entered to badger, they are tried to fox. Gary does not subscribe to Lucas's theory that many dogs worked regularly and exclusively to badger are reluctant to enter to fox.

Middleton's show successes are best described as legion, for there are few prizes that have evaded him. With over 200 'Best in Show' to his credit, however, he describes his greatest thrill as his first win at the Grayrigg show some twenty years ago with a dog called Rusty, the progeny of a bitch called Tiny mated to the inevitable Wilkinson's Rock.

I found Middleton a fascinating and interesting terrier man, totally lacking the superstitious nonsense which clouds the minds of many terrier men of Middleton's generation.

26. George Newcombe

It would be hard to dislike George Newcombe, though it would also be fair to say that Newcombe of Rillington, near Malton, is one of the most controversial figures in fell-terrier breeding today. I met him some seven years ago, at a show in North Yorkshire, amid a heated discussion on Lakeland terrier type, and even today his name arouses great controversy among fell-terrier breeders.

George had no heritage of terrier breeding in his family, though his father, a country police officer, had some experience of attempting to train Airedales for police work. George bought his first terrier after his demob in 1946: a pedigree Bedlington bitch costing £5 paid for with money collected for a homecoming present by the natives of his village. His first terrier was purchased from a Mr Hammond of Kirkby Moorside, and this purchase started off George's interest in working Bedlington terriers. At that time, many Bedlingtons were still kept by men who worked terriers, and George considered the old type of Bedlington of fifty years ago to be the most versatile terrier possible: small enough to get to ground and quick enough to be a mini lurcher. Sadly, the Bedlington has degenerated somewhat since the war-time years, and few are worked today.

George acquired his terrier *savoir faire* from Bedlingtons, and hunted rat, rabbit, fox and badger with his team. To quote George, he hunted badger until he learned better, for after seeing several dogs of various breeds take a dreadful mauling from badger, George forsook this sport, and worked fox with his terriers, and his dogs have seen service with several hunts, including the Farndale, the Glasedale, Salter's Gate, Sinnington and the Wensleydale.

In 1950, George developed an interest in Lakeland terriers, and wrote to Willie Irving, then with the Fell Hound Trailing Association, to purchase a terrier. Irving wrote several interesting letters to George, one of which stated that he did not like the puppies sired by Copper Coin, a popular Egremont-based stud – yet Willie certainly used this stud on his own bitches. Irving also mentioned that few show-bred Lakelands were worked, as few fanciers showed any interest in getting the facial furnishings of their terriers soiled or damaged. Clearly the schism 'twixt hunter and showman was well and truly established during this time. In fact, in 1950 or 1951, Willie told Frank Buck that, if Willie owned a first-rate show Lakeland, he would not even consider working it.

George bought Rillington Ruthless from Irving (Irving never had a Kennel Club prefix of his own), and set to work entering the dog (George called him Jock) to fox and badger. Few show breeders worked their dogs, but George found Jock as good as any unregistered fell terrier at finding and killing foxes, and stated that the dog marked above ground, refusing to enter uninhabited earths. Curiously enough, early in the 1950s, several miners from South Wales journeyed to Willie Irving and bought Lakeland terriers, ranging from puppies aged eight weeks old to sapling youngsters who had not lived up to their early potential. Some ten show-bred Lakeland terriers were taken back, and all proved excellent workers to fox and badger. Sadly, a similar purchase of today's show-bred Lakelands would not do quite so well as workers. It seems likely that the Lakeland terrier of the days immediately after the Second World War still had much of the working instinct of their fell-bred ancestors.

George continued to work his pedigree Lakeland with success, and produced some fiery workers. In fact, quite a few terriers seen around the working terrier shows have the Rillington Lakeland terriers in their ancestry, including John Winch's Chase and Graham Ward's bitch line. Coulson bred an extremely game, pedigree Lakeland terrier, a terrier which saw hunt service with six hunts, from one of Newcombe's bitches.

Some fifteen years ago, however, George bought a fell type of terrier from Joe Dickson of Embleton, bred down from John Cowen of Embleton's strain of fell terrier, which in turn was descended from the dogs of Sid and Harry Hardasty. At this time, Cowen's stock was really at its best, and Bracken, the purchase made by George, worked with most of the Yorkshire packs, both mounted and foot packs. Bracken proved a useful worker, but George says that the dog was not in any way superior to the best of his Rillington-bred registered Lakeland terriers.

When the Working Bedlington Terrier Club was formed during the 1970s, it seemed obvious that George should become an official of the club, and he was in fact elected to the post of chairman. However, after holding the post for some time, George began to believe that the genuine working Bedlington, the dog described by Rawdon Lee as the toughest, hardest terrier alive, had been lost for ever, killed off by the show craze that was producing poodle-like dogs in both shape and temperament. Unlike Miss Williamson, one of the founders of the Working Bedlington Terrier Club, George did not believe that the breed could be put to rights by simply improving the present pedigree Bedlington stock, for Newcombe considered that the real honest-to-goodness Bedlington blood had long been lost. Thus Newcombe broke away from the club and attempted to produce his own strain of working Bedlington by infusing the show Bedlington strains with the blood of Cowen's working fell-terrier stock. His first generation look very similar to the old Bedlingtons of the early 1900s, and all the hybrids have proved game and tractable. I wish Newcombe luck with his project, and hope he succeeds before the Bedlington becomes simply a blue or liver poodle, no better and no gamer than a lady's lapdog.

27. John Nicholson

John Nicholson is huntsman for the Lunesdale Foxhounds, a fell pack kennelled near Sedbergh in North Yorkshire. The Lunesdale country is a little different from the country hunted by the Lakeland packs, for while it is forbidding and difficult to hunt, it is not as panoramic and rocky as the land hunted by the Melbreck, the Coniston, the Ullswater and the Blencathra. In fact, rock earths are not common in the Lunesdale, and most foxes find sanctuary in earth sets of excavated rabbit warrens. These are treacherous enough, but worst of all are the badger earths that give shelter to harassed foxes: enormous excavated citadels that are undiggable and can prove to be

62. *John Nicholson, with a terrier excavated after five days underground.*

death-traps for unwary terriers. Terriers have been to ground for up to five or six days in such places, places that are so deep that even the most vociferous terrier cannot be heard. Furthermore, much of the Lunesdale country is limestone, and in limestone 'innocent' one-eyed sets, 'places to start a puppy', lead to cracks and crevices that plunge hundreds of feet into the substrata. Disregard the gentler contours of the land, the Lunesdale country is peppered with death-trap earths, sets famous for the number of terriers that have come to grief in their depths.

Nicholson, however, was born in Ambleside, in the Coniston country, where his father farmed sheep on the land near Lake Windermere. As a boy he spent much time following the Coniston Foxhounds hunted by Anthony Chapman, who was then in his prime and a great man with hounds and terriers. Nicholson admits he learned a lot from watching Chapman.

In 1950, he began hunt service, joining the Lunesdale, then hunted by Walter Parkin, a famous fell walker with a reputation for endurance. Nicholson whipped to Walter Parkin until 1963, when Walter left Lunesdale and Nicholson became huntsman of that pack.

163

John Nicholson has kept terriers since childhood, but he obtained his first terriers from 'Brait' Black of Ambleside, who bred a rugged but typey strain of black-and-tan and black-and-grizzle fell terriers, similar in type to the family kept by Jim Fleming who lived only a mile or so away from Black. Nicholson still kept dogs of this breeding until he came to the Lunesdale in 1950. At that time there were few terriers and fewer terrier men around Sedbergh. Parkin still kept his strain, bred down from Benson's controversial Red Ike, ameliorated by Buck's dogs (the Black Rock strain of Walter Parkin), but there were few other strains in the Lunesdale country.

In the early 1950s, Nicholson met Breay, who was not yet incapacitated by the diabetes and asthma which plagued his later days. Nicholson was impressed by Breay's strain of terrier, its quiet temperament until roused and its ability to find 'bait' and if need be destroy foxes. He used Breay's Bingo on some of the bitches bred from the 'Brait' black strain of terrier. Later he added other Breay-bred blood to the stock. One of the Breay strain terriers that he worked was Socks, a terrier bred by George Lothian, Nicholson's father-in-law, of Oxenholme, who also used Breay's stud dogs on his terrier strain. Socks was a good all-round worker, a steady, sensible, reliable dog who did much to create Nicholson's reputation for being one of the best terrier men in the fell packs. Socks could work a fox well without getting too badly bitten, and he 'baited' well, rarely coming to grips with his fox and damaging it. He was still a renowned dog for bolting foxes, a dog who could bolt a fox that was winded and reluctant to run. After several useful seasons with the Lunesdale, he was put to ground in a rock hole (one of the few rock holes in the Lunesdale country) in Dent, and though he continued to bay well into the night, by morning he was silent; and although Nicholson attempted to dig to him, Socks was never found. Nicholson surmises that he fell into a rock crevice, an ever-present hazard in limestone country.

One of his best terriers, Monty, a big red dog bred down from Breay's Rusty, a son of Bingo, is seven years old and still alive in kennels. Monty is a quiet, sensible dog, not a fox killer, for Nicholson does not favour the type of dog that goes in and 'worries' its fox. Monty is a superior finder, however, and an excellent stayer with a strong steady bark – the sort of dog that shifts foxes well without crippling and maiming them.

Nicholson is an astute judge of a terrier and a respected show judge in the north. He likes a moderate-sized terrier, not too big to get in, but large enough not to get knocked about below ground. He insists on a narrow chest, however, and will not use dogs he cannot 'span' with his hands. Unlike Breay, who favoured a smooth- or slape-coated dog, Nicholson favours a short wiry coat that can keep out the cold and sheds water quickly. He likes a square-headed terrier, one not too bull-terrier headed but capable of coming out of a tangle with a fox without the jaw being broken. A twelve- or thirteen-inch terrier is his ideal-sized dog, as larger terriers are of little use in this type of country.

He takes his terriers out on couples when they are nine months of age, and

164

when they seem eager to try for a fox he allows them a chance. He dispenses with preliminary entering, as there are few rat and rabbit around his home. Badgers are a problem for a terrier hunting in the Lunesdale, for the sets are not only numerous but also deep. He discourages his dogs from hunting badger as he considers a terrier must be strictly for fox to earn his keep at a northern hunt kennels.

Nicholson has no time for the pedigree Lakeland terrier, and dogs with registered Lakeland blood not too far back in their ancestry are viewed with suspicion by the Lunesdale huntsman. According to Nicholson, while registered Lakeland terriers are often game enough for the occasional Saturday fox dig, they are neither hard enough nor constitutionally sound enough to survive three days a week hunting the fells in mid winter. Furthermore, he finds most 'pedigree' Lakeland terriers are too big for the Lunesdale earths, and the long soft coats of an unplucked Lakeland are not suitable jackets to weather the elements. Most are noisy and so aggressive that they will fight each other as readily as they will a fox, Nicholson believes.

Borders are viewed in a more favourable light by Nicholson, who says that while he has not owned a Border, he has seen pedigree Borders, the property of Roger Westmorland, at work, and been impressed by their capabilities. Furthermore, he testifies that there are many Border-terrier crosses at work in the Lunesdale country and that some are incredibly good workers.

28. Brian Nuttall

(Interviewed at Sproston, on 14 November 1980)

Brian Nuttall is a quiet, unassuming man in his mid forties, who has not only a heritage of terrier keeping but a wealth of personal experience concerning terriers, their work and most branches of field sports. Furthermore, and more priceless still, Nuttall is a keeper of accurate records and working pedigrees who has a fair working knowledge of practical genetics.

He began keeping terriers when he was fourteen years of age, inheriting, so to speak, his first dogs from his grandfather, who was a gamekeeper in Lancashire. These dogs were typical of the unclassified morass of fell terrier which existed in Lancashire some thirty to fifty years ago. Some very smooth coated, resembling strong-headed black or black-and-tan fox terriers, while others were linty-coated dogs showing much Bedlington influence. Others were near replicas of today's working Lakelands. Nuttall's grandfather used this fell blood in the creation of his type of dog, enhancing the already fiery bloodline with dashes of pit bull terrier from Northumberland. Nuttall was quick to stress that these fighting dogs were not Staffordshire bull terriers, but an unregistered type of fighting dog kept by miners and farmers in Northumberland. The resulting hybrids, Nuttall's grandfather having taken two bitches to be mated to these tiny pit dogs (which Rob Robertson of North Kenton said were rarely above twenty pounds in weight and invariably black or red brindle), were used for fox, otter and badger control in Lancashire. As might be expected, the progeny were dead game but apt to be a trifle hard and mute, preferring to close with their foes and finish the fight rather than bay and corner their quarry. Nuttall states that while the stock looked very mongrelly, they all had as a common denominator a reckless courage when their tempers were roused, and he believes that, to the best of his knowledge, his grandfather never bred a quitter. From this fiery brew came Nuttall's first terriers.

Nuttall's bitches were mated to the best available dogs, and at that time the best available dogs were kept by Frank Buck and Cyril Breay of Kirkby Lonsdale. Breay's noted dog Rusty, a red dog some twelve and a half inches at the shoulder and game as a pebble, played a big part in Nuttall's breeding by mating a Patterdale bitch called Hem. Nuttall bred an exceptional worker called Worry, as game a dog as ever drew breath; and from Breay's dog Bink (a dog used on quite a few local bitches), mated to a cross-bred Border x Patterdale bitch, he bred another excellent worker called Tim.

Frank Buck's Davy (a son of Breay's Gem) a sire that played a great part in the creation of the black fell terrier of North Yorkshire and Lancashire, was the sire of one of Nuttall's best workers, a dog called Nip, a black dog with white feet and legs (marked like a collie, as Nuttall describes him). In contradiction to most books, which state that fell men would never use a terrier with white feet, many excellent fell terriers of this time, such as Buck's Tex, had these collie markings. Nip was lightly used as a sire as he was lost to ground to fox.

Nuttall's dogs have played a very important part in the creation of the smooth-coated fell terrier. Phelan's dog Poker, a dog that has worked with two hunts and acquitted itself well in both, was bred by Nuttall. Poker was sold by Nuttall as a puppy for £12 and passed to Phelan via Didricksen and Gould, finally being purchased by Phelan for £250. Likewise, Gould's dog Smitty, a dog that has proved a prepotent sire in the Midlands, is a result of mating a bitch called Jem, bred by Brian Harrison, to Nuttall's Turk. Smitty, in turn, bred some extraordinarily good workers and lookers when mated to a variety of bitches. Another Nuttall dog, Flint, the great-grandsire of my own dog Jaeger, was an excellent worker who carved a formidable reputation in the Pennines and a beautiful animal. Nuttall, however, discontinued this line for various reasons, but it was a line which could not be faulted for courage. I saw bitches and dogs from this line at work some five years ago, and only a fool could question their excellent working instinct.

Nuttall prefers smooths, and black smooths at that, for contrary to the opinion of many fell men, he believes this coat stands the weather best and cleans easily. Woolly or long coats, he says, open up when wet and allow a

63. Nuttall's brood bitch Penny, dam of Poker etc.

dog to chill badly, while roughs tend to hold the wet and become clogged with clay balls, causing a dog great inconvenience underground. He likes his dogs of moderate size, twelve inches high and twelve to sixteen pounds in weight. Unlike many Midland fell-terrier breeders, who favour large dogs, Nuttall does not decry the small terrier. One of his bitches, a small nine-inch bitch called Whip, was a wizard at fox; while Wasp, a diminutive, rat-sized bitch of three and a half pounds, served him well to fox and could bottle up a litter of cubs in next to no time.

Nuttall worked for four seasons as terrier man to the Cheshire Hounds and has a wealth of experience at entering terriers to fox. In addition to this, he keepered Wild Boar Clough in Derbyshire. Although he was an avid rat hunter as a boy and killed over 200 rats in a night with terriers, he does not enter his terriers to rat or rabbit, preferring to keep the dogs off small quarry and enter them straight to fox. His method of entering is typical, but he despises any form of baiting. He simply digs to a fox, lets a terrier bay the fox through a fork or behind a spade at the end of the dig, after which he allows the fox to escape and encourages his terrier to indulge in a fruitless though meaningful chase. This, he believes, is better training than any baiting of a

167

fox. In fact, Nuttall rarely kills foxes, preferring to allow them to escape and run free to give sport another day. Nuttall's terriers are entered to fox at about nine months to a year, and 'if they don't go to the first they go to the second'.

Nuttall's post as terrier man to the Border County Mink Hounds allows him to hunt the terriers on Saturdays. Once again he remarks on how unsuitable a long coat is for a terrier designed to hunt mink. A smooth-coated dog plunging into an icy April floodstream shakes itself dry in seconds, but a long-coated dog chills easily. He has seen icicle-clad, rough-coated dogs clatter like glass chandeliers after a dip in freezing water; and I cannot help but agree with his opinion about coat type. Terriers that enter to rat, says Nuttall, will also work a rat as freely as a mink during a mink hunt, which makes them a great nuisance.

Where breeding is concerned, Nuttall is equally methodical about his terriers and does not breed from either a dog or bitch unless and until they are proven, neither does he overbreed. His kennels, neat and well kept, consisted of some seven terriers ranging from a magnificent bull-terrier-headed bitch, muscled like a gladiator, to youngsters just starting. He refuses to outcross, preferring to add just a dash of new blood from proven stock – usually sons or daughters of his own stud dogs mated back to his own line. His record keeping is good and accurate, and such careful documentation has produced an unequalled quality of a top terrier breeder and a first-rate worker of terriers – a *rara avis* today. I can vouch for the working ability of his dogs, for like him I use tiny dashes of outside blood, and frequently resort to using Nuttall-bred stock to add to the vitality of my own strain of Jack Russell terrier. Personally I find it hard to fault this bloodline, and I can believe Nuttall's only boast, 'I have never produced a non-worker from this family.'

29. Christopher Ogilvie

(Interviewed at Coniston, Cumbria)

Christopher Ogilvie is an unusual person to be hunting a fell pack. He is not a native of the fells, for he was born in Kent, though his family (his father is a doctor) moved to live in Patterdale. Ogilvie is an enthusiastic hunter, however, with a wide experience of hounds and huntable quarry. Although he is a young man in his mid thirties, he has hunted for some seventeen seasons with the Blackcombe Beagles, the Bucks and Courtney Tracy Otter-hounds, the Lochaber, finally finishing up whipping in and eventually hunting the Coniston Foxhounds.

64. Christopher Ogilvie, huntsman and lakeland poet.

He obtained his first terriers from Maldwin Williams from Ullswater, a Welsh-bred fell type of terrier mingled with traditional fell-terrier blood. It was a useful terrier, as good as any Ogilvie has owned. Interesting fell types of terrier are certainly still bred around the Snowdonia area, but whether they are descended from Lakeland fell types or dogs from the Ynysfor strain of terrier is an unanswered question.

He left the beagles to work with otterhounds, and was given a useful terrier by Derek Shield, a policeman from Patterdale. This was a hard-bitten terrier bred from Johnny Richardson of Blencathra's strain – a game, sensible strain of terrier well suited to the task of bolting otters. One of his hardest, gamest, most sensible terriers was bred from Richardson's dogs. The bitch, Topsy, was bred by mating Maldwin Williams' Major, a dog who served at the North Tyne Kennels to Johnny Richardson's bitch, Tess. Topsy was a sensible bitch, but utterly game. She would bay her quarry well and patiently, but if the fox refused to bolt, she was capable of killing it. In spite of the fact that she saw much work, she was rarely badly bitten and lived up to the ripe old age of thirteen.

Ogilvie's present line is descended from a bitch he called Jennie, a bitch sired by Tinker, a wheaten-coloured, soft-coated dog from a strain that has worked in the Coniston country for generations. (Some of the earliest photographs of Coniston hunt terriers show wheaten-coloured dogs.) The dam of the bitch was bred by Sid Wilkinson out of his famous Rock, a line bred to the Ullswater terrier bitch, Myrt, bred by Jim Fleming of Grasmere. As might be expected with a bitch of this breeding, she proved a great finder, having an excellent nose and great sense when up on her quarry. She met her death in Scotland when Ogilvie was with the Lochaber Hunt. Chris entered her to a fox driven into a rock pile by hounds. Sadly the pile also housed a badger, and Jennie encountered it, trying for a jaw hold as she did with foxes. The result was unpleasant, but predictable, and her jaw was sheared. She died a few days later.

She bred several litters before her demise, however. One of her offspring was killed by hounds when Ogilvie kennelled the hounds in a byre while he went to tea at a farm. Something triggered off the hounds and they slew the terrier. At that time, however, a keeper near the Coniston Kennels owned a dog called Tommy, a result of mating one of the black fell terriers (perhaps of Buck strain) with a white Russell-type bitch. Tommy was a grand worker, but he was quarrelsome in kennels so was passed to Ogilvie and saw much service with the Coniston Foxhounds. Mated to Jennie, he bred Jake, Ogilvie's best terrier: a gaunt, narrow, wheaten dog with a poor coat, but a nailer to work and strong enough to finish the job if the fox refused to bolt. He resembles some of the old so-called Patterdale terriers featured in Lucas's book, *Hunt and Working Terriers*.

Ogilvie keeps Russells as well as fells, but he is not a Russell enthusiast. Most are too yappy for kennels, and he shares Richardson's opinion about the fact that, while Russells work well enough, they are not constitutionally

65. An Ogilvie hunt terrier, a duplicate of the old Patterdale type bred by Anthony Pool.

strong enough to take the hardship of a life hunting the fells. He likes narrow-chested, leggy terriers, terriers well able to work on couples, and while his own terriers are inclined to be woolly coated, Ogilvie much prefers the wire jacket of a good type of fell terrier. He keeps three types of terrier: finders, baiters and hard ones, dogs tough enough to kill. His hauls of fox are high, considering that he hunts the near-perpendicular heights leading from Ambleside to Patterdale, and takes seventy or so foxes each season.

He enters his bitches less carefully than he tries his dogs, allowing them to run loose while hounds mark to ground, for bitches are not as jealous at work as dogs and are less likely to battle with each other below ground. Ogilvie believes that, if a dog is correctly bred, it will self-enter. He cites an instance of Jet, a bitch bred from Jennie and sired by Mick, an old black Coniston terrier of a sort that has existed in the Coniston country since before 1914. Jet left kennels for the first time that day, and when hounds marked to ground, she raced to the spot, shot down the cairn and baited her fox frantically.

Dogs are never allowed to go to ground together when Ogilvie is hunting as they are likely to fight each other rather than unite against a common foe. Ogilvie is a quiet, well-spoken, taciturn man who is not only well educated and literate but a Lakeland poet of some note.

30. Pat O'Malley

(Interviewed at Stainton, Cumbria)

Pat O'Malley describes himself as a small-time terrier man and no expert, his kennels containing only three or four terriers. O'Malley was born in Mayo of a farming family. His first terrier was a small Lakeland or fell terrier of the type bred and worked in Mayo, although Scarteen terriers were supposedly common in Mayo. A slape-coated type of terrier was O'Malley's first terrier, and Pat hunted this terrier to rat, rabbit and similar small fry, but states that many farmers used their terriers to herd sheep and cattle. Funnily enough, most of the Irish terrier breeds – the Irish terrier, the soft-coated wheaten, the Kerry Blue, the Glen of Imaal – were also used for multi-purpose farm work as well as vermin control in their native Ireland.

O'Malley came to Britain some sixteen years ago to find work, and as soon as he found a 'fixed abode' he set about breeding terriers once more. His first terrier was Smut, a puppy bred by Norman Savage out of Sid Wilkinson's illustrious line that included in its working pedigree such workers as Bowman's Lil, Richardson's Tarzan and Fred Barker's Chowt-faced Rock. O'Malley chose wisely, so it seems, for he purchased the dog at six weeks old, and the day after its purchase he took it to work. That day it went to ground and began baying at a rabbit in an earth close to the site on which O'Malley was working.

Smut entered to badger at six months (Middleton says most of Wilkinson's strain have a reputation for premature entering – an enthusiasm that can be the downfall of many young terriers), but happily was not ruined by this encounter, for he learned to keep out of reach of the badger, nipping and teasing until the end of the dig, when O'Malley finally crowned through to the badger; whereupon Smut rushed in and seized the badger, holding it until O'Malley could bag it. He was a little too bulky for fox in most places, though he did work with the Ullswater, the Bewcastle and the Wensleydale Foxhounds during Maurice Bell's Sunday hunts. At the Bewcastle meet, Smut drew a fox with the fox's teeth fastened through his nose.

Flint, the brother of Eddie Pool's Wasp, the result of mating Pool's Black Jock to Gyp, a terrier of the Scarteen hunt breeding, was O'Malley's next terrier. Flint was a sensible terrier, game but with brain enough to keep out of trouble. He received an early mauling from badger, after which he held back on both fox and badger. Flint had the best nose O'Malley has ever seen on one of his terriers, and he could run buck like a hound.

Jet, bred by David Windle, sired by Sid Wilkinson's Jock (a noted game terrier, now a veteran at stud with Bill Brightmore) was his next terrier – a poor doer who never looked right as a puppy but improved dramatically after O'Malley wormed him. Like his famous father Jock, Jet was a tiger, capable of killing any fox, and he rarely allowed one to bolt. O'Malley used him in difficult places when a fox refused to bolt for hounds. He went to ground on

172

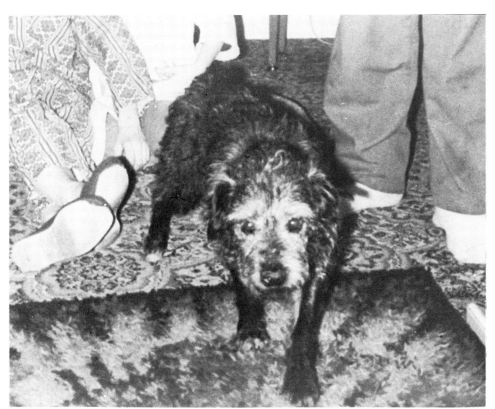

66. *Pat O'Malley's present hunt terrier.*

only two badgers, both of which tore him about badly, and O'Malley realized that the dog would never learn discretion and ceased to use him in places where a badger might be found. However, he became a remarkable dog to fox, and Roy Newton, who left the Lakes to hunt the Lochaber Foxhounds, still uses Jet with the Lochaber on any foxes that are shy about bolting.

31. *Jimmy Overs*

(Interviewed on 25 April 1982)

It must seem rather strange to the reader that Jimmy Overs, a retired head gamekeeper, a breeder of top-grade Labrador retrievers and an expert on pheasant rearing who has never had a terrier on his premises should appear in a book concerned with fell terriers. Overs, however, must rank as one of my

67. *Jimmy Overs.*

most important interviewees, for, together with his father, he was kennelman to the famous Egton Kennels owned by Mrs Graham Spence – one of the most important kennels, whose dogs were literally the missing links 'twixt fell terriers and the more fashionable Lakeland terrier which began to evolve from the working fell terriers after the meeting of fell-terrier breeders in 1912.

Overs' father was a gamekeeper near the Spence residence at Summerhill, where, following the death of Mr Graham Spence, his wife was advised by her doctors to take up an absorbing interest. Thus she began putting together one of the finest kennels of Lakeland terriers in the world, dogs of such quality that the Romanian prime minister sent to Summerhill for a male Lakeland terrier. Mrs Spence therefore employed both Jimmy Overs and his

68. Jimmy Overs' father with Howtown dog.

69. Mrs Graham Spence.

father as kennelmen to help to build and stock her kennels. The Overs family had no connection with fell or Lakeland terriers before that date, though the family had bred and worked an unregistered strain of Cairn terrier, which Overs describes as every bit as good as the fell terriers bred by the fell packs at that time.

The Overs, father and son, set about trying to buy in the very best fell and registered Lakeland terrier blood to start the kennels, and their purchases were as varied as stock from John Pool of Glenridding's fell terriers to such top-class registered terriers as Marshal (later rechristened Field Marshal) from Billy Ridley for the then substantial sum of £8.

At that time, Lakeland-terrier conformation was improving by leaps and bounds, and the dogs purchased by Mrs Spence in 1928 were a far cry from the unsightly little battlers in Clapham's book *Foxhunting on the Lakeland Fells*. The improvement, however, was certainly brought about by crossing the native fell terriers with fox terriers and Welsh terriers, and often adding a dash or so of Irish-terrier blood to the rather mongrelly unCumbrian mix. Mrs Spence tried her utmost to stop further addition of these alien breeds, writing rather vehement letters to doggy periodicals and condemning the practice in Brian Vesey-FitzGerald's collection of essays on breeds of dog. By this time, Mrs Spence had left Summerhill and its near-by Egton cum Newland, an estate from which she borrowed her Egton prefix. She settled in Howtown, in the midst of the Ullswater Hunt country, and her enthusiasm for the purity of the Lakeland terrier became even more intense.

She bred many terriers, some of which threw back to the old type of Bedlington which had been used in the creation of the original fell terrier, with roached backs, linty coats and pendulous, houndy ears. But some outstanding-looking specimens were also produced at her kennels, including, at that time, the incomparable Lady of the Lake – a bitch bred out of Tinker, a game hunt terrier, mated to Vic of Wastwater, a dog with an unbroken line of workers in its pedigree. The terriers she produced from her kennels were not only outstanding lookers, but often extraordinarily good workers. She had an aversion to terriers with even a small fleck of white on their feet (many breeders dyed the toes of their terriers to conceal this minor fault), and would not tolerate such a terrier in her kennels. She sold them as workers (minus their pedigrees, of course) to fox hunters and badger diggers. One evening at Gowbarrow, I listened to a conversation between Sid Wilkinson (whose sister married Jimmy Overs) and Eddie Pool of Glenridding, concerning these rejects of Mrs Spence, and both spoke highly of those pedigree terriers, which were then still as game and sane as their fell-bred grandparents.

In fact, Mrs Spence was a great enthusiast of the real working terrier, and often gave Braithwaite Wilson, the huntsman for the Ullswater Foxhounds, £1 (a handsome tip in 1933) to try one of her terriers to ground when the hounds put a fox 'in'. Wilson actually kept two or three of the Graham Spence Egton terriers at the Ullswater Hunt Kennels, and once said that he favoured the type more than the Bedlington-blooded terriers bred in

70. *Mrs Graham Spence with kennelman Overs, Snr.*

Glenridding (referring to the dogs bred by John Pool). No champion terrier was ever used to ground, of course, for even in those days Lakeland terrier judges were reluctant to give prizes to badly scarred exhibits. Lil, on the other hand, the full litter sister of Egton Lady of the Lake (the first Egton Champion Lakeland terrier) was a wonderful worker, a true finder, even in the vastness of Blaeberry borran, and a wonderful bolting terrier. Wilson once told a hunt follower that few better terriers were working with the fell packs than this sister of the first Lakeland-terrier champion of the Egton Kennels. Whether or not Braithwaite Wilson used the Spence-bred terriers in the creation of his own terrier strain is speculation. Sufficient to say that, when Jocelyn Lucas interviewed the 'Flying Whip', as Braithwaite Wilson had been described during his years as whip to Bowman, Wilson had a kennel of very typey black-and-tan, rough-coated terriers that were a far cry from the dogs bred by the Chapmans at the Coniston or the Porter family at the Eskdale and Ennerdale.

Mrs Spence encouraged the Overs to trap rats and try the infant terriers on those creatures before allowing the dogs to go to hunt kennels, and even allowed the hunt to meet at her Howton home, where her hospitality was a legend. When she died in 1949 she left her kennels to the Overs family. Unfortunately, since Jimmy's father had no car, visiting shows and showing dogs became difficult, if not impossible, and slowly the kennels ran down, their dissolution no doubt aided by the fact that Overs Junior fulfilled his life's ambition and left the kennels to become a gamekeeper. He took one terrier with him, and used it to good effect when a local hunt terrier could not quite reach its fox, for the Egton terriers were very narrow chested and could literally get anywhere.

That was Jimmy Overs's last fell terrier, for terrier temperament is a bit out of place on a shoot where large stocks of pheasants are reared. He still follows many hunts, including the Ullswater and the Bewcastle, and his knowledge of natural history and the habits of predators is incredible, his gift as a raconteur of those tales fascinating. After I had interviewed him and was driving back south, I felt somewhat saddened by the fact that such a stately, well-spoken, highly intelligent man should once have been typical of the owners of fell terriers but now represented one of the last of a generation whose like we shall probably not see again.

32. Douglas Paisley

(Based on accounts by those who knew him)

Bowman, wrongly in my opinion, is often said to be the most important figure in the creation of the modern fell terrier. In the Lakeland-terrier stakes my money would be on Douglas Paisley, former honorary whip and some-time honorary secretary to the Blencathra Hunt.

After 1921, the Lakeland terrier (the alternative name Patterdale terrier now falling gradually into disuse) improved in type dramatically as a result of the eugenic programme followed up by various breeders around the Egremont area, most of them almost certainly using wire-haired fox-terrier blood and/or Irish-terrier blood to bring about the improvement. Breeders like Alf John-ston, whose Oregill prefix is still carried by Alan Johnston, Alf's grandson, and Mawson helped to bring about the improvement in type, as did Tom Megeen, who collected the finest specimens available at the time. The main task of working the new breed, however – for a new breed it certainly was – fell on men like Willie Irving, huntsman for the Melbreck, and more important still on Douglas Paisley, who not only worked the new strain in the Blencathra area, a land of deep granite borrans and damp gill earths, but also showed his strain at Crystal Palace in 1929 and 1930, winning well even with dogs that had followed hounds only a few days earlier. Today, with their exaggerated furnishings, face and leg featherings, such feats would be impossible, for a day on the fells, or even worse a day in a damp, sodden gill earth, would render a modern show Lakeland totally unfit for the Kennel Club show bench. In Paisley's day it was still possible to win with workers.

In spite of stories to the contrary, and there were many who knocked the new improved Lakeland terrier, the show Lakeland of pre-1930 was a fiery dog. Most specimens were utterly game, with the same pluck and fire as their fell-terrier ancestors (see interview with Harold Watson, page 222). They were mostly quarrelsome, in fact, and Willie Irving is said to have had

179

71. *Douglas Paisley with Tinker, far left.*

several of the new breed killed in kennel fights. Whatever blood was introduced to bring about the improvement, it was certainly game blood. Long states that Paisley's dogs were some of the gamest in the fells, and several old terrier men of Egremont (still the very best place to hear fell terrier tales) confirm Long's story that two of Paisley's terriers once killed a fully grown otter. Yet it was at the pursuit of foxes that Paisley's dogs excelled.

Lucas knew Paisley only slightly, and I am indebted to stories told me by Lucas as well as to his admirable *Hunt and Working Terriers* for accounts of Paisley's dogs. Paisley's most famous dog was Tinker, the far-left terrier in the group held by Paisley, and it was this dog that Paisley used as a cornerstone of his strain, as did George Long, some of his dogs also being descended from Paisley's Tinker. Tinker was an incredible animal and tales of him drawing foxes and otters from drains are legion. He worked for some three seasons with the Blencathra and won considerable distinction hunting some of the worst borrans in the country. No earth was too deep for him, and, Lucas said, no quarry too fierce.

Bess and Sandy were two of Paisley's terriers from the same strain, and Bess was reputedly immune to pain. In 1927, Paisley put Bess to ground at a fox in an enlarged rabbit burrow in low-lying land near the hunt kennels. She met her fox, sounded twice and then remained silent. Paisley, fearing the worst, dug to her only to find her trying to draw the fox. Its teeth had met through her upper jaw, but she had never whimpered, merely struggled to get a better purchase on her quarry. Paisley inbred her frequently as he valued the raw courage this Lakeland bitch stamped into her progeny.

Paisley's dogs had a formidable reputation for raw guts – a courage that was to be the downfall of many of them, for few had what G. H. Long described as 'reverse gears', bad wounds seeming only to drive them to greater efforts. Paisley might accurately be described with Glaister of Carlisle and Irving of the Melbreck as one of the first exponents of the new improved registered Lakelands.

Sadly, few breeders of today's pedigree Kennel Club Lakelands work their dogs since the process of crawling into an earth alone is sufficient to ruin a dog's chances of winning at Kennel Club shows. Even honourable scars are not wanted on potential champions. Truly Paisley would not approve of the modern Kennel Club registered Lakeland terrier that his work helped to create.

33. John Parkes

(Interviewed at Kirkby Overblow, North Yorkshire, on 16 April 1982)

I interviewed John Parkes at his farm near Harrogate one Saturday, and spent till the early hours of Sunday morning both talking terriers and going out ratting with Parkes's team of yearling fell terriers around the farmyard.

Parkes is, to use his own expression, 'a fanatic about the Breay strain of fell terrier', and has endeavoured to keep the 'Master's' strain relatively pure. Yet he began his interest in working terriers by keeping a strain of Jack Russell bred from the terriers worked at Bramham Moor Hunt and descended from Warrior, a renowned fox-hunting terrier and a stayer to badger. Parkes was primarily a badger digger, and his interests brought him into contact with noted fell hunters such as Maurice Bell, Frank Buck and Jossie Akerigg. In such company it seemed inevitable that Parkes should forsake Russells and become a fell-terrier addict, his first purchase being from John Watkinson, who kept a strain of terrier from the Prouds of the Bewcastle Hunt. A later purchase came from Doug Parkin: a bitch called Trixie, bred by John Horner's Bing out of a fell-terrier bitch of uncertain ancestry. Trixie worked well for Parkes and became a good stayer and an excellent finder in bad places. Trixie was killed by a car on the road outside Parkes's farm, but just before that happened, Parkes had met the late Cyril Breay, who reshaped the youthful enthusiast's ideas on terriers.

72. John Parkes with some of his Breay strain of fell terriers.

Breay was at that time a little over the hill since his ill-health was finally taking its toll, not only on his constitution but also on his morale. Such was his charisma, however, that youthful hunters flocked to him for advice. Breay gave Parkes a foundation stud dog called Monty, a son of Breay's famous Rusty, and a good-class bitch called Trixie, bred by John Whaley out of Breay-bred stock. Few dogs could have served a terrier man better. Like all Rusty's progeny, Monty had fire in plenty and stayed to fox or badger indefinitely. And like all the Black Davy line, he had an incredibly good nose and could find literally anywhere. Parkes cites a curious example of Monty's finding ability. One spring, he was asked out on a cub-hunting session by a local keeper who was being greatly troubled by a marauding vixen and her cubs. They searched the area for a breeding earth, and while feathers and fur were abundant, no earth could be found. Then Monty stood beneath a tall oak tree and began to bay. At first Parkes considered the ageing dog to be going senile and took him away, but he kept returning to the tree and continuing to bay. Parkes eventually climbed the tree and found the litter of cubs plus the vixen hiding in a lair between a pile of broken twigs and a hollow in the main branch. Later, Parkes returned and measured the height of the nest. It was twenty-five feet above ground level! Monty died of old age at about sixteen years of age, so it seems reasonable to assume that Parkes used this useful male as the mainstay of his breeding scheme.

When Parkes began his search to find a suitable bitch for his stud dog, Hardasty's famous Turk had recently died (a dog distantly related through Fleming's Myrt to Breay's strain). Before his demise, however, he had bred a litter of puppies, one of which went to Harry Hines. Breay thought highly of Hardasty's Turk, as indeed he did of Harry Hardasty himself, once describing him as the best terrier breeder in the Lakes. Thus Parkes had little reservation about bringing this line into his own strain. Monty mated the Turk-bred bitch and produced a litter of three puppies: Trusty and Dusty, who died in a badger set after a week's dig during Christmas 1973, and a male puppy which Parkes called Bingo, in memory of Breay's illustrious stud dog who died in a quarry in the Lunesdale country.

Breay now gave Parkes a bitch called Bonnie, a full sister of Monty (Rusty x John Whaley's Trixie), an exceptionally hard bitch who took terrific punishment because of her courage and was to die prematurely aged before her tenth year. Parkes mated this bitch to Rock, a dog sired by Maurice Bell's Britt (rated by many as the hardest fell terrier ever to come out of Yorkshire, and incidentally a grandson of Hardasty's Turk). Rock had a dubious reputation. For courage, like all of Britt's puppies, he could not be faulted, but he proved too hard for any hunt and was retired from the newly formed Lochaber Hunt since he literally tore every fox to pieces. He also had a peculiar reaction to boots, and attacked Parkes every time his master approached in a pair of fell boots, even though he would be docile and even fawning when Parkes appeared wearing shoes.

The progeny of the Rock x Bonnie mating was ill fated. Parkes kept a black typey bitch from the mating, and had her reared by Cyril Breay, but shortly after her return to Parkes she hobbled back to the farm limping slightly. Parkes found that both her front feet had been severed by a rotary mower. He did the only thing possible and put her down immediately. He now allowed Bingo (the result of the Monty x Hines Hardasty-bred bitch) to continue the bloodline, and mated him to a bitch called Scoobie bred from Ken Harrison's Daz (a Britt-bred dog and a bitch from the Breay/Buck Skiffle bloodline). Scoobie (the property of Jack Brown) produced two puppies: Tina, who went to Parkes, and Chip, a dog who was usually worked in deep earths with a bleeper but died on badger aged seven years. During his lifetime, however, Chip achieved considerable renown and was reputed to be able to hold any badger at the end of a dig.

Such was the success of the litter that Jack Brown mated his Scoobie to the now ageing Monty, the father of Bingo, but the litter, while being useful, could scarcely be called spectacular. Doug, a blue, rough-coated male was sold as a pet, but became a bad cat worrier and had to be returned. Punch, another male, became a useful fox dog but was too keen to go for a catchhold to survive long as a badger dog. The remaining bitch, Judy, was only suitable to work to fox and of little use on badger digs. None of the second litter matched the class of Tina, the result of the Bingo x Scoobie mating.

So useful did Tina prove that Parkes mated her to Bingo (her own sire) to continue the line. Three puppies came from the union, the first being Ferodo, a superb animal, a looker who won several shows and a worker who found foxes at seven months and stayed seventeen hours during a badger dig. Sadly the dog was crippled in a car accident and had to be put down. The second puppy, Bonnie Mark II, is still with Parkes, as is the third, a beautiful, eye-catching slape-coated red dog as muscular as a gladiator and a dog of whom Breay would have been proud. I was particularly impressed with this replica of Breay's Rusty, which was, if anything, of better type than Breay's old dog.

Parkes keeps perhaps ten terriers, all Breay bred and all much of the old type bred at Kirkby Lonsdale. What is most impressive, however, is that all are kennelled together and Parkes has little trouble with kennel fights and very few deaths.

As I stated, I spent a Saturday night and a Sunday morning hunting with Parkes's dogs, and found them busy, eager ratters, keen as mustard and able to twist and weave into the recesses of a log pile. I feel that Breay would have been more than approving of Parkes's team.

Bloodlines of Parkes' present dogs:

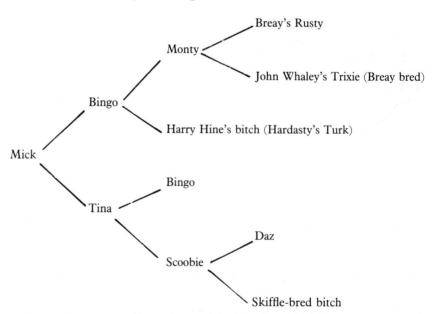

184

34. Walter Parkin

(Interviewed at Shap, on 29 December 1980)

I visited Walter Parkin, ex-huntsman of the Lunesdale foxhounds, long after a crippling stroke had incapacitated him, making him, to use the words of Maurice Bell, 'a shadow of himself'. And what a huntsman Walter was: a respected man, an expert with hounds, a serious breeder of fell types of terrier, but above all one of the great fell-walking huntsmen.

During Parkin's heyday between 1946 and 1963, this rather fragile, spare man was stamina personified, fell walking his hounds around fifteen miles a day over the awe-inspiring lunar terrain hunted by the Lunesdale Fox-hounds. In 1952, he walked sixty-seven miles (to the Ullswater Foxhounds meet and back) simply to see Joe Wear work some new hounds. Nimrod grown old came to mind as I heard Walter's wife tell tales of Walter's fell-hunting days, but then such men are bred from fell-hunting dynasties, not chance genetic sports thrown up from run-of-the-mill families.

Walter was born on 29 May 1909. Joe Bowman was his grandfather's first cousin, and thus Walter grew up in the world of fell hunting. I asked him if he knew Bowman.

'Of course,' replied Walter. 'I went to his funeral' – and then added quietly, 'But everyone did, I suppose,' for the funeral of Joe Bowman was one of the great events in living fell history. Anthony Metcalf Gibson, master of the Ullswater, injected Walter with his first dose of fell-hunting fever, for Gibson would fetch the eleven-year-old from school to hunt with the Ullswater Hounds, and thus Walter Parkin spent most of his time, until military service took him away from the fells. The year 1942 found Parkin in North Africa with the 8th Army, and he also took part in the diversionary attack that preceded the Salerno landing. At the cessation of the war he returned to the fells, and in 1946 became huntsman to the Lunesdale Foxhounds, a post that he held until 1963.

Parkin's first terriers were scruffy blue, tan, silver and wheaten-coloured, silky coated dogs similar to the terrier Gyp,* or to Nellie, the favourite of E. G. Paley in Anne Roslin Williams's book, *Border Terriers*. Such terriers are still bred and worked in the southern fells and northern Lancashire, and are called Border/Lakelands, a term that is probably oddly accurate since they are survivors of stock that undoubtedly gave rise to both Border and Lakeland terriers. Mrs Parkin, Walter's wife, described these terriers as being 'like Yorkshire terriers, only three times as big. They were utterly game, entirely from stock, bred and worked by fell packs, but not typey or of good coat'.

In the late 1930s, however, Walter's dogs underwent a metamorphosis. During this time Albert Benson bred the dog called Red Ike – a dog of

---

*See Lucas's *Hunt and Working Terriers*, p. 184.

185

73. Walter Parkin (right) with a Breay-bred fell terrier.

unknown breeding, but one can say with fair confidence that there was Irish-terrier blood not too far back in its ancestry. Red Ike was to transform the dogs of Parkin and the dogs around Coniston where Ike was to stand to stud. Ike was a dog of uncertain temper, touchy with people and quick to anger, yet the impact he made on the fell-terrier stock was considerable, and his progeny was so game that it found a market all over Britain and America. Parkin mated this dog on to several bitches of his old strain and produced some incredibly game stock, utterly fearless, with excellent noses and a disposition to stay with a fox until either the dog or fox died. This stickability did, in fact, result in the extinction of several of the Red Ike bloodlines. Later Parkin mated the Red Ike bitches to Breay's/Buck's dogs and produced what Walter described as the Black Rock strain, a family of black or red terriers with hard or smooth coats. Every male which Parkin kept from this line Walter called Rock, hence Rock I, Rock II, Rock III, which complicates the unravelling of pedigrees of some of the fell terriers bred around Lunesdale.

Parkin never bred a bad terrier from this line, though one that he bred, a black-and-tan dog from Rock III (owned by Bill Braithwaite), was extremely slow to enter, and at two years of age had little or no idea of working fox. Later something clicked and the dog, Jack, suddenly went to fox with a vengeance. While the fox lived Jack would stay, and numerous times he had to be dug out. Twice gargantuan digs were needed to excavate Jack, digs of such magnitude that the national newspapers covered the events.

Parkin never favoured a large terrier, not even for working the deep earths that abound in the Lunesdale area, and he refused to contemplate using a dog much above twelve inches and not readily spannable. He learned from experience how detrimental a loose, open, soft coat could be, and henceforth kept only broken-coated or hard-coated terriers. Blacks, reds, black and tans and blue and tans were the colours Walter favoured in his terriers.

Walter entered his dogs first to rat, but did not mind too much if his puppies ran rabbits, for 'they soon knew that fox was the game' when they were entered to their legitimate quarry. After they had entered to small fry they were allowed to run with the pack, to be entered when they were good and ready. Parkin rarely dug badger, and then only by accident, for he regarded badger hunting with extreme distaste and was reluctant to hunt these quiet, harmless creatures. In any case, his terriers were worked regularly to fox, and injuries inflicted by badgers can render a dog *hors de combat* for days afterwards.

Walter now lives in an old folks' block of flats where keeping dogs is prohibited: an odd twilight for a man who loved both hounds and terriers, and one who once nearly died trying to give the kiss of life to a hound which had eaten strychnine. As I left Walter, Maurice Bell shook his head sadly and whispered, 'Pity such a man has to grow old.' It is indeed a tragedy, for the fells are no longer producing men of the calibre of Walter Parkin.

35. *Eddie Pool*

(Interviewed at Glenridding, Cumbria, on 15 October 1981)

My interview with Eddie Pool came about in an extraordinary manner. I was kicking my heels in Glenridding, waiting to interview Dennis Barrow at the Ullswater Hunt. A child of maybe thirteen years old came walking her dog along the pavement. It was a red old-fashioned fell terrier of the type somewhere between a Border/Lakeland and with a strong hint of Bedlington. The lady with the girl, seeing my interest in the dog, volunteered the data that it was a type of Lakeland. I said 'I know,' and the girl, who became quite excited about my knowledge of fells, invited me to meet her father. This turned out to be Eddie Pool. Strangely enough, Maurice Bell had drawn up a list of people I should interview and had included Eddie Pool (an expert on Joe Wear's terriers, Maurice had said). I had scheduled my meeting with Eddie for January 1982. Fate destined that I should meet him earlier – it was a meeting for which I am profoundly grateful.

74. Eddie Pool.

The Pool family have long been native to the Lakes. Originally they were Dutch miners who came to the Lakes in the reign of Elizabeth I to prospect for metals. Strangely enough, one theory suggests that the Bedlington terrier was introduced to the north of England by Dutch immigrants, though there is nothing to substantiate it.

Pool's grandfather, Anthony Pool, a great terrier man by all accounts, worked fell terriers and crossed them with Bedlingtons to produce a really game, hardy terrier suitable for working in the fells. A glance at the photograph of the Salters Hall Wood badger dig (page 45) will show the reader the type of Bedlington (a hard-bitten sturdy dog which is a far cry from the show-bred Bedlington of today) worked in the Lake District during Pool's grandfather's day. Eddie is still a great advocate of the working Bedlington terrier, though good game stock of the calibre of yester-year is becoming increasingly difficult to find.

His first terriers were, of course, home bred, out of his grandfather's old Bedlington type of fell-terrier stock, mated to a dog belonging to Joe Wilkinson (the brother of Sid Wilkinson), a fell type of terrier which Eddie suspects had Jack Russell blood. His first terriers, Tony and Wasp, were worked hard and responded well to Pool's training programme, working with the Ullswater whenever Pool, who is self-employed, could manage a day's hunting. Wasp was eventually mated to Anthony Barker's Rock, a tough, hard-bitten dog, game as a pebble and an excellent finder and fox killer. Rock in fact made a considerable impact on the fell-terrier population around the Ullswater area. The mating resulted in a bitch puppy called Nettle, who was given back to Anthony Barker as a stud fee. Barker worked her hard and returned her to Pool when he finished hunting. The bitch eventually ran into a pile of sticks and lost an eye as a result of the collision, so Pool retired her. Nettle, however, continued dead game and eager to go until her death at fifteen years of age.

Nettle was mated to Anthony Barker's Jim, a really game terrier. She was jet black in colour, and so a bit of a rarity in the Ullswater country where most terriers are either red or black and tan. Jim, however, was a dog of good type and an excellent worker. Peggy, a bitch puppy from the union, continued Pool's bloodline. She was sold to a Mrs Granger for £6 as a child's pet, but she was a worker not a lapdog and proved unsuitable. Thus she was returned to Pool, who tried her, found her useful and in turn mated her to Joe Wear's very useful stud dog, Jock, a big, bold-looking male easily capable of killing a fox if it decided not to bolt. A strange anecdote surrounds Peggy's litter – an anecdote that may illustrate the power of divine retribution. Joe Wear had pick of the litter in lieu of stud fee and chose a big, powerful dog, typical of the type Joe fancied, and indeed bred, and of the type he liked to judge at shows. Pool's father also fancied the puppy, and when Wear sent around a friend to claim the puppy, Eddie's father palmed off another second-choice puppy instead of the one Joe had chosen. The ringer puppy sent to Joe Wear grew into Punch, a useful dog, a nailer to work, with excellent nose and the ability to finish any fox that refused to bolt. Eddie's father's puppy, however, grew into Tony, a renowned sheep worrier, impossible to break of the habit, and a costly habit at that, as Pool's father found. Tony was eventually put down because of his interest in sheep – 'interest' being a bit of an understatement, by all accounts!

Wasp II, the sister of Tony and Punch, continued Eddie's bloodline. At that time Violet Barker, Anthony Barker's sister, had a useful terrier called Mick. Pool suspects it was a registered Lakeland terrier, but has no proof. It was, however, a useful worker, really game and keen, which was in turn mated to Wasp II. The result was not particularly satisfactory, for Fly, the bitch puppy from the mating, was only slightly worked and Pool rated her no more than an average worker. He eventually mated her to Sid Wilkinson's Rock, a very potent stud in Glenridding. Nettle and Jock were the results of the union. Nettle was a fine worker, but although she was mated many times, she failed to conceive. Her brother, Jock, therefore continued the bloodline for Eddie. He was a useful worker, but was destined to die in a crag earth at Dove Crag.

At the time when Eddie Pool still had Jock he was given a bitch by Monty Fairish, the gamekeeper from Carlisle, who bred his useful though ugly strain of terrier which Pool suspected had Irish-terrier blood way back in its ancestry (see notes on Scarteen terriers, pages 133, 137). This was called Gyp, a smooth-coated tan animal, eager to work but disobedient and a devil with pheasants, cats and other livestock. In despair, Monty gave the bitch to Eddie and suggested he should try it, see if he could break its irritating habits and, if not, to dispose of it in any way he thought fit. The animal was game but recalcitrant, and Eddie had a bad time breaking the bitch of killing everything in sight. Once she settled down, however, she became a very useful dog. Her puppy, mated to the ill-fated Jock who was to die at Dove Crag, produced Pool's Wasp III, a useful bitch who was tried and found game, but only lightly worked with the Ullswater Hunt.

At this time, Joe Wear had taken a bitch to Monty Fairish's dog Mick, a highly game dog who carved quite a name for himself around the Carlisle area as being very reliable to fox – not a flashy dog, but a good, sane, sensible and steady worker who would not get himself knocked about unnecessarily. (I saw two of his progeny work in Penrith.) Joe Wear, a connoisseur of game fell terriers, certainly rated Fairish's Mick highly, for he took Jean, one of his best bitches, to Fairish's dog. A puppy from this union was mated to Pool's Wasp III and bred Pool's present brood bitch Meg.

Gyp (Fairish's gift to Pool) was also mated to Trim, a dog puppy from a Sammy Davies bitch mated to Sid Wilkinson's Rock, and Tony III, a useful Irish-terrier type of dog, badly scarred and very game, is still with Eddie. Eddie has doubts about this male. The dog is game and very hard but, like the Tony Mark II, he does not respond to discipline and is most strong willed.

Pool likes strong game dogs, powerful enough to take the hardships of fell hunting but narrow enough to get. He still has a liking for Bedlington-blooded dogs, however. He never shows, for he believes the breeding of dogs for show simply ruins the working qualities of a terrier.

36. Edmund Porter

(Interviewed at Eskdale Green, Cumbria, on 26 May 1981)

I visited Edmund Porter at the Eskdale and Ennerdale Kennels at Eskdale Green, where the kennels are overshadowed by an enormous rock scree opposite the house. Edmund is the third generation of Porters to hunt the Eskdale and Ennerdale Foxhounds, which was formed in 1883 by the enigmatic Tommy Dobson. Dobson took on Edmund's grandfather, William Porter, as a young trainee, though protégé might more accurately describe the relationship, and when Dobson died in 1910 Willie Porter inherited the pack, lock, stock and proverbial barrel. Dobson also left his amazing crop of terriers, decidedly mongrelly in appearance, to Edmund's grandfather. Many of these terriers still bore traces of the chocolate Bedlington-terrier cross used by Tommy in the late 1880s. Indeed, from time to time the Eskdale and Ennerdale still produce an occasional chocolate terrier in the litters. Arthur Irving served as huntsman under Willie Porter, and also under his son Jack Porter.

The hunt country centred on Eskdale Green comprises some of the wildest and most forbidding countryside in Britain. I visited some of the spots with Arthur Irving, who seemed curiously unruffled about hunting districts where sheer rock faces chopped off mountain spurs and virtual peaks appeared on the horizons. Most of the earths are rock earths, some deep, beneath enormous granite boulders several tons in weight. This area was a fashionable hunting ground for visiting notables from the south of England during the 'flapper' period (1920s), but it poses a difficult terrain for any huntsman, and an even more difficult job for any terrier who has its fox to ground in these borrans. Surprisingly, terriers are rarely lost in these earths, possibly because the Porter family are indigenous to the area and know every inch of the ground, but more likely owing to the fact that they are by nature good terrier men and unwilling to lose a terrier in an 'impossible' place. In fact, only one terrier has been lost to ground in this country in the last ten years.

It is an area fraught with hazards, however. Langdale is thick with adders, and Edmund's dog, Turk, a chocolate terrier from the original strain, was in fact killed after being bitten by an adder in Langdale – a bite Edmund did not notice until nightfall, by which time the venom had paralysed the brain, making veterinary aid useless. Turk was a formidable worker and also a looker, for he won Rydal Show three times.

191

75. *Willie Porter with the Eskdale and Ennerdale.*

Edmund keeps some six or so terriers, and, breaking away from family tradition, has some excellent Jack Russell types bred by Roger Bigland at the Heythrop Hunt. Edmund rates these as equally good as any fell terriers in the Lakes. He still maintains some of the original Ennerdale and Eskdale blood, however: small, rather classless fell terriers similar to some of Dobson's later blood. Edmund uses some of the N'Beck dogs for outcross (from Tyson's dogs plus a judicious dash of Alan Johnston's Oregill pedigree Lakeland strain). 'Show-type terriers are too big for these earths,' Porter said, which is curious, for it is common talk that a very large terrier is of use in these earths. Indeed, both the fell terriers I saw and photographed were under twelve inches tall, but rather up on the leg, as opposed to the Sealyham-shaped Lakeland fell terriers seen in some parts of Lancashire.

Porter enters his terriers gradually, allowing only fifteen-month-old terriers to enter to fox, for he believes terriers never forget the trauma of premature entering. Porter is also a heretic as regards entering, for he allows and actively encourages his dogs to hunt rabbits. In most cases, this would make a terrier unsteady to rabbit in an earth, but as Porter explained, the earths are largely exposed rock sets in districts where rabbits would find it too hard to exist. Thus there is no danger of his terriers picking a rabbit in these earths.

Furthermore, Edmund does not welcome a very hard terrier – one which closes with its fox and slays it below ground – though he keeps a few to kill reluctant foxes. Most of his terriers are required to bay at a fox rather than tackle and slay it, and while his terriers showed the mark of much work, no terrier in the kennels displayed the damage found on some of the terriers worked well but certainly not wisely in the south. In fact, Porter has an excellent reputation, locally and nationally, not only as a first-class huntsman but also as a terrier man of considerable repute.

76. *Edmund Porter with hunt terriers.*

37. The Proud Brothers: Eddie and Bob

The Prouds, who hunt the Bewcastle Foxhounds, are not full-time huntsmen but simply farmers who feed, clean and hunt their own hounds. They hunt an enormous country 'twixt the Scottish border and the edge of the Blencathra country: a variable country, a mixture of harsh fells, rolling uplands and forestry. The Bewcastle were originally a trencher-fed pack, each farmer keeping, feeding and bringing a hound or so to the meet. In 1924, the pack moved to kennels and came into the capable hands of Teddie Proud Senior, an incredible man, a master of hunting hounds and an expert at entering terrier to fox. Teddie Proud was a fanatical hunter who hunted rats around farms, otters, foxes and badgers, and thus his sons received expert tuition in hound management and terrier work.

Yet neither of the Prouds claims to be a serious terrier breeder, though both have very definite views on terrier work. Most of the dogs working with the Bewcastle are gift dogs, dogs bred by hunt supporters, terriers on loan, or terriers which have become too much for pet owners to handle – 'got boss of

77. *The late Ted Proud Snr (right) and Bob Proud.*

194

their owners', Bob Proud described this type of dog. Most southern hunts are offered such dogs fairly regularly – dogs which are bored and thus become touchy with people, stock worriers and cat killers out to find scope for their suppressed hunting instinct. Such dogs often make excellent hunt terriers, providing the hunt terrier man is patient and firm enough to overcome the initial training problems. Lucas's book *Hunt and Working Terriers* mentions in a chapter written by John Bell Irving a Border terrier called Sandy which was a heller with stock until it was properly entered to otter. Barry Dainty, once terrier man for the Warwickshire Foxhounds, had an excellent terrier that was given to him because it had become 'wilful'. The Prouds obtain or are offered several such terriers.

Ted Proud Senior (father of Bob and Eddie) obtained one of his best terriers from Fred Barker, who then hunted a pack of Pennine Hounds at Ousby. Barker produced an incredible strain of terrier, using his Chowt-faced Rock (a red dog of unknown origin but reputed to be one of the Patterdale red terriers bred by Bowman, though no proof exists) and the Heinemann strain of Jack Russell terrier obtained from the Ilfracombe Badger Digging Club. This dog, also Rock, was a useful all-round terrier, for Ted Proud not only hunted the dog with the pack, but dug badger with him, worked otter, ratted regularly and also shot over the dog, which was as good at finding pheasant as a top-rate springer. Certainly this red dog, Chowt-faced Rock, of unknown breeding, was one of the most important studs in the history of the working fell terrier.

Both Bob and Ted Proud Junior are a little against the Jack Russell type of terrier for work in the peaty earths of the Bewcastle country, since they consider this terrier type to be a little unsteady and scarcely hardy enough for the job. Likewise, pure-bred Lakeland terriers, terriers which have a strong trace of pedigree registered Lakeland blood, don't find favour at the Bewcastle as these are invariably quarrelsome and headstrong to the point of being hazards. Fell blood ameliorated with a dash of Border would constitute the Proud brothers' ideal, for Border blood seems to temper the fiery fell-terrier temperament. One of Bob Proud's best came from Norman Bartlett, a terrier bred by crossing a Border terrier obtained through Ted Proud Senior with one of Bartlett's strain of Jack Russell, a strain which Jeff Burman of Louth states can be traced back to the dogs of the late Arthur Heinemann. This Border/Russell Punch would go to an earth and take scent of the edges of the mouth of the earth. If he barked the Prouds could be certain there was a badger at home. Punch disliked badger intensely, as he once received a pounding from a badger when he was a puppy. Likewise, he would go to ground in a large set, avoid the badger and go straight to his fox. Also, when he bolted his fox, he would come straight out, practically on the fox's brush. He died of old age, at maybe ten years of age – a good age for an active terrier.

Another of his terriers, Black Rock, possibly sired by Eddie Pool's Tony, was another nailer to work, a great finder, a good worrier and a dog which could be hunted twice or three times a week as he was rarely knocked about by his encounters with fox or badger. Rock killed foxes almost casually, fencing, sparring, going for a throat hold and throttling the foe. Black Rock, too, died of old age, maybe aged nine or over.

Jess, an unregistered Border terrier or maybe a Border with just a hint of fell terrier (it was a leggy dog, taller than most borders), was another noted terrier at the Bewcastle. He came to the Prouds as an unentered dog, a cat worrier who had bested his owner in the personality struggle. He settled in well at the Bewcastle and became a nailer to work. When he bolted his fox he would run for hours with the hounds until the fox was either killed, put to ground or lost. He worked maybe two very hard seasons with the Bewcastle, but went to ground in an earth set and had to be dug. Day faded and night came, and the Prouds continued to dig by torch-light. At about ten o'clock at night the roof of the dig fell in and smothered the terrier.

Scamp, bred by Bill Teasdale, a good breeder of hard, game fell terriers, was a blue ragged terrier, game and reliable and a wonder at climbing grykes, capable of following his fox anywhere. He could get to his fox where another terrier would fail, and could fold his body like a snake to get into a rock hole. He lived a hectic, precarious life, but died of old age in kennels.

Bruin was a good terrier in rock (some terriers work better than others in earth holes, while others seem to do better in rock). Bruin was shy of badger and would hang around an earth, whining and yickering if a badger was at home. At fox, on the other hand, he was excellent. He was of the type known as Border/Lakeland in the north, an unregistered, rather classless type of terrier of the kind worked by the Coniston at the time of Clapham.

The present Bewcastle terrier is Punch, a superbly bred terrier, bred by Willie Gray, the Safety Officer for the Ministry of Agriculture, from a Whaddon Chase Border terrier to a Dalston fell bitch. Punch is working well at the moment (Fairish described him as one of the best the Bewcastle has had), but in spite of his breeding and potential, he was three years old before he would look at a hole, though he would hunt fox 'on top' for hours, even as a yearling. When he first went to ground he was a devil for badger, which is a bit of a nuisance to a hunt, but now he ignores badger and will pass them by to bolt a fox. Gray's dogs have an incredible reputation for gameness and nose from Thurso to the southern fells.

38. Johnny Richardson

(Interviewed at Threlkeld in January 1981)

Are there people like Richardson still being born in the fells? Somehow I doubt it, for incredible characters are becoming increasingly rare as man grows more conventional.

Johnny Richardson came from farming stock, but his interest in hunting was kindled early, hounds often being quartered at his parents' farm during the hunting season. In those days, some sixty years ago, each farm had a bed for the huntsman and a boiling pot that could boil porridge and flesh for the visiting hounds. Even as a child Richardson was a great walker, a prowess that was to serve him well later, in rather curious fashion as it happens.

War interrupted his hunt service, and in 1939 he joined the Highland Light Infantry and was posted to North Africa. At the offensive on Tobruk 1941, he was captured and sent to a prisoner-of-war camp at Vara Sabina in Italy, but managed to escape and survive for fourteen months by foraging along the Appenines, living on grapes and fruit in summer and filching sheep, poultry and even frozen turnips when winter came. He describes this trip down the Appenines to the American British invasion advancing up Italy as 'not easy' – an incredible understatement. He never reached the Allied armies, however, for he was recaptured in Calabria, together with a French escapee, and put in a civilian prison cell in Tivoli. He sojourned here for a month, together with suspected partisans, black marketeers and petty criminals whose relatives brought in fresh food which the Italians shared with Johnny. After a month he was returned to Vara Sabina by the Germans, who had the foresight to confiscate Richardson's shoes to ensure he stayed in the coach taking him to the prisoner-of-war camp. He arrived in Vara Sabina shortly before midnight, but the next day the camp was the centre of an American bombing raid that all but levelled both camp and town. Thus he was again moved, together with whatever survivors of the raid could be rounded up, and taken to Florence, where yet again he escaped, this time living in the hills among a cosmopolitan band of partisans, comprised of Czechs, Russians and Frenchmen as well as Italian outlaws. For some weeks he lived with Italian families, families not especially sympathetic to the British but by now a little anti-German and very tired of the war. Eventually he joined up with the advancing British and American armies. It is a colourful history for a colourful character; but to return to Richardson the terrier man rather than Richardson the escapee.

The Richardsons always kept fell terriers, and Johnny had his first when he was a five-year-old. This terrier was Scamp, scarcely a typical child's pet, for it was a doughty animal bred by George Bell who hunted the Blencathra Hounds for nineteen seasons and who received his terrier foundation stock from Jim Dalton, who hunted the Blencathra for thirty-six seasons between 1894 and 1939. Dalton's dogs were quite typey, and judging from a photo-

78. Johnny Richardson with Titch.

graph taken *c.* 1900 were a far cry from the typical turn-of-the-century type of fell terrier. The terrier in the photograph (page 54) is certainly a very good show-type specimen, and in all probability has been tidied up with smooth fox-terrier blood. The terriers were game, however, and very sensible (a quality Richardson prizes greatly, rating sense as important as gameness in a hunt terrier), and so Richardson has inbred to this line to this very day.

Scamp, his first brown-red fell terrier, was in turn mated to a dog called Rock, a game but quiet terrier owned by Thomas Rawlings, a dog which had worked for six seasons with the Eskdale and Ennerdale Hounds. Richardson chooses his studs carefully. Not only will he not use a dog unless it is dead game, but he refrains from using dogs that are nervy, unsteady with stock, wildly flamboyant when up to a fox or tending instantly to close with its prey and receive a mauling for its trouble. Many of Richardson's terriers, dogs which went through three days a week hunting experience, were only slightly marked. For this reason, he is chary about using the currently fashionable registered Lakeland-terrier blood now so widely introduced to improve type in fell terriers. Richardson concedes that such dogs are often game, but too game for their own good, perhaps. When up to a fox they behave wildly and are not up to the rigours of a Blencathra hunting winter and walks on couples for twenty miles a day.

The result of this union between Scamp and Rawling's Rock was Spider, a doughty bitch that saw considerable service with the hunt and worked three days a week for six or seven seasons. She was mated to a renowned worker, Dobbin, the property of Porter of Borrowdale, a famed worker to fox, dead game but extremely sensible, a dog which entered earths with caution and care, engaging his fox cleverly and rarely suffering damage from the encounter. He was also a dog which could run loose and was extremely steady with livestock – a quality that no Lake District hunter could fail to find desirable. All in all, Porter's dog was the beau idéal of most fell-pack huntsmen, and Dobbin's son, the result of his mating to Spider, was an even more renowned stud dog and worker.

Tarzan, the dog Richardson bred from Spider and Dobbin, was an incredible animal: a small, neat red dog, but not so much a looker as a famous worker to fox. He was steady to badger, ignoring them, as all Richardson's dogs are encouraged to do, but was a nailer to fox and an excellent finder of foxes even in the deepest borran. Hunt supporters who remember this dog state he was never known to 'lie'. Such was his fame that he became one of the most potent sires in the Lakes, and his progeny must be numbered in dozens if not hundreds. 'Prich' Bland of the Melbreck used a grandson of this dog to start his own strain of terriers, terriers which are still found at the Melbreck, and such was the worth of this small red terrier that Bland still uses blood from the original Tarzan to mate to his strain. Breay once described this dog as one of the most important sires in the Lakes – a dog that literally founded a dynasty were Breay's own words.

The line was continued at the Blencathra Hunt by mating Tarzan to a half-bred Border/fell bitch Tess, and the progeny, Tess II and Tinker, were bred and walked at High Lodore, Borrowdale. Tinker was a useful, sane terrier, good to fox and sensible, but possessed of a peculiar habit. When he was badly bitten – and it must be remembered that Richardson's dogs work three and sometimes four days a week in some of the worst country in Britain – he would return to his place of work, lie up a while and recuperate at the house of his birth. Yet as soon as he was fit and well, he would seek out Richardson, either at the kennels or at the place where the hounds were working. It was a considerable feat for a dog, when one considers the Blencathra country to be well over 240 square miles in area. Richardson rated this dog highly, as highly as he did Tarzan, yet the dog seemingly made little impact on the pedigrees of fell terriers in the Lakes.

Tinker was in turn mated to a Russell type of bitch (Richardson does not use the term 'Russell type' but simply refers to the type as a white terrier). This was Judy, the property of Todd of Darlington, a name which appears in many fell pedigrees. They produced Nettle, a tan-and-white bitch, and Titch, a black-and-tan dog puppy. Later outcross blood of a Russell type was imported from Harry Carr of Dungannon, dogs tried and tested for the last eighty years in Ireland. From this infusion of bloods comes Richardson's present strain: white terriers, but fell-bred whites, not, as Richardson insisted, Jack Russells.

The Blencathra huntsman goes for small, useful-sized terriers, twelve inches at the shoulder or less, and contrary to the opinion of southern terrier men, few, if any, Lakeland hunters like the enormous stilt-legged terriers once reputed to be used in the fells. Sense, courage and constitution are the qualities Richardson rates more highly than type or colour. He favours rough coats, and anyone who has been on the fells near Blencathra in winter will see why, for a smooth-coated terrier is unhappy at the best and more often than not dead from exposure at the worst. I found Richardson similar to his terriers, a quiet, unassuming man who radiated sense and stamina. He was a delight to interview.

39. Tom Robinson

(Interviewed at Cockermouth, Cumbria, on 24 February 1982)

I interviewed Tom Robinson of Cockermouth on 24 February 1982 with Eddie Pool, after Eddie had described the Robinson family (Tom and his father) as having forgotten more about working fell terriers than most people ever get to know.

Robinson, a powerfully built man in his mid fifties, is one of a long line of

79. *Mowdie Robinson and Joe Armstrong.*

fell-terrier breeders and, like most Lakelanders, is of farming stock, though after the First World War his father forsook farming for mole catching, poisoning and trapping moles around Cockermouth. Tom's father was called 'Mowdie' Robinson, 'Mowdie' being a Lakeland name for a mole. He bred a useful, if rather unsightly strain of fell terrier: a mixture of Bedlington, fell, Border and Lakeland blood Tom described the type, though it is possible that most fell terriers at the turn of the century would have resembled it.

Bedlington blood was introduced into this strain from time to time, and many of the terriers produced by Robinson Senior were blue, shaggy coated animals. In fact, some of the very best Bedlington terrrier blood – used for work rather than show – was bred on the west coat of Cumberland just after the Second World War, and Kitchen of Egremont produced some incredibly game, gutsy terriers by mating his fell terriers to the game strain of Bedlington. As late as the 1930s, Welsh miners were going to the west of Cumberland to get the best strains of Bedlington for badger digging.

Tom's first terrier was a dog bred by his father, 'Mowdie' Robinson. This was a dog called Grip, an ugly, shaggy, blue dog more Bedlington than fell, Tom described him, but a great rat hunter and excellent rabbit hunter and a nailer to fox or badger. In spite of many maulings, maulings which removed most of Grip's teeth, he lived to a ripe old age and died a fireside death. He was considerably luckier than Tom's second dog, a game, red, hard-coated fell called Boss, a cracker to work but lacking discretion, for he received many bad maulings from badger and was finally killed by a badger during a dig some four miles from Cockermouth.

Boss was mated to a rough-looking Bedlington fell terrier than would have passed for a pure Bedlington or a leggy Dandie Dinmont, but out of this unlikely mating came Mist, quite a typey terrier, but a superb finder and an excellent stayer. Mist worked one day with the Coniston, hunted at that time by the Quixotic and quick-tempered Ernie Parker, a master of the art of hunting hounds but never one to suffer fools gladly. Mist found in a borran after followers had tried their terriers without success, which so impressed Parker that he demanded Robinson bring Mist to be mated with his own dog Turk, a crusty, quick-tempered dog but an excellent worker and one who could both find and finish a fox. In return, he would give Ernie a puppy. Such was Parker's dynamism that few refused his demands, and Robinson mated Mist to Turk the next summer. The rest of the union was Darky, a dog that went to Ernie Tyson of Grasmere and became a foundation stone for many fell-terrier strains.

One of Robinson's most noted dogs was Rags, a scruffy red dog whose appearance justified his name. Rags was a game dog, but apt to lie too close to his fox for comfort and a heller for badger. Once, at Helm, he went to ground in an old quarry face and became stuck. He gave tongue readily for an hour or so while Robinson shifted ton after ton of rock. At last the rock floor on which Robinson was standing fell in and Robinson had to abandon the dog as the crater which appeared on the floor was apparently bottomless. He went home heavy hearted at the loss of the dog, but next day Jimmy Bewley, a good terrier man who may have been responsible for the first black terriers in the Lake District, went to the quarry and heard a muffled scratching. Bewley shifted one large rock at the surface and the terrier walked free. Bewley was awarded an RSPCA gold medal for his efforts.

Tom Robinson's next terrier, again from his father's rough, unrefined cross-bred strain, was Bink, a terrier which had an unsuccessful start in life and refused to enter to any quarry. The terrier was shy and nesh – an irritating defect one had to admit – and Tom's father decided to drown the puppy, but Tom begged for the bitch and she turned out to be an outstanding worker. The number of supposedly failed fell terriers which have blossomed into superb workers is legion. The lesson is that perhaps no terrier should be dubbed a failure until it is four years old.

In 1946, Tom entered hunt service at the Ullswater and worked as a whip for Joe Wear. Tom entered Tear 'Em, Joe Wear's most famous dog, a big powerful, rough-coated, black-and-tan terrier with a massive head. Wear never owned this dog, but had it on loan from Jim 'Gilie' Fleming of Grasmere. Robinson described Tear 'Em as a hooligan of a dog, vile-tempered, disobedient and wilful to the point where Fleming had almost given up in despair. Tear 'Em was a villain with other dogs and would kill any dog or bitch that offended him. His first weeks at kennels must have been catastrophic, as a fractious terrier soon comes to grief when faced with twenty couple of hounds. However, he entered quickly to fox. Hounds had run a fox to an L-shaped earth, and the fox was crouching just behind the bend, dusting any terrier that came up to him. Four terriers were tried and all four received a savage beating as soon as their heads went round the corner. At last Robinson decided to try Tear 'Em, deeming it no great loss should Tear 'Em be damaged or daunted by the encounter. Tear 'Em approached the fox carefully – rather a novelty for a dog of this disposition – and received a stinging bite for his troubles. He erupted and killed his fox in minutes, refusing to come out when called, crunching every bone in the fox with his enormous head. Robinson moved on with the hounds and minutes later was joined by a highly ecstatic, bloody Tear 'Em. Tear 'Em never looked back after this.

At Jericho, a minute hamlet near Troutbeck, Tear 'Em entered an earth and all hell broke loose. Fearing for the dog, John Pool (father of Eddie Pool) and Robinson dug like fiends, and came upon Tear 'Em breaking up his third fox. Magically he was scarcely marked by the affray.

80. Butcher and Badger in couples in the foreground.

Robinson left the Ullswater in 1948 to do military service and returned five years later to take up hunt service under Hardasty at the Melbreck. Hardasty had his superb terriers, which bred the illustrious Turk, the most prodigious stud during the 1960s, yet Robinson still kept his own strain of terrier infused with Wear's Tear 'Em strain. Pat, his most prolific dam, mated to Teddy, a black-and-tan grandson of Tear 'Em, produced two puppies which went to Joe Wear, while another mating, to Edmund Porter's Patch, a dog of poor type but a superb worker, rated by one of the Eskdale and Ennerdale supporters, produced Myrt, a good if not a great worker. Myrt, mated to Eddie Pool's Tony, a hard, tough, brawler of a dog, produced a bitch called Mist, Robinson's present brood bitch. Mist in turn mated to Cheggie Swanson's Roy, a top-class stud dog worked by Roy Newton, a Lakelander who went north to hunt the Lochaber, a hard, newly broken Scottish country.

Robinson's greatest claim to fame, however, came with the dig to Badger and Butcher in a bad place above the Brotherswater Hotel. After a few days, Butcher emerged, but fourteen days later the corpse of Badger was excavated. This dig was celebrated in verse by Mr and Mrs Walter Curry which is sung at social evenings throughout the Ullswater country. Here is the ballad which they wrote:

BADGER AND BUTCHER

Twas early spring in '48
And the hounds were running strong.
The rugged hills o'er Kirkstone pass
Re-echoed with their song.
Well Reynard knew the fate in store,
In vain he doubled back.
No trick he knew could now avail
'Gainst that famed Ullswater Pack

But fate that guards o'er man and beast
Came now to succour him.
A cleft stood open in the rocks
And Reynard dashed within.
But once again did fortune frown,
Death followed in his wake,
For Butcher and Badger they were there
To put his life at stake.

What happened then is only guess.
No man will ever know.
But the sun went down and darkness fell
With the terriers still below.
For fourteen days and fourteen nights
The Dalesmen fought the fell
With dynamite and crowbar and words unprintable.

J. WEAR, HUNTSMAN, ULLSWATER FOXHOUNDS.
WITH RESCUED TERRIER, "BUTCHER."

Mid snow and ice with frost and gale,
They worked, they sweat, they swore.
They turned the inside from that fell
A thousand tons and more.
And when it seemed all hope had gone
And fourteen days had passed,
There seemed no life in that prison grim
And it seemed no life could last.

With crumbling rocks on every side
A final effort made,
And Butcher crawled into the light
Alive and undismayed.
But Badger paid the price in full,
A price all brave hearts scorn.
So here's a toast from Dalemen all
Good hunting where he's gone.

40. Jack Smith

(Interviewed at Midhopestones, Stocksbridge, Yorks, on 12 September 1981)

Jack Smith is a publican who lives in Midhopestones, near Sheffield, and besides being an outstanding hunter and a first-rate terrier breeder, is a fascinating raconteur with a host of incredible and entertaining stories of his experiences.

Jack has always been in contact with working terriers, for his father, a Lancashire-bred gamekeeper, was also a terrier man who bred fell types of terrier and exchanged terriers with Cyril Breay at Kirkby Lonsdale. In fact, Jack's father's strain closely resembled the dogs bred by Breay and Buck in the early 1960s. Most of Jack's father's dogs were black or red, and just now and again a wheaten-coloured terrier appeared in the litters. For some reason he did not like chocolates, though Breay's strain often produced terriers of this colour. Smith Senior told Jack that chocolates were constitutionally unsound, and not only were such dogs slow to mend after a mauling from a badger or an infected fox bite, but many chocolates were anaemic and very bad doers. Yet, in spite of Smith Senior's antipathy to the colour, chocolates still appear in the strain he created.

It was inevitable that Jack's first terrier should be one of his father's strain, possibly a Breay-bred terrier, Whiskey, a strongly built, straight-legged black terrier. Jack worked him hard and Whiskey became a first-rate badger and fox-digging dog, and above all an excellent finder. Jack rates finding and nose highly, as most dogs will bolt or stay to a fox even in a deep earth, but it takes an exceptional dog to find in such a place.

Jack's strain of terrier having started with Whiskey, he mated this dog to two related bitches: Buzz, a fawn, slape-coated bitch, and Brandy, a tight-coated red. Shortly after these bitches produced their litters, Whiskey went to ground in a fairly straightforward set, but was killed by a badger during the dig.

By dint of line breeding Brandy's puppies to the sire's line, Jack produced Mantle, a useful bitch and a first-rate brood. At that time, Jack became acquainted with Wally Wyld, the terrier man for the Grove and Rufford Hunt who owned Kipper, a black male bred by Breay, a brother of Breay's famous Rusty. Jack took Mantle to be mated by a son of Kipper, a black replica of his sire bred down from Skiffle, a daughter of Black Davy, the swop puppy from Frank Buck (see account of Breay's and Buck's breeding, pages 103–116). From this breeding came Ranter, a black and tan, hard coated terrier who proved to be one of the most potent sires among the fell terriers of

82. *Oliver Gill's Beano, a son of Smith's Ranter, sold in 1979 for £350, a record for a fell terrier.*

207

83. *One of Jack Smith's bitches emerging from an earth.*

the time. Ranter served numerous bitches and bred literally hundreds of workers and show winners, the most notable of which was Oliver Gill's Beano, a red male sold to White for £350 after a very successful show career. Ranter literally stamped his type into his progeny and produced many near-replica males.

After a very successful show career and a hard life badger digging, Ranter became prematurely aged and from the age of eight had spells when he was decidedly unwell. A vet's examination revealed that he had his heart on the wrong side of the body – a curious genetic fault, though Jack believes the frequent maulings from badgers could have caused the organs to move. Ranter died suddenly during his tenth year after producing some of the best working terriers of his time – a good-looking dog, a famous worker and a truly remarkable stud dog.

Jack's own strain are faily typey, and his ideal dog seems to be a hard slape-coated, straight-legged, fourteen-inch, sixteen-pound terrier with a strong-muscled jaw. He is against the introduction of pedigree Lakeland terrier blood, and mentions that he has seen several 'bonny' pedigree bred fell terriers who would not even sniff at a dead fox. Likewise, Jack does not like Border terriers and states that, though many claim to own a good Border terrier, he has yet to see one.

Jack therefore line breeds to proven fell-terrier lines and avoids close inbreeding. He experienced some difficulty when he bred just a little too closely to the Whiskey line. A bitch stuck in whelp and required help to deliver her puppy. Jack fished inside the bitch and produced a spherical monstrosity with one leg, a hideous freak resembling a science-fiction mutant rather than a working fell terrier. Since that time Jack has been more than careful in his breeding programme – though if most serious fell terriers breeders were to tell the truth, they also would admit to having bred some similar monsters while trying to establish a strain. The author has produced some sickening abnormalities in breeding to his own terrier strain.

Jack starts his strain at six months of age, taking them out with the adults to watch a dig. He does not artificially enter a dog on bagged quarry as he is fundamentally against baiting, believing that such practices will cause the cessation of all field sports. His dogs are stock steady to rabbit and will pass them by in an earth to get to a fox or badger. He tries his puppies to rat when he can get them, but rats are few and far between in the Stocksbridge area. Otherwise he simply starts his puppies to fox when they show that they are willing.

He has hunted fox and badger from the Midlands to the Scottish borders, working his dogs in a variety of different types of earth, ranging from the formidable Lakeland borrans to peat earths to the even more formidable earths found in worked-out mining districts. He was at one time the York-shire representative of the Fell and Moorland Working Terrier Club for rescuing trapped terriers, but is now of the opinion the club has drifted away from its original aims. Smith keeps a team of ten terriers and puts out dogs and bitches to his brother lest his strain should possibly become extinct through losses below ground, disease or, worst of all, theft. This last hazard is an increasing problem in the modern working terrier scene, one is sorry to say.

41. Barry Todhunter

(Interviewed at Threlkeld, January 1981)

Barry Todhunter is the son of Robert Todhunter of Hesket Newmarket, and grandson of a noted terrier-owning gamekeeper on his mother's side. With such a background it would be surprising if the lad had not taken to hunt service. In fact he obtained a post as whip to the Lunesdale at the age of fifteen, thereby becoming the youngest whip in the country. Barry whipped in for two seasons with the hunt under the tuition of John Nicholson, and Nicholson could not speak too highly of the lad. After these two seasons he took up an appointment as whip for the Blencathra under the tuition of huntsman Johnny Richardson, and has subsequently held that post for some nine seasons. At twenty-six years old, few young men of his age have such experience, either with hounds or terriers.

He obtained his first terriers from his father's bitch, Rip: a pair of bitches, Rip and Tess, out of a Sid Wilkinson x Ennerdale and Eskdale-bred bitch mated to a dog from Cheggie Swanson of Cockermouth, who keeps an old and tested line of terriers. Rip started young and became a very sensible bitch and her coming to grief in a flooded rock pile adjoining a flooded gill, a gill that actually diverted itself into the earths, was a great loss to Barry. Tess, the sister of Rip, was a slower starter, but now has become a reliable and sensible worker. She was two and a half years old before the task of going to ground finally clicked, but she has made up for it since.

Not surprisingly, since Barry is whip for the Blencathra, he owns a few of the Johnny Richardson-bred terriers, primarily bred from Richardson's red fell strain mated to Grip, the property of Stan Mattison, who whipped in to the Blencathra before Barry took up the post. He has also worked white terriers (not Jack Russells, for, like Richardson, he does not use the term Jack Russell for terriers born to two fell-terrier parents) bred from John Nicholson's (Lunesdale) Nettle mated to Arthur Will's Teddy, a useful fell type which may have some Border terrier blood.

A few years back he came by a smooth, black-and-tan terrier, bred originally by Roger Westmorland but sold as a pet (Westmorland breeds the original Breay/Buck strain of terrier). The terrier changed hands when the girl who owned the terrier died, and Barry hunted the dog for two seasons with the Blencathra until it went to ground on a fox driven to ground near Keswick and was killed, possibly by badgers. While Barry admits that he has seen good smooth-coated dogs, and very good ones at that, he favours a hard wiry jacket that can resist the icy wind and damp of a Blencathra winter.

He hunts a hard country, a country of exposed, wind-swept slopes, of gill earths that can drown a dog – a country of seemingly bottomless borrans. It is a country that has seen off four of his most useful terriers in eleven seasons, some being killed by badgers no doubt, but the majority coming to grief in

84. Barry Todhunter at the Lowther Show in 1982.

deep earths or being drowned in borrans connected to icy gills. Constitution is everything in such places, and like Johnny Richardson, Barry is shy of using fell terriers that show signs of being bred from registered Lakeland terrier stock. While such dogs suit many hunters, Barry simply cannot accept that they are tough enough to take up to twenty miles a day, run on couples, or hardy enough to endure a succession of very bad days hunting in icy weather.

He enters his terriers on rat or rabbit and puts them to fox when they are ready, usually when they are a year or so old. He discourages a dog going to badger, and he has seen his dogs shoot out of an earth backwards if there is a badger at home. He stresses that he is employed to control foxes and not to hunt badgers. Winch considers Todhunter to be a relic of the old type of fell hunter, iron hard constitutionally and totally dedicated to hounds and terriers.

42. Robert Todhunter

(Interviewed at Hesket Newmarket, Cumbria, on 17 October 1981)

The Todhunters have been connected with hunting for some time. Indeed, the very surname means hunter of foxes. Mrs Ida Todhunter, wife of Robert Todhunter, was the daughter of a gamekeeper who bred a strain of slate-grey rather rangy terriers with obvious Bedlington terrier ancestry. Curiously, even these terriers threw up the occasional white Jack Russell type of terrier in their litters, puppies which, to contradict the tales told by many writers of terrier books, were not put down, for they found a ready market among terrier men, particularly the rabbit-hunting fraternity. George Long says that it was a popular belief among fell hunters that the white terriers born from fell litters made superior rabbiting dogs.

Ida's father, Mr Bartle, was a great friend of Douglas Paisley, who not only hunted with the Carlisle Otterhounds, but also with the Blencathra Foxhounds. Mr Bartle regularly used Paisley's terriers to ameliorate his own terrier strain and to improve the temperament of his dogs. These Bedlington-blooded terriers were fractious dogs, quick to enter but equally quick to fight, and to fight with great savagery at that. One of Ida's first memories is of her mother trying to drown off two grapplers in the water barrel.

Her father's dogs were great ratters and were encouraged to work this quarry regularly. She recalls an incident when some rats, several dozen or so, were migrating between two stacks of corn stooks, and her father's dogs set about the horde, working until they were reeling from exhaustion.

Mr Bartle used Paisley's dogs on many bitches. She describes Paisley's

85. Robert Todhunter, 1982.

dogs as being 'quiet and rather shy with strangers and so quiet about the house you didn't know they were there . . . They entered quickly, however, and when they came on foxes they were devils to work.' This is confirmed by several people who knew Paisley, for in spite of the obvious fox-terrier crosses involved in the creation of his terriers, Paisley's dogs were extremely placid and even reluctant to fight. In fact, Paisley was known to draught highly aggressive dogs, no matter how game they were.

The addition of Paisley's dogs to Bartle's strain improved what was a rather gaunt appearance and produced a more compact, neat and heavily boned type which worked just as well, as is verified by the fact that Bartle worked his dogs with the Blencathra Hunt for several seasons.

The present strain of fell terrier bred by the Todhunters comes originally from Coniston. In 1970, Mr Todhunter approached Gary Middleton of Kendal and chose and ordered a puppy. The pup was, however, killed in a kennel fight at Middleton's kennels, but Middleton honoured his word and obtained a puppy from a policeman in Coniston to replace one ordered by the Todhunters. This bitch, Rip, became a renowned worker, entering first time to a fox driven by the hounds into a bad place: an earth into which a stream was running. (Maurice Bell states that he is always reluctant to enter a terrier into such an earth, as the stream flowing into the fissure can emerge some four miles or more away.) The bitch entered quickly, and after a fierce struggle bolted the fox. She was then taken into hunt service at the Lunesdale by their son, Barry Todhunter, who had by then taken up hunt service as a whip at the kennels.

Rip was mated in turn to a strong, typey black-and-tan Lakeland type of fell terrier, the property of William ('Cheggie') Armstrong of Cockermouth. This dog, Roy, was not only a very typey animal, but an incredibly game dog to fox. He features in quite a few modern fell terrier pedigrees. The result of this first union was two black and tan fell terrier bitches, one of which joined Barry Todhunter at the Lunesdale and later at the Blencathra, the other, a bitch called Pip, being kept by Robert.

Pip worked regularly with the Blencathra (Robert is a member of the hunt committee) and proved a doughty worker to fox. She came unstuck when she entered a rock set in Borrowdale to bolt a fox that had put in into an earth obviously holding badgers. They heard her baying a few times, but then she fell silent. By nightfall she had still not appeared, and later in the night the land was swept by a bad blizzard, the sort that no one who has not hunted the high ground near the Lakes can appreciate. As the blizzard abated, Todhunter Senior noted that the water was flooding into the earth, and though they dug with a spade, bar and earth-mover for several days, the bitch was never recovered.

The progeny of Pip, sired by Cyril Tyson's dog Mocky – a very typey animal bred down from Hardasty's Turk with liberal additions of Alan Johnston's Oregill strain of Lakeland – were about twelve months old at the date of the interview and literally begging for work. The puppies were of normally placid disposition, but a week before their son's Jack Russell, smeared with fox blood and scent, had leapt into the back of the car where the sapling puppies were crated. They galvanized into life and seized the Jack Russell through the bars, screaming with rage as they did so.

The Todhunters enter their terriers when they are ready, which may to the uninitiated seem a trite comment, but such is the way with an experienced terrier man. Puppies are encouraged to hunt rat, rabbit and stoat, and when they are ready they are allowed to try for fox. 'They forget rabbits when they are bitten,' said Robert Todhunter. Failures seem rare in Todhunter's dogs, perhaps because of this careful entering.

The Todhunters are equally successful at the shows, and their dogs have won more than their share of prizes at the Rydal Hound Show (Terrier Section), and have claimed many places at Harrogate. Robert Todhunter judges quite regularly, and makes his choice from dogs of the correct type rather than dogs which bear fearful lacerations – a commendable practice today when many judges pick out a dog, assessing it only by the number of scars and unhealed wounds it carries.

'Many terriers are too smart to get badly knocked about by quarry,' says Robert Todhunter. This is a sensible comment from an experienced terrier man, especially when one considers that many of the terribly mauled terriers seen at some terriers shows have been thus mutilated mainly through the ignorance of their owners, who enter two terriers at once in an earth and thus deny a dog the room to manoeuvre during an encounter with fox or badger.

43. Cyril Tyson

(Interviewed at Lamplugh, Cumbria, on 26 May 1981)

Lamplugh, where Cyril Tyson lives, is a tiny village some five or so miles from Egremont. He began keeping terriers as a lad, for the family had a history of terrier keeping, Cyril's father having worked a few white-bodied terriers of a type between the old-fashioned Sealyham and the fox terrier.

In 1947, Cyril became firm friends with Harry Hardasty, then huntsman for the Melbreck, a hotbed of classy Lakeland terrier types ever since the dogs of Willie Irving. It was Hardasty's custom to breed fairly large batches of terriers and then, as one would do with hounds, put them out at walk with suitable farmers and hunters, getting the best back once they were ready for work. Tyson walked several from him, one of them being a black-and-tan dog called Bill, a strong powerful dog with guts to spare (guts that became his undoing, as it transpired). Bill was a goer, a dog who worked with three hunts and who was a renowned stayer to fox. Bob Ferguson, whom I met by

86. *Cyril Tyson.*

chance while trying to find a place to park my car in Egremont, recalls this dog as being one who would die rather than quit. Bill was eventually mated to Spider, a nondescript if useful bitch bred by Grip, a Blencathra Kennels dog. From this union came Midge, a brood bitch who was to play an important part in the creation of the modern working Lakeland.

At that time, Hardasty had an incredible sire at the Melbreck Kennels, a red dog that was to become one of what I shall label the four pillars of the modern Lakeland terrier. This male, a battle-scarred dog of outstanding type who worked as well as he looked, bore the common Melbreck name Turk, and was perhaps descended from the dog of Irving also called Turk (a grandson of Alf Johnston's Copper Coin), though this is speculation, based on a conversation with Arthur Irving, and the dam of Hardasty's Turk, according to Tyson, came from Scotland. Turk mated numerous bitches and bred some excellent progeny, but, curiously, Tyson came by his Rocky by the merest chance. Cyril had taken Midge to be mated to the Turk and had a litter of puppies aged eight weeks from the union. One day Tyson was out walking near Egremont when he chanced on a lad leading a classy eight-

87. One of Tyson's top winning terriers.

217

month-old terrier of outstanding type and obviously also of unusual courage, for even though it was still so young, the lad was being pushed into getting rid of the puppy since it was causing havoc as a cat killer. Tyson traded a pup in Midge's litter for the eight-month-old dog, and this peculiar barter led to Tyson acquiring one of the most famous studs in Lakeland history, a dog which gave rise to several dynasties. It was used by Maurice Bell to produce Britt, a worker of the highest order who produced numerous families of working terrier in Scotland. Winch's Chanter was also bred from this dog via a bitch called Tatters (a daughter of Sid Hardasty's Rusty), and Chanter was responsible for a large number of the red Lakelands found in Durham.

So far as pedigree goes, Rocky is doubtful. Supposedly, and Tyson (a man keen to keep records) is vague about this, Rocky was the result of mating Turk to a bitch of near 'pedigree' (registered Lakeland terrier) blood, but Tyson is honest in admitting that this was never really proven or disproven. However, Rocky was obviously of the type produced by Hardasty's Turk, as photographs reveal, yet it is curious that one of the most influential studs in the fell-terrier world should have a doubtful origin.

Rocky, mated to Midge, produced Tyson's Mantle, which, when mated to Winch's Chanter (Rocky x Tatters), produced Tyson's Moll, a worker and a looker who became the dam of most of Cyril's present stock. Tyson then used one of Alan Johnston's Oregill-strain pedigree Lakeland terrier males on Moll to produce the bitch Mocky, a top-winning bitch in the Lakes.

Tyson enters his dogs by Fabian tactics, starting them off at sparrows and graduating through rats to cubs and adult foxes. Indeed, he has worked terriers at the Eskdale and Ennerdale, the Melbreck, the Lunesdale and the North Lonsdale. Normally his dogs see adult foxes at between eighteen months and two years old. Cyril avoids badger if he can help it, as he finds Lakeland terriers are far too hard for badger and suffer badly when used for badger digging. In fact the Fell and Moorland Working Terrier Club came about as a result of an ill-fated badger dig. Tyson had run a fox to ground in a large set and entered his dog Bill at the fox. After a lengthy dig – and 'lengthy' in the Lakes usually means days – Tyson came on the suffocated corpse of Bill. Apparently, if the dog could have been dug quickly and received expert aid, he might have lived. Thus, in 1967, Tyson called a meeting comprising Mary Tyson, Rawlinson, Riddick, George Bell, Bob Ferguson, Johnston and Wilson. Cowen was unable to attend the meeting, but became one of the founders of the club, later to be known as the Fell and Moorland Working Terrier Club, a club designed and shaped to provide a rescue service for trapped terriers. Tyson also designed the motto and the badge, and gave the club its title.

More recently he has formed a more insular club, the Cumbria Terrier Club, a group not connected with the Fell and Moorland Club, specifically designed to cater for the needs of terrier men in the Lakes. In fact the club is limited to members inside the borders of Cumbria. This club, too, runs shows and provides an expert terrier rescue service.

Pedigree of Tyson's present dogs:

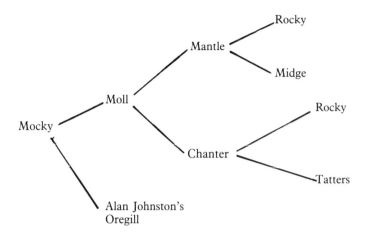

44. Graham Ward

(Interviewed at Consett, 14 March 1978, 21 August 1981)

Graham Ward is a quiet unassuming construction worker who, according to Winch, an authority on the northern working terrier, has a kennel of some of the finest red fell terriers in the world.

Ward comes from a mining family which had no interest in working terriers, though his grandfather kept a string of whippets which were run at the now illegal best-of-three rabbit contests popular at the turn of the century. Ward's interest in terriers was kindled by Harry Emberson of Leadgate, who worked a tiny nondescript Manchester terrier type of dog called Penny – a first-class worker to fox and badger, a terrier that rarely tangled with a foe but had sense enough to bay and keep out of the way.

Ward's first terrier, Peg, cost him 7s. 6d (37½p), a reasonable price for a nondescript collie-marked black-and-white terrier. Ward was eleven at the time, and like most boys of that age put a great deal of work into training and entering the terrier. However, shortly after Ward's thirteenth birthday, a Border terrier dog followed Graham's mother home. Ward reported the dog, an obviously pure-bred puppy of maybe ten months old, and began training it. Like most Borders the dog took quite a long time to enter – six months, in fact – but by now Graham had become apprenticed to Bob Robertson and Charlie Anderson, two noted Durham terrier men, and under their expert tuition Ward's Border terrier became an outstanding worker. Robertson,

88. *John Winch and Mrs Graham Ward with some of the Hardasty-bred fell terriers.*

who died some four years ago, was antipathetic towards Border terriers and refused to keep one, but he once described this terrier, called Piper, as one of the best all-round terriers he had ever seen, a dog which could bolt a fox, or kill it if need be, and stay to badger for hours, nipping, barking, teasing, but seldom getting badly bitten.

Ward mated this Border to his strange-looking Jack Russell type of terrier, Peg, and produced a black puppy, Rip, an even better worker than either the sire or the dam. Ward worked Rip regularly, every week-end in fact, or at any other time Ward could get off work. Rip was a good sound terrier who lived to a ripe old age and died scarcely marked in spite of his hectic life with Ward. His principal quality seemed to be his ability to stay to quarry for hours, giving tongue non-stop to guide the diggers to the fox or badger.

At that time Robertson was seeking outcross blood for his Irish-bred Jack Russell strain and went to the famous Breach Kennels owned by a Miss Sixton to get his outcross. Miss Sixton owned a large kennel of Jack Russells, and most people seemed very happy about the terriers they obtained from her. Jim Blake of Burnley, who bought three terriers at the same time as Robertson, told me in 1968 that he found these Breach-bred Jack Russells to be self-entered dogs which required to be restrained rather than encouraged. Robertson mated the Breach-bred bitch to his Irish-bred Jack Russell Tinker (an incredible terrier to fox, badger, otter and a legend in the Newcastle area), and bred Penny, a gutsy little terrier bitch, game to anything, with an excellent nose.

Penny mated to Rip, the crossbred Border terrier, and bred Piper – a dog which was owned, worked and entered by F. Lowes – a good powerful male, game as a pebble and with all the sense of his Border terrier namesake. Ward

220

was reluctant to lose this bloodline as, in spite of its mongrel ancestry, it was extremely game and could be worked anywhere. When he eventually started up in Lakeland or fell types of terriers, he kept the dog Piper in mind and brought him into the fell strains.

Ward took quite a long time to choose his foundation fell bitch and visited Buck at Leyburn and Maurice Bell at Hawes before purchasing a dog from Cyril Tyson at Egremont. Tyson at this time was breeding a bright-red Irish-terrier type of fell terrier bred down from Harry Hardasty's Turk, perhaps the most famous terrier ever to work with the Melbreck Hunt. This Melbreck strain, derived from Jim Fleming's famous dam Myrtle, was not only superb at work, but also unbeatable at terrier shows throughout the Lakes. Ward was obviously impressed by his visit to Tyson's Egremont Kennel.

Ward purchased Printer, a fine red dog, from Tyson in 1968 for £10 and began his own strain of red fell terrier from this dog – a dog that carried at least three lines to Hardasty's Turk. At this time, Tyson's stock was out-standingly good looking and came under fire by breeders of less typey terriers for being show dogs rather than work dogs. Ward found such criticism ridiculous since Printer not only looked good but was also a good worker: hard as flint, a good stayer with an excellent nose. Printer was superbly bred, his sire being Cowen's Rock, a dog that had seen considerable work both privately and with the Melbreck, and his dam Mantle, not only a looker, but also a first-class work dog, a finder, a stayer and also a bitch that could finish her fox if it seemed unlikely to bolt.

Ward mated Printer to Penny, the Russell type bred from Robertson's Tinker and the Breach-bred bitch, and produced Mel, a good-looking fell type with an Irish-terrier type of coat, straight front and the first of the magnificent heads for which Ward's strain is now famous. Mel was mated to Chanter, John Winch's stud dog, a Hardasty-strain terrier Winch had obtained from Tyson, and produced Mandy, the dam of all Ward's best terriers.

Likewise Piper, the result of the union between Rip and Penny, was mated to F. Lowe's fell terrier, Mandy, a Hardasty strain fell terrier with a dash of Rillington-strain (George Newcombe) pedigree Lakeland terrier, and pro-duced Dandy, a red fell terrier with one of the best heads to be found on any fell terrier in either the Lakes or the rest of the country for that matter.

Ward's strain is therefore a potent blend of Jack Russell, Border and red fell terrier from the Melbreck strain, and while the strain are lookers and win well in the north of England, Ward is quick to stress that his dogs are first and foremost workers – a statement he is quick to prove when chided by bad losers at shows. His stock is predominantly red Irish-terrier-coated dogs with enormously powerful heads and straight fronts. Winch considers them to be the type nearest to Turk, the beau idéal of all Lake District fell terriers, and only recently Ward refused £600 for one of his adult terriers.

Ward stated his future plans to be to breed a strain of good-headed blacks

221

of the stamp of Dandy since he considers that the present blacks have poor heads and too much Border terrier about them.

45. Harold Watson

Harold Watson, the present chairman of the Lunesdale Foxhounds, was born in 1907 of a family of butcher farmers in Patterdale. His first terrier was a rather nondescript fell terrier, a greyish black and tan who came to him when the child was eight years old and became his constant companion. Children's dogs are given a special sort of attention and respond accordingly. Such was the case with Harold's animal, for Sandy, a dog of no particular breeding, became a first-class worker, not over game and certainly not as hard as the typical fell terrier of Harold's youth, but one with an amazing nose that enabled the dog to find anywhere, even in known terrier death-traps like Blaeberry Borran and Dove Crag. Sandy bolted numerous foxes from such places and died at the age of ten of causes unknown, though Harold says the dog swelled like a balloon before expiring.

In 1924, Bowman ceased to be actively involved in terrier breeding and disposed of most of his terriers. Lil, a white Russell type born from the union of two of his red fell terriers, went to Sid Wilkinson, but Fury and Grip, dogs which received considerable publicity during Bowman's reign at the Ullswater, were given to Harold Watson to work. Fury was one of Bowman's most famous terriers: a red, harsh-coated Irish terrier type which Bowman referred to as a Patterdale. Watson, on the other hand, rates Grip as his best, a game, box-headed dog, utterly fearless, a good finder, a bolter and, when necessary, a dog that could kill foxes.

Grip was mated to Gyp, a Patterdale dog bred by Fred Barker, late of Ousby, and sired by Chowt-faced Rock out of an Ilfracombe Badger Digging Club white terrier of the sort worked by Arthur Heinemann. Grip took a fearsome beating that season, and once, while out with the Ullswater, killed a fox in a deep earth, receiving as a reward for his labours a bite that went through his muzzle and the roof of his mouth, a wound that caused him to pump blood, as a surfacing whale pumps water and air, when subject to any exertion. Yet that afternoon he broke loose and killed another fox in a deep earth in spite of his wounds. The result of the union between Grip and Fred Barker's Gyp was a litter of four puppies, including Peggy and Fury. Fury went into hunt service with Joe Wear and was one of his foundation stock terriers when he took over from Wilson at the Ullswater. She worked eight seasons with Wear and was trapped numerous times, once for six days.

In 1924, when hounds marked a fox about Rydal Water, George Chapman and Robin Logan tried five or six terriers to shift it, but it thrashed every one. Fury entered and killed quickly and efficiently – so efficiently, in fact, that Anthony Chapman insisted that Wilson mate Fury to Chapman's Crab, a wonderful worker, a good finder and a famous Coniston terrier. Fury worked a barn for rats that summer after a farmer had complained to Harold he was overrun with rats. 'Overrun' proved the right expression, for Harold killed 404 rats that day, using Fury and a stick. At the end her mouth was so swollen she could scarcely shut it and she was so exhausted she could scarcely totter home. Yet, in spite of this mauling, she whelped a litter of twelve puppies to Crab. One of these puppies went to Wear, another became Braithwaite Wilson's Crest which did much work with the Ullswater. Wilson apparently showed this elegant black-and-tan terrier to Lucas. Watson kept one puppy himself: a black-and-tan bitch called Peggy.

At that time, Harrison Tweedie, manager of the Anderson Banana Company, owned a superb Lakeland terrier (a refined fox terrier type of dog which won at Cruft's in the early 1930s – Watson is unsure of the date). This dog mated in turn a registered Lakeland terrier bitch and bred Rastus, a slape-coated dog that was unsuitable for show because of his lack of coat. In spite of his fancy show pedigree heritage, Rastus was a killer, wildly game, fierce with sheep, a bad cat killer and a dog which retaliated when Watson punished him for a misdemeanour. At this time it was fashionable to decry the more elegant Welsh-terrier type of Lakeland being created by the Lakeland Terrier Association. Todd of Kendal wrote his 'Terrier Song' as an indictment about the way breeders were producing terriers, mentioning that a noted Cruft's Champion was 'chased down the road by a mouse'. Watson showed Rastus to Douglas Todd and explained that the dog was sired by one of these noted Cruft's champions. Todd laughed, but predicted a decline in courage and working ability of the show-bred Lakeland terrier – and proved to be no false prophet in his utterance, unfortunately.

THE TERRIER SONG

Now there's many a song about hunting,
Packs and huntsmen are honoured by name,
But there isn't a song about terriers
Which in Lakeland have gained lasting fame.

Chorus:
So always remember your terriers,
Protect them from wet and from cold,
For the love of a tyke for his master
Can never be measured in gold

Whether it's Fury or Trixie or Nellie,
Or Rock, Jock or Turk it's the same,
One quality you'll find among them,
And dalesfolk call it 'dead game'.
And whether he's rough or smooth-coated,
He'll tackle badger, otter or fox,
Run a drain or creep into a soil-hole,
Or squeeze through a grike in the rocks.
  Chorus:

He'll yield not one inch though they maul him,
He'll fight to the death on his own,
Though sometimes he'll be imprisoned
By a rush-in of soil or of stone.
And then the brave lads of the valleys
To save him will toil day and night,
And join in a Hallo of triumph
As he blinks back to God's blessed light.
  Chorus:

Now at Cruft's famous show down in London,
They have Lakelands that aren't worth the name.
If you showed 'em a fox or an otter
They'd fly for their lives without shame.
They're not built to creep or do battle,
But to sit on a chair in a house,
And they do say that one recent champion
Was chased down the road by a mouse!
  Chorus:

So here's to our gallant laal workers,
Not beauties, perhaps, but they'll do.
With gameness they've also affection,
And make you a pal good and true.
And when your terrier, in old age, is dying,
And the world all about you seems sad,
A lick on the hand will console you,
For a truer friend man never had.
  Final Chorus:
    D. P. Todd, Kendal (Tune: 'Laal Melbreak')

Peggy was mated to Rastus and bred Grip, a dog Watson reared but sold to a badger digger in Gloucester, where it was killed by repeated maulings from badgers. Before its demise, however, it mated Nettle, the property of Joe Wilkinson (Sid Wilkinson's father), rated as one of the best Lakeland terriers alive in the 1930s. One of the puppies from Grip and Nettle went to a fishmonger in Penrith, but became such a terror with cats and livestock that his owner was glad to sell him. He was bought by Tom Megeen, manager of

89. Grip, killed by badger in Gloucestershire.

the Cumberland Bus Company, no hunter but a man determined to collect a kennel of the best-looking Lakeland terriers in the world.

Towser, the fishmonger's dog, did not settle in kennels too well and killed one of Megeen's champions and maimed another. Megeen despaired, for a dog with intense hunting instinct must, when kept in the boredom of a show-dog kennel, be a devil to manage. He gave Towser to Willie Irving at the Melbreck, who worked a team of the best-looking Lakeland terriers in the fell packs. Towser became the grandsire of Irving's famous Turk. (This Turk is not to be confused with Irving's other Turk, sired by Copper Coin and bred in 1949.)

Harold Watson saw the foundation of the highly successful Lunesdale Foxhounds. Up to 1927, an ardent hunter called Tommy Robinson hunted a small pack of foxhounds, calling them the Sedbergh and Lunesdale Foxhounds, but in 1927, for some reason, he gave up the pack. In 1929, he mentioned to Bowman, who was chopping wood in front of the Ullswater Kennels (he had been retired from hunt service some five years before) that he was intending to start up again. In 1930, Robinson, Harold Watson and Harold Hodgson went to Willie Porter, a generous type of huntsman, and were given five hounds which were brought home in the boot of the car after they had eaten a cake Robinson had won at the hunt raffle. Later three of the hounds, Merryman, Magic and Murray, were given the hunt by the Ullswater Foxhounds. Later still Trixie joined the kennels from the Ullswater after Braithwaite Wilson had decided to put her down because she 'ran both

225

ways' (which means back-tracking in fell-pack parlance). She became a famous brood bitch. From this small beginning came the magnificent hounds hunted by John Nicholson.

Watson saw the age of greatness on the Lakeland hunting scene, and knew Parkin, Parker, Wear, Braithwaite Wilson, the Irvings and Dalton. He knew Breay intimately, and from what he saw of his dogs believed them to be superb if the earths were not too deep, but rather weak if the earths were enormous. Furthermore, he does not think Breay's dogs were thick enough coated for the Lunesdale country and mentioned that he had seen them shivering with cold while waiting for a fox to bolt. This is curious, since Hinchcliffe, chairman of the Pennine Foxhounds, once told me that Breay's dogs and their progeny were at their best in deep borran earths in freezing conditions. It is not easy to pick a way between the opinions of masters in matters of history.

46. Roger Westmorland

(Interviewed at Troutbeck, Cumbria, on 22 February 1982)

Roger is well known for his working Border terriers, a strain descended from Dandyhow Brussel Sprout, a predominant sire among Border terriers. His first love, however, is the working fell terrier. Hunting is in his family, so it seems for his father-in-law was a close friend of Richard Clapham, whose book *Foxhunting in the Lakeland Fells* (1921) did much to bring this area of the world to the attention of the hunting fraternity.

In spite of his name, Roger Westmorland is not a native of the Lake District, for he was born in Wighill in Yorkshire of a family of foresters and farmers. His father kept terriers, not in any great number, but mainly of Border/Lakeland type, to keep down rats and foxes around the farm. It was not his father who influenced his interest in terriers, however, but one Herbert Ibbotsen, a blacksmith with a passion for hunting who lived a matter of a mile or so from Westmorland's home. Ibbotsen kept a rough-and-ready type of fell terrier, not refined enough to be called a Lakeland, and two of these, Tangy and Taffy, became Westmorland's first terriers.

Roger was nine at the time, but sporting terriers have a knack of opening up the countryside to a child, and before his tenth birthday Westmorland was well on his way to becoming a seasoned rabbiter, using ferrets, two terriers and a very antiquated and illegally carried .410 shotgun. Both terriers had bolted foxes from artificial earths well before Roger was ten years old, but his most vivid memory is of his first badger: a badger dug shortly before his eleventh birthday using Tangy, Taffy and a rabbiting spade – a fair feat for a

90. *Roger Westmorland's Squeak, Biddy and Turk.*

child. He told me how he carried the badger home to Wighill like a great white hunter. It was to be the first of many badgers he was to dig.

Later he mated Tangy to a good-class black fell terrier owned by a joiner in Leyburn, a terrier bred by Frank Buck, who lived in the same district, though it was to be years before Westmorland met Frank Buck. Tangy bred a variable litter, ranging from light-coated black fells of the type bred by Buck to open-coated Border/Lakeland types, some of which Roger kept and used for badger digging in the Bramham Moor Hunt country. This period of his life, digging with Bramham Moor hunt servants, shaped his attitude to hunting and brought about Roger's passion for orderly, well-managed badger digs involving as little cruelty as possible to the badger and as little damage to the terrier – a commendable attitude of which some of the younger sporting enthusiasts have perhaps lost sight, one is sorry to say. I certainly share Westmorland's sentiments that the wilder elements of the sporting terrier fraternity have done and will do much to bring about the cessation of hunting.

Later Westmorland became an under-keeper, but retained his interest in hounds and terriers by part-time terrier work with the Bramham Moor and the Bedale Hounds. Later he also put in some service as part-time terrier man with the adjacent pack, the West of Yore, and during a lull in the hunting with the West of Yore he met Frank Buck, who was trying a young terrier to ground. Buck owned a hard, tough little terrier at the time: an excellent worker called Nip, a dog capable of bolting a difficult fox by dint of barking and nipping in and out at him without sustaining undue damage in the process. Westmorland was very impressed with the dog, but above all by Buck's expertise in handling the terrier throughout the dig. Few terrier men north or south of Wensleydale had Buck's know-how during this time, and Westmorland learned much from him.

Through Buck he then met Breay, and Breay continued Westmorland's education concerning terriers. What his encounter with this pair did, however, was to convince Roger that Breay and Buck had better, gamer, steadier and more reliable dogs than his own. Furthermore, Westmorland became infected with Breay's fetish for line breeding and continued to practice this method on his own strain of terriers.

His first Breay-bred terrier was Judy, the result of mating a granddaughter of Blitz with Bingo, a tried and tested line that had been worked hard by both Buck and Breay. Judy became a useful worker to fox, badger and otter, but her most outstanding feature was her ability to climb rock cracks like a cat.

Westmorland never bred from this bitch, for in her second year she went to ground in a shake hole in Leck Fell, an opening in the limestone worked often by Breay and Buck, both with some success. But, as Westmorland says, shake holes change shape after every fall of rain. Judy went to ground on a fox in this shake hole, and though she bayed for some minutes, the sound of barking grew fainter and finally silence prevailed. Westmorland dug for a while, but failed to locate the terrier.

His next Breay-bred terrier was Loppy, bred by Fred Jenkinson, an excellent terrier man and a good dog breeder. Loppy was fairly ugly: a big, black, fourteen-and-a-half-inch fell terrier with rolling gait and huge Bedlington-terrier types of ear. Nevertheless, in spite of his curious shape, he could get anywhere by dint of folding those long legs. Loppy worked well to fox, badger and otter for Westmorland and enjoyed considerable fame as a working terrier in the north. He would bolt his quarry if possible, but if a fox refused to bolt he could finish it quickly and efficiently for he had a bite like a steel trap. During his seventh year, however, Loppy went to ground on a fox in Potts Valley when the Lunesdale Hounds had run it to ground there. Loppy, alas, ignored the fox and closed with a badger instead. This country is bad for badger – so bad, in fact, that Nicholson, huntsman for the Lunesdale, breaks his dogs to badger. It would have been better if Loppy had been broken to badger, for after a hard three hours' dig involving spade, pick and crowbar, Westmorland unearthed the dog. He was still alive, but his throat had been lacerated and his jaws broken. Loppy died shortly after Westmorland got him home. During his sixth year, however, he had mated a Breay-bred bitch and sired Slim, a tall, rangy terrier, fourteen and a half inches at the shoulder but slender enough to get anywhere. Jim French once saw this terrier get through the bars of the Cotswold Hunt Kennels. Westmorland believes that it eventually came to rest at a kennels in Swansea and became foundation stock for most of the tall elegant black fell terriers in South Wales. Few dogs have made a greater impact on the Welsh fell-terrier scene than this son of Westmorland's Loppy.

Westmorland has taken part in some gargantuan digs. On the day of Slim's departure for the south, Westmorland received a phone call from a farmer in Cartmell Fell. A badger had cut loose on his wife's hens and had returned to its lair in a one-eyed rabbit warren. 'An easy dig,' was the farmer's comment, but those are famous last words for a terrier man, since one-eyed sets are often notorious death-traps for terriers.

Westmorland arrived and found the badger had, indeed, gone into a rabbit warren that was enlarged somewhat but nevertheless a rabbit warren. Further down the bank, however, was a deserted badger set, its sides littered with overgrown mounds of excavated earth, and it was into this set that the rabbit warren led. After a hectic eight-hour dig, Westmorland tore out a huge boulder, eighteen feet below the surface, and found the dog had bottled up some five badger which bolted and were crawling around Westmorland's feet. Most hunters are highly sceptical of laymen who come to them with tales of an 'easy dig'.

Westmorland was in on the famous dig that ended the life of Bingo, the illustrious fell stud dog bred by Buck out of Topsy and worked by Breay. Bingo was a superb worker and a nailer to fox, and by the end of his third season he had become legend in the Lunesdale country. One day, however, during Bingo's fifth season, hounds put a fox into a bad place in Garsdale quarry, a filled-in shaft that had followed a lode into the heart of the limestone. Five terriers, three hunt terriers of Nicholson's breeding and two lay terriers, were tried at the fox but failed to shift it and were badly mauled for their trouble. By noon it was decided to try Breay's Bingo, who entered, bayed, closed with his fox and became silent.

After dusk came, Breay arrived to collect Westmorland, and they began to shift mounds of rock to get into the lode working. So bad was the place that Breay insisted Westmorland should tie a clothes line round his waist to allow any diggers to excavate him in turn if things became very bad. Roger crawled down the passageway until the line gave out, then made fast the line. Breay, a cautious man, insisted Roger should withdraw. Then, thirty feet on, Roger's lamp illuminated a stone fall under which the fox and Bingo had fought it out. Bingo was dead with his top jaw broken asunder, the fox a few yards on with its bottom jaw taken off in its death struggle with the terrier. Westmorland brought out both the dead dog and the now dead fox. During the spell Roger had been to ground it had begun to snow and the land was now a striking white colour in the moonlight. It was a sad ending for Bingo.

During Breay's last years, Rusty, Bingo's son, became too much for the now ailing master. He was a fiery dog, utterly game, also a cat killer and such an inveterate hunter that he would run nose-down across the fells, ignoring Breay's cries to return. Breay was now ill with diabetes, and seriously ill with asthma as it happened, and he gave Rusty away to someone in Lancashire as a pet. Rusty was ill designed to be anyone's pet, however, and he returned to

Roger's kennels. Roger kept him a month or two, and on the death of Bingo returned him to Breay once more. On Breay's death, Rusty returned once again to Troutbeck. He took a fearful mauling from a fox in a peat hag that winter and died quite suddenly and quietly in Roger's kennels.

Roger still breeds a Breay line. Some time back, Breay's Tina, a chocolate bitch of good quality with an excellent nose, was mated to Hardasty's Turk and bred a tan bitch, Biddie. Biddie was, in turn, mated to Rusty, and bred a bitch Roger sent to a friend in Kent. This, in turn, was mated to Slim, and Roger's kennels are bred down from this mating.

In the summer of 1982, Frank Buck helped to look after Roger's dogs for a short while, and a litter was born during his stay. A white-legged puppy, the image of Frank's Tex, turned up in the litter – proof, perhaps, that Roger has not departed from the line breeding programme of Breay and Buck.

47. John Whaley

(Interviewed at Mallerstang, Cumbria, on 17 July, 1981)

John Whaley works a hill farm in Mallerstang a stone's throw away from where Cyril Breay once lived, in a house called 'The Thrang'. In fact, young John's earliest memories are of skinning sheep's heads at his father's butcher's shop, and hanging a bag of the heads (priced between 1½d and 3d, or approximately ½p and 1p) on Breay's gate as he travelled to school in the mornings.

Whaley did not obtain his first bitch directly from Breay, however, but from Frank Buck at Harmby. Buck was using a stud dog called Mick at the time – a little-used male, a full brother of Blitz and a litter brother of Crete, a bitch given to Major Burdon as a stud fee, and so named because Crete was invaded on the morning Buck handed the stud puppy over to Burdon. Buck had mated Mick to a bitch called Rip (a bitch which finished its life as a pet with Frank Buck's mother). Whaley's pup, Stump, which was a fairly popular name for fell terriers during the war years, was a powerful-headed, slape-coated, black-and-tan bitch, as can be seen in the photograph. This once again lends weight to the argument that the enormous bull-terrier types of heads one commonly sees on so-called Patterdales was introduced into the strain by the Burdon stud dog in 1940.

Stump became a famous bitch in the Mallerstang district – so excellent, in fact, that Breay once referred to it as perhaps the best bitch he had ever seen work to fox. Whaley was a loner, however, preferring solitary digs to following the Lunesdale Foxhounds with Breay. Yet Stump found much work in the Mallerstang district, and not only excelled herself as a worker but became an excellent brood bitch.

91. John Whaley.

In Hawes, seat of Maurice Bell's Wensleydale Foxhounds, lived a good foxhunter called Iverson, known as 'Mollie Art' Iverson (his mother was Mollie, his father Arthur, hence 'Mollie Art' – a common method of nick-naming in the countryside Herriot describes in his book *All Creatures Great and Small*), and Iverson owned a similar Breay/Buck type of terrier, also called Stump: a very hard dog to fox, but a sane, sensible worker. Stump produced two puppies to her namesake, and these, Dusky and Darky, were sold to a keeper called Mason from Lancashire, who worked a bad patch of country that was hell on terriers and eventually killed off Dusky and Darky while they were at work to fox. Both were excellent workers, and there is some quite firm evidence that both influenced fell-terrier bloodlines in that area before their deaths.

Whaley next took Stump to Breay's Monty, a son of Blitz and a full brother of Buck's Tex, who was in the process of becoming a legend in the Penhill area of Wensleydale. Monty was a handsome, useful and very versatile dog, a good bolter and a dog which could easily kill any fox which refused to bolt.

Stump produced two noted puppies from Monty, puppies which were now ideally bred according to Breay's line-breeding calculations, since they contained at least two lines to Blitz, the cornerstone of the Buck/Breay bloodline during the 1940s. One of the puppies, Major, a good-looking, rough-coated dog of the Monty stamp, became quite an important stud in the

North Yorkshire, south Durham area, and many lines are descended from him. The other puppy, Trixie, a good all-round worker, became, according to John Parkes of Harrogate, one of the most important later brood bitches in the strain, a game bitch, a busy hunter, a good finder below ground, and a bitch which would stay to a fox till the crack of doomsday if need be. Mated to Breay's Rusty (Bingo to Tig), she produced some useful puppies, some of which went to Warwickshire to breed a useful strain of red, slape-coated terriers still to be found near Kineton. Others from this line were to be absorbed into the family of Russells bred by Barry Dainty, who stayed at the South Warwickshire Hunt for only a short time, but whose Russell dog, Pedlar (Taggart x a daughter of my own Russell dog, Rupert) mated a few of the Whaley type of Patterdale, and bred some incredibly good badger-digging dogs. I later brought some of these Whaley fell-bred Jack Russells back into my own strain.

Trixie was now mated to a Breay type of terrier: a dark-red, slape-coated terrier closely resembling Rusty and having several lines to Blitz. This terrier, Rock, owned by Josie Akerigg, was a good dog to ground, had a very favourable record of work with the Lunesdale Foxhounds, and became a moderately important sire. He sired a black-and-tan bitch which Whaley called Dak: a strong, game bitch with a good nose, and a wonderful worker of vermin around the farm.

Dak was taken to Ken Shepherd's dog at Windermere, a good-looking, reliable dog, game as a pebble to fox or badger – though Whaley experienced doubts about the dog's ability to the latter quarry later in the evening I met him. Ken's wife brought in the dog to show Whaley, and to Whaley's horror a huge, boar badger, fat as a pig, ambled out of the kitchen and crawled on to his lap. It was a disconcerting experience, but the boar badger was, in fact, Brocky, the animal hero of Sylvia Shepherd's (Ken's wife's) book of the same name. Ken's dog was game to badger below ground, but regarded Brocky as a harmless if exasperating bed-fellow.

From Dak and the Shepherd terrier came John's present bloodline as well as a bitch now in the kennels of Frank Buck of Leyburn, a terrier which Frank considers to be one of the hardest, most useful fell terriers he has in his kennels.

Whaley believes that the original Breay/Buck strain is the best in the world, though he is aware of the decline in the standard of the breed, both in terms of physical stamina and sadly as workers since Breay died. He waved me good-bye, saying that Breay would turn in his grave if he could see the monsters that turn up around the shows and whose owners refer to them as Breay types of terrier.

48. Sid Wilkinson

(Interviewed at Patterdale, Cumbria, 1981)

I interviewed Sid Wilkinson on Halloween 1981, with Eddie Pool acting as my guide to the Ullswater Hunt country. Few people have influenced the breeding working strains of fell terrier more than Sid Wilkinson. Sid obtained his first terrier from Bowman in 1924, the year that Bowman retired from service with the Ullswater Hunt. The terrier, a tan-and-white bitch called Lil, was an outstanding worker and worked for several seasons with the Ullswater. Sid is vague about the breeding of this bitch, but believes she was simply a sport born from two fell types of terrier of the kind worked by farmers and lead miners in the Ullswater country, for Bowman obtained many of his most reliable terriers 'on loan' from these lay hunters.

Lil was mated to yet another Patterdale-bred terrier, Crab, the property of Braithwaite Wilson, who took the Ullswater Hunt over after Bowman retired. Crab was line bred from Betty, Braithwaite Wilson's famous brood bitch, a rather untidy, woolly coated strain of terrier, completely free from what Wilson described as the 'taint' of registered Lakeland blood. He once told Lucas, the author of *Hunt and Working Terriers*, that the days of the real old type of fell terrier (which Braithwaite Wilson referred to as a Patterdale since this type of dog was fairly common in the Ullswater country) were numbered. The craze for showy, registered Lakeland terriers was going to be the death of the hard-working little fell terrier, and so he deliberately kept his strain relatively pure. To illustrate its toughness, his bitch Betty was once stuck fast in a rock crevice in Cross Fell for three days in blizzard conditions before it could be rescued. Hounds had put in a twenty-pound vixen of a type then called a greyhound fox, and Wilson had entered Betty. Betty had killed her vixen, lying up on the carcass and gnawing it for sustenance.

It is worth noting that Wilson boasted his strain was free from Bedlington blood, while, in the near-by village of Glenridding, John Pool was breeding some very game terriers by infusing fell blood with good working Bedlington stock. Braithwaite Wilson himself accepted that Bedlingtons were game enough, but did not believe they could stand the hard Ullswater winter. Truly Sid chose a most suitable strain to perpetuate the bloodline.

From this union (Lil x Crab), Sid produced some interesting offspring. Tony, a fell type of puppy, he sold to John Pool of Glenridding. This dog became a first-rate fox-killing dog, but was also able to work a long net with the dexterity of a spaniel. It was his sister Nettle, however, that was used to continue Wilkinson's bloodline. Nettle was a really game, sensible worker: no fox killer, but a sane bitch and a good finder and bolter. She saw service with the Ullswater when Joe Wear arrived at the hunt as a 'whip'. Nettle was battle-scarred and frequently went to ground, yet she died of old age, a senile veteran of thirteen at Sid Wilkinson's fireside. Nettle was mated several

233

92. Sid Wilkinson with Rock.

times, and her line finally went to Joe Wilkinson, who mated his bitch Nettle (a descendant of Sid's Nettle) to a dog, Egdon Rock, the property of Mrs Graham Spence, who had collected her fine kennel of terriers from registered-stock, typey terriers but game and useful dogs. Some of these terriers were utterly game, yet very hard and bad to cats. One of them, Rip, the result of mating Egdon Rock to Nettle, went to Penrith as a house pet, but caused such havoc among the neighbourhood cats, turning them up and killing them by a dextrous spinal bite, that he was given to Willie Irving, who worked him with the Melbreck Hunt. Rock (Joe Wilkinson) was also a villainous cat killer, and after his hunt-service days was pensioned off at a farm of Sid's brother. Even as a battered, crotchety veteran, he succeeded in wiping out every cat on the Wilkinson farm.

Wilkinson's Rock mated several bitches, one of which was Charlie Clark's black and tan, a result of mating an unregistered bitch to Arthur Irving's Robin, a strong powerful pedigree Lakeland terrier bred down from Willie Irving's illustrious bloodline. A puppy from this union, a bitch called Nettle II, arrived at Sid Wilkinson's kennels. Nettle was a doughty worker,

93. *Wilkinson's Nettle.*

game as they came and an excellent dog at bolting fox, with a wonderful nose for finding on the deep borrans that harbour foxes in the Ullswater country. At that time the gamest stud in the Patterdale district was Anthony Barker's Rock, a famous worker, hard as nails, a good finder and a tremendous fox killer who once slew three foxes in one day's hunting. This dog, descended from two white terriers from the Ilfracombe Badger Digging Club and the hardbitten red dog called Chowt-faced Rock, proved a fortuitous choice of stud, for the result of the union was Sid Wilkinson's Rock, a strong red dog who came to be one of the greatest studs in the working terrier world.

Rock was an odd mixture. He was a good looker who won well at the shows, in spite of the fact that Hardasty's Turk, a dog of peerless beauty, was also doing the working terrier show rounds at the time. Wilkinson openly admits that Rock was outclassed by the Melbreck dog, also a red, which he describes as one of the most perfect terriers he ever came across, and Rock was frequently placed second to Hardasty's Turk. Curiously, it is a little-known fact that both these pillars in the world of working fell terriers were related, both being descended from Jim Fleming's Myrt, a bitch who served with the Ullswater Hunt under Anthony Barker's aegis during the years of the Second World War. Like Turk, who gave rise to a dynasty of terriers, Rock too became the sire of many families of working terrier.

Trim, Eddie Pool's most famous dog, was one of the first of Rock's puppies, a tremendous finder with an uncanny nose, a dog that Todd, author of 'The Terrier Song' (see Harold Watson), once described as the best all-round terrier he had ever seen. Todd rated this dog highly, and tales are still told of Trim in the Ullswater country. Wilkinson described the dog as having the strongest head he had ever seen on any fell terrier. Middleton's strain, a strong powerful strain of black-and-tan terriers, as noted for work as they are for their show qualities, is also descended from Wilkinson's Rock. Middleton admits that his strain received frequent transfusions from Wilkinson's dogs, for Middleton is quite certain that Rock was the greatest sire of fell terriers ever born. Two later Rock-bred puppies actually came to Middleton by the strangest quirk of fate. Some grandchildren of Rock (via a bitch from the dog mated to Johnny Richardson's famous Titch, a leggy black-and-tan terrier) were sold as pets to Derby, where they were given no work and settled into a life of domesticity. Settled, however, was hardly the word, for terriers of this breeding (a breeding which had some of the most famous dogs in the Lakes in its pedigree) are ill suited to the boredom of city life and became overweight, destructive, uncontrollable lumps of flesh. The disillusioned owners asked Wilkinson to have the liabilities back, but the pair had to be tranquillized before they could be taken on the train to the Lakes. Wilkinson received the obese pair with dismay, and Middleton took them off his hands. Within days the pair were killing rats, and both became useful show terriers once they were 'fined' down by judicious deprivation. I believe Middleton also made useful hunt terriers out of them.

A dog from identical breeding became Wilkinson's famous sire, Jock. Jock proved to be a tremendous worker, really game and a very good fox killer. Even as a mature dog, however, he was a villain with other dogs, particularly big dogs, and would launch himself with almost suicidal glee at any large dog or bitch he saw. Sid Wilkinson had developed an almost crippling arthritis by this time and found Jock a bit too much to handle. Thus he was passed to Bill Brightmore's kennels, where he still lives at the time of writing. He is a well-known sire of workers, however, and Pat O'Malley's dogs, the dogs of Jimmy Robinson and Dennis Barrow's Turk were of his getting.

Undoubtedly Wilkinson's Rock was one of the most important studs in the breed. At Lowther I questioned the owners of some twenty-two top-class red fell terriers, all of which had at some time or other won Best in Show awards. Eighteen of them could be traced back to Sid Wilkinson's Rock.

49. John Winch

(Interviewed at Consett, over a period of five years)

I consider John Winch to be *the* authority on the northern working terrier and freely admit that he has acted as sage, mentor and guide in my researches into the history of the various strains. Winch's theory that Irish-terrier blood played an important part in the development of the fell terrier is no longer disputed, but when, in 1968, Winch first put the theory forward few breeders believed him.

Winch comes from a family of terrier breeders. His father, a fitter by trade, bred Border terriers, and his grandfather produced good-quality Sealyhams, Bedlingtons and Irish terriers in addition to top-grade Border terriers.

Winch is a barrister, but his life has been sufficiently chequered to merit comment. He left school at eighteen and did military service in the army, intending to study law when he left. In those days, however, intending solicitors were required to put up £500 for their education and keep themselves for five years. Winch's family were unable to find this sort of money, so he took up employment as an earth-mover driver on a construction site and studied for his law exams in the evenings. In the late 1960s, he took an exam with the Chartered Institute of Transport and won £25, and it was here that his contact with working terriers began. With his £25 in hand, he placed an advertisement in the *Field* to obtain a real Jack Russell terrier of what he believed to be the best type, and received a reply from a Mrs Nicholls of Taunton, who sold him two rough-coated terriers called Pobble and Fly.

Winch entered both easily and quickly, and after a spell of terrier free-lancing, working both badger and fox, he became terrier man (part time) with the Braes of Derwent Hunt. Pobble and Fly worked well for the Braes,

94. John Winch, an authority on northern working terriers.

238

being typical Somerset Jack Russells, not keen on headlong and damaging tackles with fox and badger, but excellent dogs at nipping, baying and bolting foxes. After being terrier man for the Braes for two seasons, Winch decided, however, that he wanted harder, more typey terriers.

At this time Graham Ward, a friend of Winch who encouraged John to join the Fell and Moorland Working Terrier Club and to take over the Durham area to look after their interests, had already brought the Tyson-bred Hardasty stock to the Durham area, and Winch was impressed by the good sharp lines of Tyson's original stock. In 1970, Winch went to Egremont and purchased Fury, a daughter of Tyson's Rocky. Fury worked with Braes for a season and freelanced at fox and badger. She was a natural stayer, fearless but sensible, and rarely got herself badly mauled, though Winch says she was eager to get stuck in. She was an excellent bolter, and throughout her work years she never killed a fox.

Later Winch bought Chanter from Tyson, a bright-red male sired by Tyson's Rocky out of Tatters, a Melbreck-bred bitch bred by Sid Hardasty (Harry Hardasty's brother), bred down from the same Gillie Fleming line that had produced Turk. Chanter was wild, unruly and undisciplined when Winch bought him, keen to run head down and 'deaf out' Winch's cries. He entered to fox easily, however, and while he never lost his fiery disposition, settled down to work quite readily. Chanter was a game, hard terrier, reluctant to come off his fox once he engaged it. Furthermore, when he killed his foxes, he pulled his victims out of the earth. He killed two foxes during a dig with the Braes of Derwent and drew the vixen (Winch has the mask stuffed above his living-room door) after a six-hour session to ground. He suffered badly after these battles, as he was never a constitutionally strong dog, but a day or so later would always be eager to go again. At Bladon he went to ground in what Winch thought to be an easy set – and found his fox, but after a while the baying grew very faint and Winch had to call out the Durham members of the Fell and Moorland as well as Tyson from Cumberland to dig Chanter out of the set. The dig lasted three hard, tiring days, and picks, shovels and earth-movers were used. On the third day of the dig the earth-mover tore out a huge bite of earth and Chanter came out in the bucket. Chanter died of old age at thirteen, having sired four litters and earned a working certificate with the Braes of Derwent Foxhounds.

Chanter lived long enough to mate G. Ward's Mel, a daughter of Printer and Penny, and bred Ward's brood bitch Mandy. He also mated his own half-sister Fury and bred Rip, a game, easily entered terrier who sadly proved sterile.

Winch believes that certain strains of registered Lakeland terrier are still able to work and work well. In 1974, he bought Magic from Alan Johnston of Egremont's Oregill Kennels and started to work it. Magic entered to rat more quickly than Winch's unregistered fell terriers, but before he could try her to fox, she became involved in a fight in the rear of Cyril Tyson's van and died as a result of the mauling received. Winch's next purchase was from

John Cowen of Embleton, a red dog from the Hardasty line, but in spite of the fact that the dog was dead game and totally fearless, he became too big and Winch sold him to a badger digger in Pontefract. Turk's courage proved his downfall for he tackled a badger head-on and died as a result of the battle.

His next purchase was Spider, a bitch bred from registered stock from the Newcombe Rillington line mated to Alan Johnston's Henchman, but the bitch developed a hip infection and saw little work. In 1980, however, he bought Kim, a black fell terrier bred by John White of Glencoe out of a home-bred bitch mated to a son of Buck's Davy. Kim was bought from White of Glencoe for £100 and a gold sovereign ring by McDonald and became a very useful worker. However, he lost most of his teeth and half his jaw after a tackle with fox, and Winch bought the dog for £20. Kim has mated Ward's dogs and bred some useful black working terriers.

Winch became president of the Fell and Moorland Working Terrier Club in 1972, after Cowen of Embleton, who helped form the club, had resigned. At the time of writing, Winch is still president, and has continued to be the area representative for the Durham area since 1968.

50. Wally Wyld

(Interviewed at Walesby, Notts., on 10 October 1981)

I visited Wally Wyld at his home for the purpose of interviewing him concerning his own fell terrier breeding programme and for gathering information for a chapter on Cyril Breay, for Wally Wyld was a great friend of that Kirkby Lonsdale expert and one of the few people in whom Breay would confide.

Wyld is an engaging, likeable person, modest, quiet, with none of the boastful nature one sadly tends to associate with present-day terrier men. He is, however, not only a first-class terrier man and a renowned digger, so stories tell, but also a keeper of authentic written records of his own and Breay's dogs – a fact for which we should be eternally grateful, for few fell terrier breeders are quite so meticulous about their strains of terrier as to keep accurate and truthful records of their wards.

Wyld has always had terriers, and his first memories are of his father, who worked as a miner, boarding-house proprietor, wheat-delivery man and ice-cream vendor, saving up half a crown from his pocket money to buy a nondescript white undocked terrier puppy, a puppy that cost a further 2s. 6d

95. *Mrs Wally Wyld with Kipper and a Kipper son.*

(12½p) for the local vet to dock: This puppy eventually mated by accident to a local Border terrier, Lothario, and bred a single brown puppy that the infant Wally kept; and though the dog displayed interest in going to ground at fox, Wyld showed no interest in digging, preferring to keep his dog at rat and rabbit. This is curious, as Wyld now has a reputation at his own Grove and Rufford Hunt and other hunts for being a great man with a spade.

Wyld eventually, however, met up with Machin, a keen badger digger whose sister became Breay's second wife. Machin kept a very useful strain of loose-coated fell terrier, more famed for their sagacity than for their blind courage, and hence extremely useful as badger-hunting dogs. Wyld said Machin frequently took as many as eight badgers in the course of a day's hunting, and always took his quarry alive and unharmed, releasing them elsewhere when the owner of the land asked for the badgers to be removed. Wyld recalls two of Machin's dogs, Moley and Whiskey, as being two of the finest dogs to badger he had ever seen. Machin would sometimes keep his dogs leashed until the end of the dig, a time when 'all' the badger were bagged, and ask if his pair could try to see if any badgers had been over-looked. By this time the earths would be full of scent, and even the excavated earth mounds tained with badger musk, yet Moley and Whiskey would often find another couple of badgers buried behind the stops of loose soil – a rare test for a terrier.

One day, however, in 1963, Machin took Wyld to the Vale of Lune Terrier Show, and there Wyld met Breay of Kirkby Lonsdale. Later that year he bought Kipper, a brother of Breay's famous Rusty, for £8 and the strain began here. Kipper was a large, bold black terrier, hard as iron, game as a pebble, but sensible at work, and probably the best terrier Wyld ever had. Kipper had ample opportunity to be tested, as next year, 1964, Wyld and his cousin Ken Wyld were offered the posts of part-time terrier men for the Grove and Rufford Hunt, Nottingham (the Grove was a hunt that once boasted some of the finest working fox terriers in the world, including, for example, Grove Nettle). Kipper self-entered at seven months, for, running free, he slipped up a pipe and laid into his fox like a fiend, closing with it after a 180-yard scrabble up the drain. So impressed was Wyld with this terrier that he bought Fly, a half-sister of Kipper, from Breay. Later that year he came by another puppy from Cyril Breay, a daughter of a Frank Buck-bred bitch, Skiffle, a daughter of Black Davy, and this was in turn mated to Kipper. Wyld, a discerning terrier man, was less than satisfied. The bitch which Wyld kept was called Trixie. She was undersized for a fell terrier, though that makes a useful terrier in Grove and Rufford country, and was slow to start, and it was eighteen months before she would look at a fox. (Curiously enough, a number of bitches bred by Breay were extremely slow to start, such as the two kept by Brockley and Eric Taylor.) At two years of age, however, she entered like a wildcat, becoming useful for a while, but then growing dangerously hard. After a year with the Grove and Rufford, she met up with a fox in a drain and attacked it with great ferocity, but the quarry retaliated and took out Trixie's eye. Wyld summed up the situation and promptly gave the bitch to a sporting farmer called Harold Holmes.

Holmes had a useful black dog in his kennels, of breeding unknown perhaps, but a known nailer to fox and badger. This he mated to Trixie (one-eyed Trixie), and bred a neat black puppy also called Trixie, insisting that Wyld take the puppy back. Wyld was over-stocked at the time, so he gave the puppy to a non-sporting pet owner in Tuxford who tired of the animal after two years and returned it to Wally. It had seen no work and had run riot, but she entered first time to a fox run to ground by the Grove and Rufford Hunt. Wyld, however, was still over-stocked so he gave the bitch to yet another sporting farmer.

Another Breay-bred terrier was purchased by the Grove and Rufford huntsman at this time: a red dog called Boney, which worked for a season or so with the hunt. Boney was mated to Trixie II to produce a useful hunt terrier bitch called Tinker. This bitch was mated in turn to the now famous Oliver Gill dog Beano, a typey, showy animal bred from Jack Smith's Ranter (incidentally sired by a son of Kipper), mated to a bitch from the renowned hunter Charlie Dickenson. Beano's puppy, a bitch puppy called Moley (after Machin's dog), a near replica of Beano in fact, was still at kennels when I visited Wally Wyld.

Wyld is still enthusiastic about Breay's strain of terrier, and he cannot speak too highly of the courage of these dogs. He is, however, terrier man to the Grove and Rufford Hunt, and the Midland earths are too small for the type of terrier Breay found useful in the borrans and peat earths of the Lunesdale country. The earths found in the Grove and Rufford country are invariably enlarged rabbit warrens, and a dog of Breay's strain would find it impossible to work such places. Wyld now uses a strain of rough-coated Jack Russell derived from a terrier he bought from Sheffield – a house wrecker with a streak of touchiness with strangers. Even so, Wyld keeps his fell strain alive, and still speaks with fondness of his times with Breay.

'In times gone I spent all my times in the Lakes. Since Mr Breay has died, however, I rarely visit the fells,' were his words to me as we parted.